OECD ECONOMIC SURVEYS

1998-1999

BELGIUM/LUXEMBOURG

ORGANISATION FOR ECONOMIC CO-OPERATION AND DEVELOPMENT

ORGANISATION FOR ECONOMIC CO-OPERATION AND DEVELOPMENT

Pursuant to Article 1 of the Convention signed in Paris on 14th December 1960, and which came into force on 30th September 1961, the Organisation for Economic Co-operation and Development (OECD) shall promote policies designed:

- to achieve the highest sustainable economic growth and employment and a rising standard of living in Member countries, while maintaining financial stability, and thus to contribute to the development of the world economy;
- to contribute to sound economic expansion in Member as well as non-member countries in the process of economic development; and
- to contribute to the expansion of world trade on a multilateral, non-discriminatory basis in accordance with international obligations.

The original Member countries of the OECD are Austria, Belgium, Canada, Denmark, France, Germany, Greece, Iceland, Ireland, Italy, Luxembourg, the Netherlands, Norway, Portugal, Spain, Sweden, Switzerland, Turkey, the United Kingdom and the United States. The following countries became Members subsequently through accession at the dates indicated hereafter: Japan (28th April 1964), Finland (28th January 1969), Australia (7th June 1971), New Zealand (29th May 1973), Mexico (18th May 1994), the Czech Republic (21st December 1995), Hungary (7th May 1996), Poland (22nd November 1996) and Korea (12th December 1996). The Commission of the European Communities takes part in the work of the OECD (Article 13 of the OECD Convention).

Publié également en français.

BELGIUM

Table of contents

●●●●●

Boxes

OECD 1999

Tables

Figures

LUXEMBOURG

Table of contents

●●●●●

Box

Tables

Statistical annex and structural indicators

Figures

This Survey is based on the Secretariat's study prepared for the annual review of Belgium and Luxembourg by the Economic and Development Review Committee on 12 October 1998.

•

After revisions in the light of discussions during the review, final approval of the Survey for publication was given by the Committee on 4 December 1998.

•

The previous Survey of Belgium and Luxembourg was issued in April 1997.

BASIC STATISTICS OF BELGIUM

THE LAND (1996)

Area (1 000 km²)	30.5	Major urban areas (thousand inhabitants):	
Agricultural area (1 000 km²)	13.4	Brussels	948.1
		Antwerp	933.0
		Liège	589.9
		Ghent	491.7

THE PEOPLE (1997)

Population (thousands)	10 181	Total labour force (thousands)	4 320
Inhabitants per km² (1995)	332	Total domestic employment (thousands):	3 710
Net natural increase	11 000	Agriculture	84
Net migration (1995)	13 400	Industry and construction	942
		Other	2 684

PRODUCTION (1997)

Gross domestic product (billion BF)	8 676	Gross domestic product by origin, at market	
Gross domestic product per head (US$)	23 831	prices (per cent):	
Gros fixed investment:		Agriculture	2.0
Per cent of GDP	17.8	Industry and energy	26.1
Pae head (US$)	4 230	Construction	5.0
		Other	66.9

THE GOVERNMENT (1997)

General government (per cent of GDP):		Composition of the House of Representatives	
Current expenditure	50.5	(number of seats):	
Current revenue	50.1	Socialists	41
Gross debt	121.8	Christian-socials	41
		Liberals	39
		Others	29
		Total	150
		Last election: 21.5.1995	

FOREIGN TRADE (1997)

Exports of goods and services (per cent of GDP)	72.9	Imports of goods and services (per cent of GDP)	68.4
Main exports (per cent of total), SITC (BLEU):		Main imports (per cent of total), SITC (BLEU):	
Iron and steel products (67 + 68)	7.5	Iron and steel products (67 + 68)	4.9
Chemical products (5)	18.0	Chemical products (5)	15.2
Machinery and equipment (71 to 77)	13.2	Machinery and equipment (71 to 77)	17.2
Textile products (65)	4.2	Textile products (65)	2.6
Transport equipment (78 + 79)	15.1	Transport equipment (78 + 79)	12.6
		Energy (3)	7.1

THE CURRENCY

Monetary unit: Belgian franc	Currency units per US$, average of daily figures:	
	Year 1997	35.7584
	November 1998	34.7042

Note: An international comparison of certain basic statistics is given in an annex table.

BASIC STATISTICS OF LUXEMBOURG (1997)

THE LAND

Area (km^2)	2 586	Major city, thousand inhabitants:	
Agricultural area, 1996 (km^2)	1 264	Luxembourg, 1.3.1991	75.8
Woodland, 1994 (km^2)	886		

THE PEOPLE

Population (thousands), 1.1.1997	418.3	Employment (thousands):	
Inhabitants per km^2	162	Total domestic employment	226.5
Net natural increase, 1.1.1997	1 794	Dependent employees:	209.9
Net migration, 1.1.1997	3 672	Agriculture	1.6
		Industry and construction	54.6
		Services	153.7
		Employers, self-employed persons	
		and domestic help	16.6

PRODUCTION

Gross domestic product (billion LF)	587	Gross domestic product by origin, at market	
Gross domestic product per head (US$)	39 244	prices (per cent):	
Gross fixed investment:		Agriculture	0.8
Per cent of GDP	22.9	Industry et energy	15.7
Per head (US$)	8 992	Construction	6.5
		Other	77.0

THE GOVERNMENT

Per cent of GDP:		Composition of the Chamber (number of seats):	
General government consumption	12.4	Christian-socials	21
Central government current revenue	31.6	Socialists	17
General government gross debt	6.4	Democrats	12
		Others	10
		Total	60
		Last election: 12.6.1994	

THE CURRENCY

Monetary unit: Luxembourg franc	Currency units per US$, average of daily	
	figures:	
	Year 1997	35.7584
	November 1998	34.7042

Note: An international comparison of certain basic statistics is given in an annex table.

BELGIUM

Assessment and recommendations

Growth has been robust

The Belgian economy has performed fairly well over the past couple of years, with buoyant growth and low inflation. After a slowdown in 1996, real GDP growth picked up in line with developments in neighbouring countries and, at 3 per cent in 1997 and probably only slightly less in 1998, has been somewhat stronger than projected at the time of the previous EDRC examination of Belgium in January 1997. As business fixed investment has remained buoyant and private consumption and residential investment have strengthened, the driving force of the expansion has progressively shifted from net exports to domestic demand. The revival of private consumption has reflected not only stronger job creation and an acceleration in disposable personal income, but also a fall in the saving ratio, as consumer confidence has rebounded, possibly as a result of remarkable progress in fiscal consolidation and better prospects in the labour market.

Inflation is subdued and the current-account surplus large

Unlike in previous cycles, the wage-price performance has remained relatively good during this upswing. The end of the 1995-96 real wage freeze has been followed by only a modest acceleration in wage increases and compensation per employee. Several factors, both domestic and foreign, seem to have contributed to this result, including: the introduction of the law on employment and competitiveness which limits, on an *ex ante* basis, the maximum increase in compensation per employee in the private sector to the expected weighted average increase in the three reference countries, *i.e.* Germany, France and the Netherlands; the credibility of monetary policy; a declining but still significant output gap, estimated by the OECD Secretariat to be around 1¼ per cent in 1998; and very subdued import prices as a result of the East Asian crisis and the fall in oil prices. CPI inflation has recently been at around 1 per cent. The current-account surplus has widened to nearly 5 per cent of GDP, one of the largest in the OECD area.

**But
unemployment,
in all its forms,
remains high**

Labour market conditions have improved. This has been the result of cyclical factors, higher job content of growth, and administrative measures. The latter have resulted in an important shift of older unemployed from the normal unemployment benefit programme to special programmes which are not included in traditional measures of unemployment and the labour force, and they have therefore accelerated the decline in joblessness. The standardised unemployment rate has fallen by more than a full percentage point over the past couple of years, to 8.9 per cent in August 1998 – a rate below the EU average but well above the OECD average and still high by historical standards. The claimant-based unemployment rate (national definition) has followed a similar path, falling to 12.5 per cent in October 1998 – a level that is still higher than the structural rate estimated by the OECD Secretariat. Since the beginning of 1996, the decline in registered unemployed has been due in part to an increase in older unemployed not claiming normal unemployment benefits. The latest available data show, however, that over the past 12 months the total of registered unemployed and older unemployed has dropped by 5 per cent. A broader concept of labour under-utilisation, which adds the older unemployed and all other people in special unemployment-related programmes to unemployment as usually defined, shows that the rate of "broad unemployment" fell from 25 per cent of the broad labour force in 1994 to 24 per cent in 1996 and 23 per cent in 1998.

**The outlook is
relatively
favourable,...**

Despite concern about the global economy, the outlook for Belgium remains relatively favourable. Given the limited importance of trade and financial links with emerging markets, the direct impact of problems in those areas on Belgian exports will be small. More generally, the impact of weaker export markets outside Europe should be partly cushioned by continued vigour in the euro area, including in Germany and France. The appreciation of the Belgian franc in effective terms included in the projection erases only partially the 1996-97 depreciation; and, with a cost-price performance broadly in line with that of foreign competitors, Belgian firms are expected to remain internationally competitive. On the domestic side, after being contractionary for several years, fiscal policy is now likely to be broadly neutral, and no major tightening of monetary conditions is expected over the projection period. Finally, there are no major constraints on the acquired strength of domestic demand as the expansion remains remarkably free of tensions, the output gap is still significant, and the low employment rate provides additional leeway, especially if further structural measures enhancing employment are taken.

... although, due to the global financial crisis, the downside risk and uncertainty are significant

All considered, real GDP growth is projected to slow moderately – to around 2¼ per cent in both 1999 and 2000 – with a markedly lower rate of growth of exports. Private consumption could lose some of its recent buoyancy, but it will continue to be underpinned by the strength of disposable personal income. Similarly, while decelerating somewhat, business fixed investment is expected to remain relatively dynamic as a result of the high rate of capacity utilisation, good profits, and low interest rates. With economic growth somewhat above the potential growth rate, the output gap would partly disappear and the unemployment rate approach the estimated structural rate. Due to the restraining effect of the law on employment and competitiveness and subdued import prices, serious inflationary pressures are unlikely to arise. The major risks and uncertainties concern the international environment. If the global financial crisis were to worsen further with the dollar falling well below the level assumed in the projection, the effects – both direct and indirect – on the Belgian economy could be sizeable, mainly because of weaker net exports not only to emerging markets and the United States but also to neighbouring countries, and slack business investment as a result of falling orders and a drop in firms' confidence. On the other hand, if international financial markets were to settle down and no further decisive measures were taken to increase the potential growth rate of the Belgian economy, the balance of risk on inflation would appear to be on the upside, as improved labour market conditions might induce households to reduce their saving ratio and spend more than projected.

Appropriate economic policies have qualified Belgium for EMU

The overriding goal of the authorities has long been to allow Belgium to participate in Economic and Monetary Union from its inception. This goal has been achieved largely thanks to a sound monetary policy and a strict fiscal policy which have interacted positively. The policy of closely linking the exchange rate of the Belgian franc with the Deutschemark has been very successful, boosting confidence in the currency and progressively reducing interest differentials with Germany to nearly zero, thereby significantly facilitating the correction of the budget deficit. This, combined with a medium-term strategy of fiscal consolidation which has been steadfastly pursued even at times of unfavourable conjunctural conditions, has resulted in a fall in the general government deficit from around 7 per cent of GDP in the early 1990s to 2 per cent in 1997, well within the Maastricht criterion; and the cyclically-adjusted deficit is estimated to have fallen from over 7 per cent of potential GDP to less than 1 per cent – one of the better performances in the OECD area. At the same time, the public debt-to-GDP ratio, although remaining extremely high, has declined from around 135 per cent in 1993 to 122 per cent in 1997, reflecting not only progress in fiscal consolidation, but also privatisation and asset management operations – including capital gains on official gold sales.

But the debt-to-GDP ratio must be reduced rapidly and the "quality" of public expenditure improved

Although Belgium has recorded some remarkable macroeconomic achievements over the past few years, there are a few major unresolved problems: the debt-to-GDP ratio is still very high; the composition of public expenditure is unbalanced; and structural reform remains insufficient, with a large number of persons on welfare. A rapid reduction in the debt-to-GDP ratio is a priority of the Belgian authorities. They are committed to keeping the primary surplus (*i.e.* excluding interest payments) at around 6 per cent of GDP over the medium term. This is welcome, since it could be expected to bring the overall general government budget into surplus already in a few years' time and reduce the debt/GDP ratio to 60 per cent by 2015 or earlier. Given that Belgium's overall deficit is already less than 2 per cent of GDP, this commitment might be more stringent than the EU's Stability and Growth Pact. But, in order to avoid having to take corrective budgetary measures in an economic downturn, it would be appropriate to aim for a somewhat higher primary surplus when the economy is overheating. Another fiscal challenge is the need to improve the "quality" of public expenditure. The burden of fiscal consolidation having fallen disproportionately on public investment, this item has averaged 1½ per cent of GDP over the past decade and is among the lowest in the OECD area; on the other hand, social expenditure has remained above the EU average and the OECD average. To prevent the physical infrastructure from deteriorating, and possibly to improve it, it would seem desirable to increase public investment while at the same time restraining social expenditure. Hence, there is a need to reduce all passive spending on unemployment, to accelerate the reform of public sector pensions, and to keep health expenditure under control even if the "norm" limiting its annual growth in real terms to 1.5 per cent is dropped (see below).

To boost non-inflationary growth and reduce the large number of persons on welfare, the pace of structural reform must be stepped up

Due to rigidities in the labour and product markets, there is a risk that inflationary pressures might emerge while unemployment is still high. Stepping up structural reform would simultaneously increase non-inflationary potential growth, expand job creation and reduce the large number of persons on welfare. But progress in structural reform has been relatively slow in the past couple of years, and a number of important policy recommendations included in the OECD Jobs Strategy have not been considered. EMU and fiscal consolidation have been at the top of the policy agenda, and in the recent period the government has focused its efforts on the preparation of the EU National Action Plan for Employment. Within this framework, the Belgian authorities have continued to emphasise cuts in employers' social security contributions – focused on low-skilled workers – combined with "active measures" such as training and guidance. Employers' contributions are to be cut by a total of over BF 100 billion over the next six years, representing a reduction in the average labour cost of 3.4 per cent. As a counterpart, the social partners are expected to take measures to improve training and enhance employment; and the *plan d'accompagnement des chômeurs*, which is Belgium's main initiative in the area of active labour market policies, is to be strengthened. Several other important measures have been taken, as the authorities have pursued their efforts to improve labour market outcomes while preserving social peace and preventing the emergence of a class of "working poor". At the same time, they acknowledge that technological progress, globalisation and EMU will require more adaptable labour and product markets, more regulatory reform, and more reliance on market forces.

Progress has been slow in increasing wage flexibility...

Despite the end of the 1995-96 wage freeze, the increase in wages has remained modest. But this very welcome wage moderation at the macroeconomic level has been achieved in the context of the law on employment and competitiveness, and may have brought with it potentially large harmful long-term effects arising from rigidities introduced by this law at the microeconomic level. The law should be phased out before these slow-building and difficult to detect microeconomic effects undermine potential growth. To prepare for this and avoid jeopardising wage moderation at the macroeconomic level, the focus of attention of employment policy should be put not only on reducing non-wage labour costs but also on freeing the wage formation process, especially at the low-wage end of the labour market. Over the longer term, the preferable solution to the problem of employing low-skilled workers is to raise their productivity through education, training, and life-long learning towards levels consistent with socially acceptable wages. Over the short to medium term, however, the creation, through normal market forces, of an important number of permanent low-skilled jobs as well as more entry-level jobs for the young may require wages and labour costs to fall to match the level of productivity of workers currently unemployable. As noted in the 1997 *Survey*, several provisional measures could facilitate the transition to a more flexible wage formation process, allowing downward wage adjustments at the microeconomic level and a widening of the wage structure: the social partners when negotiating collective agreements should lower the minimum sectoral wage to the statutory minimum ("*salaire minimum interprofessionnel*"); greater use could be made of "opening clauses" allowing firms, under certain circumstances, to negotiate with their work force to pay below the minimum set in collective contracts at the sectoral level; and existing exceptions from the statutory minimum wage could be generalised to employers hiring various target groups – such as older persons, youngsters, or long-term unemployed. As mentioned below, these measures to increase employment opportunities for low-skilled workers should be accompanied by in-work benefits to maintain the income of the workers involved. More generally, employees' power in wage determination would be reduced by easing job protection rules and discontinuing the practice of administrative extension of collective agreements.

... and more needs to be done to strengthen incentives to work...

As little progress has been recorded in reforming unemployment and related benefit systems, most of the recommendations presented in the 1997 *Survey* remain valid: the duration of earnings-related unemployment benefits should be reduced, while co-operation and co-ordination with regard to availability and job-search controls between the federal body administering benefits and the regional placement services should be tightened. But, above all, benefit sanctions in case of refusal of suitable work should be applied much more strictly. The age limit for early retirement – currently at 58 – should be increased and ways should be explored to tighten or phase out special unemployment-related programmes – such as *"pré-pensions"* and *"chômeurs âgés"* – with the help of active policies, including, when appropriate, subsidised jobs.

... and improve active policies

With a view to facilitating the return of some of the older persons currently in special unemployment-related programmes to the active labour force, mandatory participation in the *plan d'accompagnement* should be broadened to include persons aged over 46; and to enhance its effectiveness, contact with job seekers should be more frequent and ways should be found to reduce problems arising from the special Belgian administrative set-up which, in this area, requires a distribution of responsibilities among the federal government, Communities, and Regions. Moreover, as many older inactive persons with obsolete skills are probably largely "unemployable" – *i.e.* can hardly be expected to find a job regardless of their wage level – the development of special subsidised jobs (such as Smet jobs) may be the only way to return them to the active labour force, to perform work of social interest. Similar programmes for other target groups of persons who would otherwise also be "unemployable", such as youngsters with no job experience and lacking the required work attitude, have already been introduced on a rather limited scale. These programmes, which normally should provide only temporary jobs and be combined with training efforts, could be extended progressively.

Equity considerations should be addressed through a reform of taxation and social protection

The Belgian authorities attach great importance to keeping poverty at a low level. Over the longer term, the best way to avoid creating "working poor" is to improve the skills of the labour force. On-going efforts to reform the education system should thus be pursued. In the immediate future, however, since the wage cuts required to price low-skilled workers and people who have prematurely withdrawn from the labour force back into the market are deemed unacceptable for social and equity reasons, they should be combined with a reform of taxation and social protection based on the introduction of employment-conditional (or in-work) benefits to help assure a socially acceptable standard of living while preserving incentives to work. While equity considerations are important, job creation is even more so, since it is the key to a low rate of poverty based on work rather than passive income transfers, and hence more sustainable over the longer term and more conducive to social cohesion.

Improving competition in product markets would also help

For social and political reasons, increasing wage flexibility and redressing incentives to work has proved a difficult and slow process. To raise employment opportunities and ease acceptance of reforms, policy efforts should also concentrate on improving competition in product markets, especially in the service sector. For instance, entry conditions in the distribution sector should be liberalised since the current licensing procedure for the establishment of shops acts as an excessive barrier to entry, favouring incumbent shop owners without necessarily advancing societal objectives in such areas as urban planning. Moreover, rules on shop-opening hours should be relaxed further. Also, the electricity sector needs to be put on a solid competitive foundation which will require a breaking up of Electrabel's strong dominance in the area of production and distribution, or, at the very least, introducing regulations to make the access to the transmission grid open and fair. These are two areas where the scope for improvement seems especially large, and where deregulation holds the promise, not only of improving consumer choice, but also of creating a significant number of jobs. This would facilitate the task of making the labour market more flexible which, in turn, is a crucial condition for reaping the full benefit of product market reform.

The health care system delivers good quality services at reasonable costs...

The Belgian health care system is dominated by a compulsory, comprehensive and universal public health insurance, with the management of the system essentially entrusted to non-profit organisations – *i.e.* mutual sickness funds or *mutualités* – and the role of the government limited to regulation and partial funding. At 7½ per cent of GDP, total health spending in 1997 was essentially the same as the European and OECD averages; and, on the basis of various indicators, it would seem that the overall health status of the Belgian population has improved significantly over the past decade, and is about average compared with that of other Member countries. Finally, broadly speaking, Belgium does not seem to be confronted with a problem of waiting lists, either for access to medical practitioners, or for hospital in-patient care.

... but it suffers from structural problems

The combination of comprehensive solidarity-based insurance, modest co-payments, a largely fee-for-service system, and independent medical practice, while very attractive for patients and practitioners, creates a weak or distorted pattern of incentives which is not sufficiently countered by government control and self regulation by the medical profession. This makes the system vulnerable to abuse and inefficiency, with an over-supply of doctors, dentists, physiotherapists and hospital beds, resulting in unnecessary medical acts. These structural shortcomings may help explain that it is in the health sector that public spending has risen most rapidly over the past 10 to 15 years; and that to restrain its growth the authorities had to move progressively away from a fee-for-service system and introduce, first, fixed budgets or *forfaits* for specific medical acts, and then, a strict global "growth norm", limiting the annual rate of growth of health spending to 1.5 per cent in real terms, to be achieved in particular by greater use of lump-sum financing. But this "norm" was imposed as a temporary measure. Without it, the trend growth of health expenditure is likely to remain strong as a result of the introduction of new expensive medical technology and the growing impact of population ageing; and, owing to the commitment to pursue fiscal consolidation, the need to avoid increases in non-wage labour costs, and the authorities' reluctance to increase co-payments, there is little scope for boosting revenue. To maintain the system will entail continuing with structural reforms.

The Belgian authorities are taking corrective measures, but they may not be sufficient...

Given the special characteristics of health care – notably the difficulty that consumers have in making informed choices – the authorities want to reform the system within the existing framework of largely non-market arrangements, relying on *concertation* among the major players under the supervision and ultimate management of the government. The stated aim is to ensure that the Belgian health care system will continue to reconcile the principles of solidarity, quality of care, and freedom of choice at a reasonable cost (compared with other OECD countries). Some of the measures being introduced – notably a wider use of *forfaits*, reliance on "peer reviews", and the introduction of a central medical file ("*dossier médical centralisé*") backed up by comprehensive medical data banks – seem promising. Through a reduction of unnecessary medical acts, they could lead to significant savings. Measures have also been taken to contain the supply of health care. Other measures – such as better information and the *responsabilisation* of all parties – may also be tried but, unless they are combined with concrete guidelines or cost/price incentives, can hardly be expected to play a major role. Whether the current approach, as a whole, will be sufficient, over the longer term, to broadly equate expenditure and revenue will depend, among other factors, on difficult-to-quantify technical and medical considerations – such as the scope for a wider use of *forfaits* for specific medical acts, and the related potential savings. It is also uncertain whether the Belgian system of *concertation*, which worked reasonably well in the past when health expenditure was being allowed to grow rapidly, can be relied upon to curb expenditure strongly and allocate it efficiently among competing claims.

... and may have to be complemented by more market-oriented initiatives...

If the choice were made to introduce more market-oriented initiatives these should focus on redressing the pattern of incentives, while taking care to avoid excessive weakening of the principle of equity or equality of treatment in the public health care system. Of course, decisions on the efficiency/equity trade-off require value judgements which ultimately belong to the socio-political realm. Nonetheless, if the sustainability of the Belgian health care system is in doubt and difficult decisions need to be taken to reduce consumption, more appropriate incentives would significantly facilitate the adjustment. Moreover, insofar as risk-based private insurance and *forfaits* already exist in the Belgian health care system, a further reduction of the set of medical services covered by the compulsory health insurance scheme (with greater latitude for additional coverage by *mutualités* or private insurance), combined with the introduction of capitation payments to curb the growth of spending under the existing fee-for-service system, would be more a question of degree than of principle.

... including a reassessment of the role of for-profit insurance companies and the well as stepping up preventive medicine

To allow private for-profit insurers to provide an efficient complement to public compulsory insurance would require a level playing field in the provision of health care insurance, a situation which currently does not exist since the *mutualités*, which also offer supplementary health insurance, are not subject to various taxes paid by private insurance companies. Moreover, the role of *mutualités* should be reconsidered: the provision of medical care might be more efficient if they were allowed to compete on the basis of contribution rates – possibly with no right to reject applicants, in order to avoid "cream skimming" – and if they were prevented from owning or controlling hospitals and pharmacies to avoid conflicts of interest. Finally, preventive medicine should be stepped up, drawing in particular on the results of public health surveys which should be conducted on a regular basis.

Summing up   The macroeconomic performance of the Belgian economy has, in many respects, been remarkable over the past couple of years: growth has picked up, inflation has remained low, the current-account surplus has widened, and employment has increased. Moreover, fiscal consolidation has continued at a sustained pace, and Belgium has qualified for EMU – the overriding priority of the Belgian authorities. But these achievements should not lead to complacency: the debt-to-GDP ratio is still extremely high and must be reduced rapidly; the "quality" of public spending needs to be improved, partly because the burden of fiscal consolidation has in the past fallen disproportionately on public investment; and, although the economy is moving closer to its potential, the number of persons on welfare remains large. Within the Belgian framework of social consensus and equitable income distribution, the focus of attention of labour policy should be on returning low-skilled workers to the active labour force through better skills and qualifications, stronger incentives to work, and a more flexible wage formation process to price them back into the market. Progress in this direction would be significantly enhanced by more competitive and dynamic product markets: especially in the service sector the scope for reform would seem considerable. The favourable conjunctural situation provides a window of opportunity to step up the pace of structural reform, which would lay the ground for continuing strong non-inflationary growth and for a sustained increase in employment opportunities.

I. Recent trends and prospects

Overview

The macroeconomic performance of the Belgian economy has been rather good in 1997 and 1998. Economic activity has generally been robust, with few tensions or imbalances – the main exception being the labour market, where there has, nonetheless, been a noticeable improvement. The driving force of the expansion has progressively shifted from net exports to domestic demand, and this trend is expected to continue in the near future. Real GDP growth may have been nearly 3 per cent in 1998, and is projected at around 2¼ per cent in both 1999 and 2000. Job creation has already accelerated, and the unemployment rate has begun to decline but remains higher than the structural rate (NAWRU). Over the coming two years, unemployment, although falling, will remain high, and a large number of persons will continue to be inactive in special welfare programmes, such as those for early retirement and older unemployed. Consumer price inflation has declined markedly and, partly as a result of subdued import prices, is set to rise only moderately as the expansion matures. At 4¾ per cent of GDP, the current-account surplus is well above the EU average and one of the largest in the OECD area.

Robust economic activity

The expansion gained momentum in 1997 and the first half of 1998, but the conjunctural indicators of the National Bank of Belgium and other provisional data point to a significant slowdown in economic activity in the second half of the year, with weaker exports. Nonetheless, real GDP growth, which reached 3 per cent in 1997, may have been nearly as strong in 1998 (Table 1). With a potential growth rate estimated by the OECD Secretariat at around 2 per cent, the output gap has progressively shrunk, to an estimated 1¼ per cent in 1998. The upturn was initially fuelled by external demand. A sizeable depreciation of the Belgian franc in effective terms, coupled with a relatively good cost-price performance and strengthening activity in neighbouring countries, led to a surge in foreign

Table 1. **Demand and output: recent trends and projections**

Annual percentage change, 1990 prices

	1995 current prices		1997	1998	1999	2000
	BF billion	Per cent of GDP				
A. Demand and output						
Private consumption	5 071	62.9	2.1	2.8	2.1	2.2
Government consumption	1 182	14.6	0.8	1.1	1.6	1.6
Gross fixed investment	1 430	17.7	5.4	4.9	3.8	3.4
Final domestic demand	7 683	95.2	2.5	2.9	2.4	2.4
Stockbuilding[1]	33	0.4	−0.3	0.2	0.1	0.0
Total domestic demand	7 716	95.6	2.2	3.2	2.5	2.4
Exports of goods and services	5 395	66.9	7.1	6.1	5.3	5.4
Imports of goods and services	5 042	62.5	6.3	6.6	5.8	5.7
Foreign balance[1]	352	4.4	0.9	−0.1	−0.2	−0.1
GDP at constant prices	..	..	3.0	2.9	2.3	2.3
GDP price deflator	..	..	1.4	1.3	1.4	1.4
GDP at current prices	8 068	100.0	4.5	4.2	3.7	3.7
B. Memorandum items:						
Private consumption deflator	..	..	1.8	1.0	1.2	1.4
Private compensation per employee	..	..	2.1	2.1	2.2	2.0
Total employment	..	..	0.5	1.4	0.8	0.7
Unemployment rate (per cent)[2]	..	..	12.5	11.7	11.5	11.3
Breakdown of gross fixed investment						
Public sector	116	1.4	19.2	6.6	2.0	2.0
Private sector residential	437	5.4	4.9	3.6	3.5	3.0
Private sector non-residential	877	10.9	4.2	5.3	4.1	3.8
Interest rates (per cent)						
Short-term	..	..	3.4	3.6	3.0	3.1
Long-term	..	..	5.7	4.8	4.2	4.4
Current balance (per cent of GDP)	..	..	4.7	4.8	4.7	4.7

1. Contribution to growth of GDP.
2. National definition.
Source: OECD Secretariat.

orders, particularly for intermediate goods, which typically are in strong demand in the initial phase of a cyclical upturn. Since late 1997, however, foreign orders have weakened, while business fixed investment and private consumption have gathered strength, taking over as the driving force of the expansion.

Since the cyclical trough at the beginning of 1993, the strength of the Belgian economic expansion has been very similar to that in neighbouring countries, and in particular Germany, France and the Netherlands (Figure 1). On the other hand, its composition has been somewhat different. While, until recently, private consumption in Germany and France has remained hesitant, perhaps hindered by actual and prospective fiscal consolidation, in Belgium, it has strengthened, as the general government deficit has fallen well below the Maastricht ceiling, fears of further fiscal tightening have been largely allayed, and consumer confidence has surged (Chapter II). Nonetheless, private consumption and real GDP growth in Belgium have not been as rapid as in the Netherlands.

Business investment, although somewhat volatile, has been the most vigorous component of domestic demand in the current expansion, buoyed by improved profits, demand factors, and historically low interest rates (Figure 2). In addition, the rate of capacity utilisation in the manufacturing sector has reached unprecedented high levels.[1] But the overall increase in investment conceals substantial differences at the sectoral level, with investment in manufacturing losing much of its early dynamism (except in certain industries such as chemicals and textiles), and investment in services surging, particularly in banking. While investment has been strong, it has clearly fallen short of the exceptionally high level reached during the investment boom in the second half of the 1980s,

Figure 1. **The business cycle in Belgium and three neighbouring countries**[1]

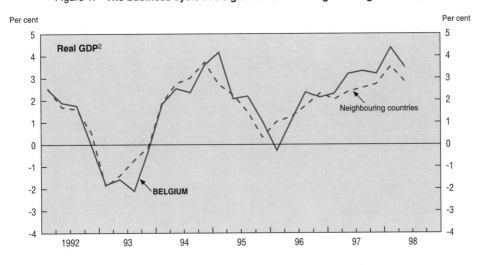

1. Germany, France and Netherlands (weighted average).
2. Percentage changes from previous year, seasonally adjusted, volume.
Source: National Bank of Belgium and OECD Secretariat.

Figure 2. **Investment:[1] comparison of two business cycles**

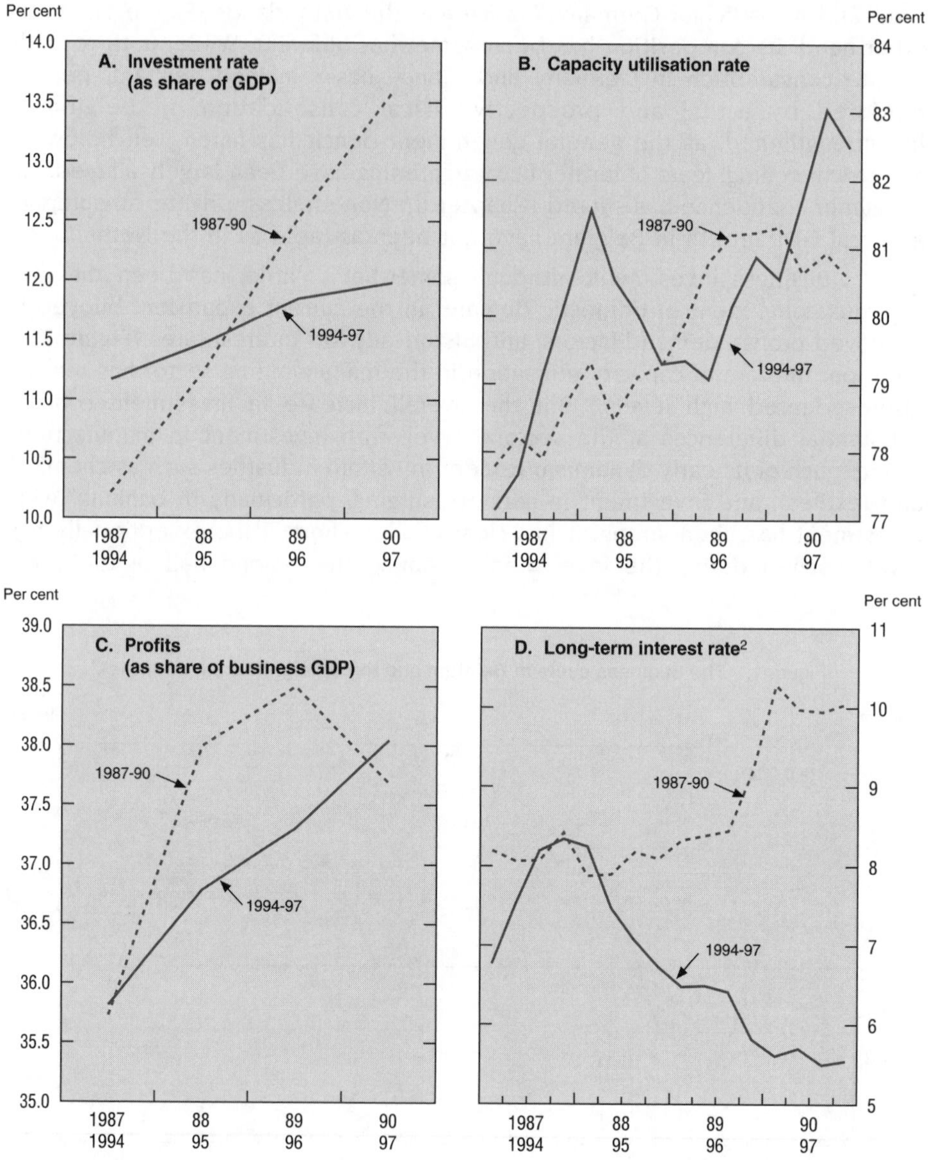

1. Business fixed investment.
2. Yield on government bonds (10-year).
Source: OECD, *Main Economic Indicators* and OECD Secretariat.

despite the fact that real interest rates are lower in this expansion than in the previous one, and capacity utilisation is higher. This performance may partly be explained by profitability which, while rising, is still below the record levels of the end of the 1980s (Figure 2C).[2]

Since the second half of 1997, the expansion has become more broadly based as private consumption and residential investment have picked up markedly. Consumption has apparently benefited from the slow but continuing improvement in labour market conditions as well as from progress in fiscal consolidation. Consumer confidence increased significantly following the presentation of the 1998 budget, as it became apparent that no further significant fiscal tightening was to be expected. This "feel good" factor, combined with substantial capital gains on financial assets and lower interest rates, has affected households' spending patterns. Car sales, one of the most cyclical components of private consumption, rose sharply in 1997, and remained strong afterwards – even allowing for the effect of the biennial Brussels' Motor Show (Figure 3). The saving ratio, which has been on a declining trend since reaching a high of 20½ per cent in 1993, fell to 15.2 per cent in 1997 and may have fallen further in 1998 – to slightly below 15 per cent.

Figure 3. **Consumer confidence and car registrations**

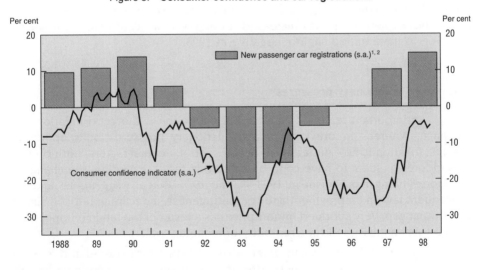

1.   Average of monthly figures. Percentage change over two years.
2.   1998: Average of the first nine months.
Source: OECD, *Main Economic Indicators.*

With falling mortgage rates, better consumer confidence and improving labour market conditions, residential investment, after dipping in 1996, rebounded in 1997 and 1998. Housing construction has also been supported by a temporary reduction in VAT for some specific housing categories, which was introduced for 1996 and 1997, and was later extended to the first half of 1998.[3] Since builders speeded up construction to meet this deadline, residential investment is likely to have shown a corresponding lack of buoyancy in the second half of the year. Owing to fiscal consolidation, the volume of government consumption hardly increased in 1997 and 1998, and employment in the government sector was virtually stable. On the other hand, public investment, after falling sharply for a few years, rebounded by almost 20 per cent in 1997 and its growth seems to have remained strong in 1998, as sales of buildings were greatly reduced. Moreover, local authorities stepped up investment, taking advantage of their improved financial situation following the partial privatisation of the *Crédit communal*. Despite these increases, public investment – at only 1½ per cent of GDP – remained low both in historical terms and compared with other OECD countries.

Export demand, which was the driving force of the expansion, started weakening in late 1997. This can be partly ascribed to the specialisation of the Belgian economy in the production of intermediate goods – a characteristic which becomes less supportive of growth as the expansion progresses. But it has also reflected the impact of the crisis in emerging markets on Belgian exports, a crisis of which the indirect impact, although still relatively small, has progressively grown. While overall exports have flagged, the growth of imports has accelerated, due to the strengthening of domestic demand. For 1997 as a whole the contribution of net exports to growth increased, to nearly 1 per cent of GDP; it seems, however, to have turned slightly negative in 1998.

Little or no inflationary pressures

An important feature of the current expansion is the good inflation performance. Whereas in previous cycles inflationary pressures built up during upturns, inflation is now under much better control. Several factors, both domestic and foreign, seem to have contributed to this result, including: the change in the index-linking mechanism in 1993-94, the 1995-96 real wage freeze and the subsequent law on employment and competitiveness; a declining but still significant output gap; very subdued import prices as a result of the fall in oil prices and the East Asian crisis; and the credibility of monetary policy.

The trend decline in consumer price inflation, which started at the beginning of the decade, has continued. After falling to a very low level in early 1998, inflation accelerated a little in the wake of a more rapid increase in food prices, before falling back to under 1 per cent in October (Figure 4, Panel A).[4] Increases in

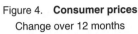

Figure 4.   **Consumer prices**

Change over 12 months

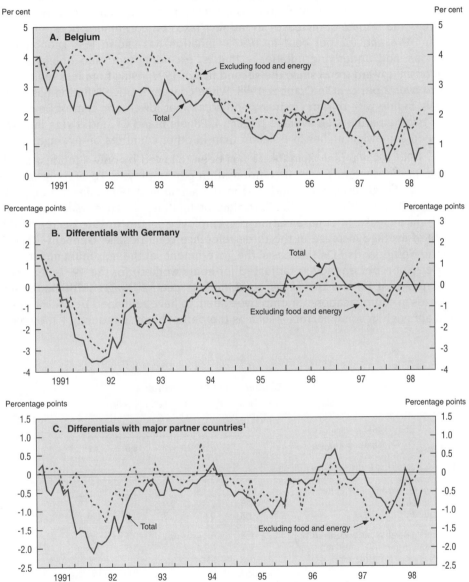

1.   Weighted average, as a function of the geographical structure of the imports and exports of Belgium with Germany,
     France, Italy, the United kingdom and the Netherlands in 1991.
Source: OECD, *Main Economic Indicators* and *Foreign Trade Statistics*, Series C.

service prices and rents have continued to slow, the latter reflecting lower interest rates and subdued real estate prices. Deregulation, notably in the telecommunications sector, has also contributed to downward pressure on prices. However, excluding the impact of increases in indirect taxes on consumer prices – 0.5 per cent in 1996 and 0.2 per cent in 1997 – inflation has shown less pronounced variations; and underlying inflation – that is, excluding food and energy – has been on an upward trend since the second half of 1997, rising from less than 1 per cent to over 2 per cent in October 1998. While consumer price inflation has been broadly in line with that in Germany and somewhat lower than that of Belgium's major trading partners on average (Figure 4, Panels B and C), underlying inflation has been somewhat higher in Belgium than in other countries on average.

The 1995-96 real wage freeze has been followed by only a modest acceleration in the wage rate and in compensation per employee. To prepare for the transition, the government introduced in the summer of 1996 a law on employment and competitiveness. The law aims at limiting, on an *ex ante* basis, the maximum increase in compensation per employee in the private sector to the weighted average increase in the three reference countries, *i.e.* Germany, France and the Netherlands.[5] On this basis, the government set the maximum increase in compensation per employee (adjusted for hours worked) for the 1997-98 period at 6.1 per cent for the two years combined. In general, wage settlements and increases in compensation per employee seem to have remained below this legal limit, although in some sectors – such as the petro-chemical industry – they have

Table 2. **Labour costs in enterprises**[1]

Percentage changes compared with the previous year

	1991	1992	1993	1994	1995	1996	1997[2]
Gross wage per full-time employee	7.8	5.6	4.8	3.0	3.1	1.8	2.5
Increase resulting from:							
Indexation	3.5	2.7	2.6	1.4	1.5	1.4	1.5
Wage increases under collective							
agreements	2.3	2.3	0.9	1.4	0.0	0.0	0.8
Wage drift	1.8	0.6	1.3	0.2	1.6	0.3	0.2
Employers' social security contributions	0.3	0.1	0.1	−0.5	−0.5	−0.4	0.2
Compensation per full-time employee	8.1	5.7	4.9	2.5	2.6	1.4	2.7
Productivity per full-time employee	1.8	2.0	−0.2	3.1	1.8	0.3	3.0
Unit labour costs[3]	6.2	3.6	5.1	−0.6	0.8	1.1	−0.3

1.   Private and public enterprises. All data are calculated without taking account of the possible influence of the statistical adjustments whereby the three national accounts' approaches are reconciled.
2.   Estimates.
3.   Per unit of value added, at constant prices.
Source: National Accounts Institute and National Bank of Belgium.

reportedly exceeded it. On average, both the wage rate and compensation per employee increased by a little over 2 per cent in 1997 – compared with 1 per cent in 1996. On a full-time basis, compensation per employee accelerated from 1.4 to 2.7 per cent, but as productivity also accelerated markedly, unit labour costs in the private sector decreased slightly – by 0.3 per cent in 1997, compared with an increase of 1.1 per cent in 1996 (Table 2). Hence, despite the end of the wage freeze, wage-cost developments have been broadly in line not only with those in the three reference countries, but also with those in Belgium's partner countries on average.

A large current-account surplus

Belgium's current-account surplus widened in 1997: at 4.7 per cent of GDP it was well above the EU average – 1.5 per cent of GDP – and the sixth largest in the OECD area. The increase in the surplus largely reflected a stronger trade balance: exports picked up in response to more buoyant economic conditions in EU countries – which account for some 75 per cent of Belgium's exports – and to a significant improvement in cost-price competitiveness. Unit labour costs in a common currency (in manufacturing) declined significantly in 1997 for the second year in a row, as the Belgian franc in effective terms continued to depreciate while, as just noted, the cost-price performance of Belgium was broadly similar to that of its trading partners (Figure 5). The impact of the East Asian crisis in 1997 was limited, given that Belgium's exports to these countries (including Japan), represent only some 5 per cent of total exports. Nonetheless, exports of goods to Southeast Asia and Japan fell by 15 per cent in the fourth quarter of 1997, and the growth of exports to China decelerated sharply.

While exports lost some buoyancy as 1997 progressed, imports strengthened as a result of the pick up in domestic demand, and especially in consumer durables. Earlier on, imports had been underpinned by the high import-content of exports and transit trade. Import prices, and particularly primary commodity prices, increased in 1997, owing to the decline of the Belgian franc in effective terms; however, export prices rose almost in parallel with import prices, reflecting the large share of re-exports and the typical passing-on of higher costs of primary imports. Moreover, towards the end of the year, energy prices fell sharply. As a result, the terms of trade worsened only slightly.

Among the other items of the current account, net investment income credits increased further in 1997, partly as a result of the continuing build-up of net claims on the rest of the world and the appreciation of the dollar and sterling – in which a large proportion of the stream of inward investment income is denominated.

Figure 5. **International cost competitiveness**[1]
Index 1989 = 100

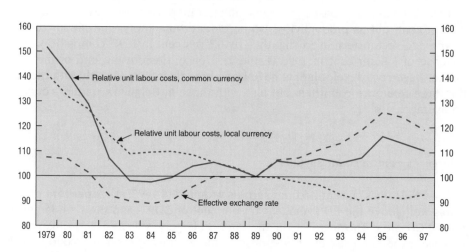

1. In manufacturing.
Source: OECD Secretariat.

In 1998, largely as a result of a decline in energy prices, the terms of trade are expected to have improved somewhat. Hence, despite a growing adverse impact of the crisis in emerging market economies on the volume of Belgium's exports, the trade surplus may not have changed greatly. With the other items, on balance, showing little variation, the current-account surplus may have widened only slightly, to 4¾ per cent of GDP.

But high unemployment

Policy measures and problems in the labour market are discussed in Chapter III. This section briefly reviews recent developments.

The economic expansion has begun to improve labour market conditions in a significant way, although a precise assessment is hampered by several policy measures and administrative decisions – such as incentives for part-time work, direct job creation by the *Agences locales pour l'emploi* and, in particular, a shift of older unemployed to special programmes entailing their exclusion from the traditional indicators of the labour force and unemployment. Available indicators show that recruitment has picked up since early 1996; and since the beginning of 1997, a growing proportion of enterprises have experienced shortages of skilled workers, and the number of unfilled vacancies has started to climb. Employment increased by ¹/₂ per cent in 1997, and may have increased at a much faster rate in 1998 – over 1 per cent. A special feature of this expansion has been the very rapid increase in temporary work: nearly 20 per cent in 1997 and the first half of 1998 (after 7 per cent in 1996 and 18¹/₂ per cent in 1995).[6] The most noticeable increase in employment has been amongst the under-25s and the over-50s.

Growth may have become more labour intensive, especially in terms of persons per output, as a result of wage moderation and cuts in employers' social security contributions which favour the substitution of labour for capital. Policy measures to encourage work sharing may also have gone in that direction – especially in the public sector. Part-time working has developed steadily and is moving closer to the European average. Private enterprises have shown little interest in government measures to promote collective reductions in hours worked.[7]

Unemployment has been on a declining trend since early 1996. The standardised unemployment rate has fallen by more than a full percentage point over the past couple of years – to 8.9 per cent in August 1998. While this rate is below the EU average, it remains historically high and well above the OECD average (Figure 6). The unemployment rate (national definition)[8] has followed a similar path, falling to 12.5 per cent in 1997 and to 11.7 per cent (partly estimated) in 1998. The NAWRU is estimated by the OECD Secretariat at around 11 per cent and at 8 per cent by the Belgian authorities. Caution is needed in interpreting the indicator because of calculation difficulties (mainly owing to the fact that the Belgian authorities have intervened frequently in the wage formation process), and even more so in a small and very open economy. Apparent regional differences in unemployment in Belgium – an unemployment rate of 7.7 per cent in Flanders, 17.2 per cent in Wallonia and 19 per cent in Brussels – mask major sub-regional divergencies. This and other indicators – such as the continuing high proportion of long-term unemployment and the disparities in unemployment rates according to gender and educational achievements or experience – suggest that unemployment remains largely structural.

The decline in recorded unemployment has, to some extent, reflected administrative measures, so that "broad unemployment" has evolved less favourably. For instance, since the decision, at the beginning of 1996, to ease the conditions under which older unemployed[9] may be exempted from job search and hence can shift from the normal unemployment programme to the special programme for older unemployed (*chômeurs âgés non demandeurs d'emploi*), the number of full-time unemployed receiving a benefit (*chômeurs complets indemnisés*) has decreased by some 76 000[10] but, over the same period, the number of older unemployed has increased by 60 000.[11] A broader concept of labour under-utilisation ("broad unemployment"), which adds people in special

Figure 6. **Unemployment rate:[1] an international comparison**

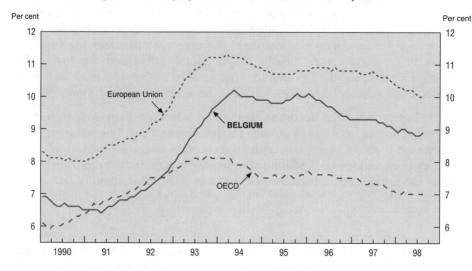

1. Standardised rate.
Source: OECD Secretariat.

unemployment-related programmes to unemployment as usually defined ("narrow unemployment"), shows that in this respect conditions changed only slightly in 1997 and 1998.[12, 13] As the decline in "narrow unemployment" and in "other unemployed" was partially offset by the increase in "people in special programmes" – particularly *chômeurs âgés* – "broad unemployment" barely edged down, still representing 22½ per cent of the broad labour force (Table 3).[14] All forms of unemployment and inactivity among working-age persons – regardless of whether they receive a social security benefit or not – are of course reflected in the overall rate of employment – the broadest indicator of the degree a country uses its potential labour force.[15] At 57 per cent in 1997, the employment rate in Belgium was one of the lowest in the OECD area (OECD, 1998), but the negative deviation from the OECD average has narrowed appreciably in the last few years, from 7.9 points in 1990 to 3.1 points in 1997.

A relatively favourable outlook

Several considerations suggest that, despite the turmoil in world financial markets, real GDP growth in Belgium should remain robust. First, given the

Table 3. **Unemployment and special programmes**[1]

Thousands

	1982	1990	1993	1994	1995	1996	1997	1998
I. Narrow unemployment (*population active en chômage*)	490	365	511	554	555	545	541	505
II. Other unemployed	80	230	214	178	159	131	112	103
Seasonal unemployed (*chômeurs temporaires*)	57	25	48	36	35	32	37	29
Part-time unemployed (*chômeurs à temps réduit involontaire*)	23	205	166	142	124	99	75	74
III. People in special programmes	163	430	420	405	395	420	428	447
Exempted from job search: For age reasons (*chômeurs âgés*)	0	72	75	74	74	95	114	131
For social reasons, training and studies (*interruption de chômage*)	0	51	46	42	41	43	33	28
Special leave (*interruption de carrière*)	0	49	58	54	51	52	56	67
Early retirement (*pré-pension*)	109	163	146	141	134	134	129	125
Direct job creation (*remise au travail*)	54	95	95	94	95	96	96	96
IV. Broad unemployment (I + II + III)	733	1 025	1 145	1 137	1 109	1 096	1 081	1 055
As a percentage of the broad labour force[2]	17.3	22.7	24.9	24.8	24.1	23.7	23.2	22.5
Memorandum items:								
V. Other unemployed and people in special programmes (II + III)	243	660	633	583	554	551	540	550
VI. Broad unemployment in full-time equivalent	596	835	944	954	909	915	925	902

1. Registration basis, end-June data.
2. Labour force + exempted from job search + special leave + early retirement.
Source: OECD Secretariat and Ministry of Employment and Labour.

limited importance of trade and financial links with emerging markets, the direct impact of problems in those areas on Belgium's exports, although still growing, may remain small. More generally, the impact of weaker export markets outside the euro area should partly be cushioned by a relative vigour in this area – Germany and France included. Also, the exchange rates used for the projection imply an appreciation of the Belgian franc in effective terms which does not fully erase the depreciation recorded in 1996-97. This, combined with a cost-price performance broadly in line with that of foreign competitors, should allow Belgian firms to remain internationally competitive. Moreover, after being contractionary for several years, fiscal policy is now likely to be broadly neutral, and no major tightening of monetary conditions is expected in the euro zone over the projection period (Chapter II). Finally, although starting already four years ago, the expansion in Belgium remains remarkably free of tension, the output gap is still significant, and the low employment rate could provide additional leeway to boost non-inflationary growth, especially if further structural measures enhancing employment were taken (Chapter III).

Real GDP growth is projected to slow only moderately – to around 2¼ per cent in both 1999 and 2000. Weaker exports may slow economic activity somewhat although, given the openness of the economy and the consequent dampening effect on imports, the contribution of the foreign balance to growth may not change greatly and may remain only slightly negative. While decelerating, domestic demand should remain the driving force of the expansion. Business fixed investment is expected to continue to grow at a satisfactory rate as a result of the high rate of capacity utilisation, good profits, and low interest rates. Private consumption is also projected to stay relatively dynamic: in addition to the "feel good" factor related to progress in fiscal consolidation and improving labour market conditions, it will be supported by sustained growth in real disposable income.

With economic growth somewhat above the potential growth rate of the Belgian economy – estimated by the OECD Secretariat at around 2 per cent – the output gap should shrink further and nearly disappear in 2000; and the unemployment rate should continue to fall. Owing to a declining but still significant output gap, the restraining effect of the law on employment and competitiveness, and subdued import prices, serious inflationary pressures are unlikely to arise. The increase in compensation per employee and in the private consumption deflator may be only around 2 per cent and a little less than 1½ per cent, respectively, in 2000. The current-account surplus is projected to remain at around 4¾ per cent of GDP.

The major risks and uncertainties attaching to this projection concern the international environment and – at this stage – would seem to be on the downside. The Belgian economy could incur severe losses if the global financial crisis were to worsen further, with the dollar falling well below the level assumed in the projection. This would entail weaker net exports not only to emerging countries and the United States but also, and perhaps more importantly, to neighbouring countries, as economic growth in the euro zone would slow markedly. Also, business investment would slump as a result of falling orders and a drop in firms' confidence. On the other hand, if international financial markets were to settle down and, on the domestic side, no further decisive measures were taken to increase the potential growth rate of the Belgian economy, there could be some risk of inflationary pressure, as improving labour market conditions might induce households to reduce their saving ratio and spend more than projected.

II. Economic policies

The overriding goal of the Belgian authorities has long been to meet the Maastricht criteria and thereby to participate in the Economic and Monetary Union (EMU) from its inception. Through a medium-term strategy of fiscal consolidation, which has been steadily pursued even at times of unfavourable conjunctural conditions, the general government deficit has been reduced from around 7 per cent of GDP in 1992 to 2 per cent in 1997, well within the Maastricht criterion; and the cyclically-adjusted deficit has been reduced from over 7 per cent of potential GDP to less than 1 per cent, one of the better performances among OECD countries. At the same time, the public debt-to-GDP ratio, although remaining very high, has declined from around 135 per cent in 1993 to 122 per cent in 1997. On the monetary side, the policy of closely linking the exchange rate of the Belgian franc with the Deutschemark has been a remarkable success: it has contributed to boosting confidence in the currency and progressively reducing interest differentials with Germany to nearly zero, thereby significantly enhancing the process of fiscal consolidation. On the other hand, with EMU and fiscal consolidation at the top of the policy agenda, structural reform has been relatively slow in the past few years, and the scope for further progress in this area remains important, especially in the labour market and in product markets.

The following paragraphs, after briefly reviewing monetary policy and monetary conditions, consider the broad lines of budget policy and progress in fiscal consolidation. Structural measures in general are discussed in Chapter III, while initiatives related to the health care system in particular are considered in Chapter IV.

Monetary policy

Despite the recent international financial crisis, the period since early 1997 has been characterised by growing confidence in the timely introduction of the euro, continuing strength of the Belgian franc within the European Monetary System, and a pronounced trend decline in European long-term interest rates. In this relatively favourable environment, and since the sizeable current-account surplus of the Belgian-Luxembourg Economic Union (BLEU)[16] has been broadly matched by spontaneous financial outflows, the intermediate goal of monetary policy – i.e. a stable exchange rate vis-à-vis the Deutschemark – has been relatively easy to achieve, without explicit policy measures (Figure 7, Panel A). Nonetheless, through its liquidity management, the National Bank of Belgium has occasionally supported – notably in February and March 1997, from July to October 1997 and from February to April 1998 – spontaneous but short-lived rises in Belgian money market rates above corresponding German rates. Despite these slight tensions, short-term interest rate differentials between the two countries have generally remained rather small, with rates edging up as in several other continental European countries (Figure 7, Panels B and C). In early October 1997, in the context of accelerating economic growth and after a marked rise of the exchange rate of the dollar, the National Bank of Belgium raised its interest rates at the same time as the central banks of Germany, France, the Netherlands, Austria and Denmark. In the view of the Bank, this represented a switch from a relatively expansionary stance of monetary policy to a more neutral position, in order to prevent any resurgence of inflation. On the other hand, Belgian long-term rates have trended down and somewhat faster than corresponding German rates, so that the differential has shrunk. The recent turmoil in international financial markets has had relatively little impact on Belgium, although the long-term interest differential with Germany – which had stabilised at around 10 basis points in the first half of 1998 – has widened anew, to around 30 basis points. Also, Belgian equity prices have recorded a significant downward correction, before erasing a part of their losses, broadly in line with other continental financial centres.

At less than 4½ per cent, the yield on Belgian government bonds is currently at an historically low level and one and a half percentage points lower than at end-1996. As the depreciation of the Belgian franc in effective terms recorded in 1997 has not been fully offset by its recent appreciation, overall monetary conditions would seem to have eased – even though, as noted, short-term interest rates have edged up and, as a result of a reduction in inflation, long-term interest rates have declined less in real than in nominal terms. The impact of such a monetary easing on the real economy, however, may be less clear-cut than in certain other countries. While in a small open economy like Belgium a depreciation of the nominal exchange rate in an environment of price stability, like the present one, can be expected to have a significant positive impact on net exports and growth, the impact of lower long-term rates is more uncertain and may even be negative. Owing to the very large (direct and indirect) holdings of government bonds by households, a decline in the yield on these securities, in real terms, represents a fall in disposable income which may negatively affect private consumption and household spending in general.[17] All in all, monetary conditions seem broadly appropriate in view of domestic conditions – i.e. low inflation and moderate growth.

Figure 7.   **Interest rates and the exchange rate**

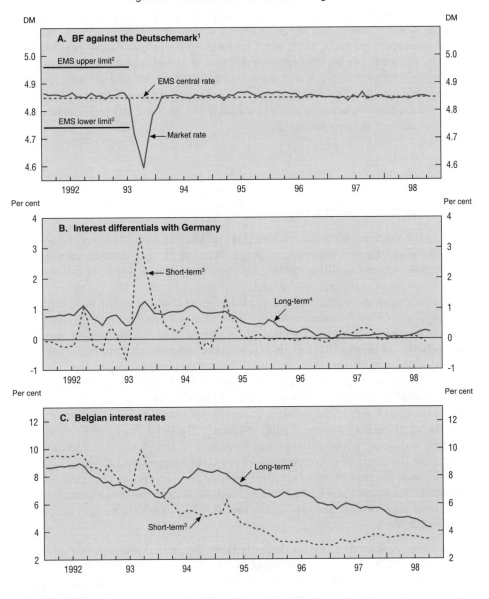

1.   DM per BF 100.
2.   On 2 August 1993, the upper limit was raised to DM 5.63 and the lower limit was decreased to DM 4.17.
3.   Three-month Euro-BF.
4.   Long-term government bonds (10-year).
Source: National Bank of Belgium and OECD Secretariat.

Given the unsettled conditions in world financial markets and the positive outlook for inflation, monetary and financial conditions in the euro area, on balance, seem unlikely to change much in 1999-2000. Nonetheless, as the economic expansion matures, both short and long-term interest rates may edge up towards the end of the projection period – a development which would be broadly in line with Belgium's domestic requirements. More generally, owing to the very high degree of synchronisation of Belgian economic cycles with those of its neighbouring countries, a monetary policy set at the EMU-wide level should pose no major problems for Belgium.[18]

Budgetary policy

Progress in fiscal consolidation

The medium-term goal of meeting the Maastricht criteria in the fiscal area was formalised by the 1992 Convergence Plan, which was introduced when the current government coalition came to power in an environment of deteriorating macroeconomic conditions and a widening budget deficit. The Plan set annual targets for the progressive reduction of the general government deficit to 3 per cent of GDP in 1996 – compared with a deficit of 6.9 per cent in 1992. To ensure that under reasonable macroeconomic conditions the 1996 target would be reached, the Plan was based on three major features or "norms": the social security system must be in equilibrium;[19] fiscal receipts must display "unit elasticity", *i.e.* they must increase in line with nominal GDP; and primary expenditure of the federal authorities must not increase in real terms. The Plan also set annual targets for all subsets of the general government, that is the Federal government and the social security system (the so-called "Entité I"); and the Communities, Regions and local governments (the so-called "Entité II"). To enhance implementation, the Federal government and the Communities and Regions agreed in 1994 to do their utmost to reach their respective targets. In the 1996 *Accord de coopération*, Communities and Regions agreed to respect the targets proposed by the *Conseil supérieur des finances*, which are that the Entité II budget should be balanced in 1999.

The various norms have broadly been respected and the budget deficit declined to 3.2 per cent of GDP in 1996, *i.e.* close to the 3 per cent target set initially by the Convergence Plan. In the meantime, it had been decided that the year when candidates for Monetary Union were supposed to have brought their deficits down to a maximum of 3 per cent would be 1997. But macroeconomic conditions, on balance, have been less good than expected since 1992, and to offset their negative impact on the budget and keep the deficit reduction on track, the government had to introduce repeated packages of corrective measures, with a total budgetary saving estimated by the Belgian authorities at a little over 6 per cent of GDP.[20] In late 1996, the Belgian Government presented a new convergence programme covering the period 1997-2000. The new plan stresses the need to keep the primary surplus at around 6 per cent of GDP (on the basis of the Belgian definition) in the medium term.[21] In the context of this new plan an additional package of corrective measures representing over 1 per cent of GDP was included in the 1997 budget,[22] bringing the total corrective effort since 1992 to some 7 per cent of GDP. The lasting impact of this effort on the budget, however, will be significantly smaller than this, since an important pro-portion of the corrective measures have been of a one-off or non-recurrent nature. This was especially the case in 1996 when over a third of the savings were estimated to stem from one-off measures. In 1997, macroeconomic conditions finally improved markedly, and the general government deficit fell to 1.9 per cent of GDP, representing an improvement of 5 percentage points compared with 1992. At the same time, the primary surplus rose to 5.8 per cent of GDP, above the target set in the 1997 budget and one of the highest in the OECD area.[23]

Reflecting the decline in public debt as a percentage of GDP and the marked decline in interest rates since the early 1990s, which was on very substan-tial public debt, broadly one-half of the improvement in the budget deficit over this period has been accounted for by a reduction in net interest payments as a per cent of GDP, the other half being accounted for by an increase in the primary surplus (Figure 8). In addition to lower interest rates and a lower debt ratio, the reduction in net interest payments has also reflected a more active debt-management policy – especially in 1993-94 when half of the long-term debt denominated in Belgian francs was refinanced at interest rates which, on average, were 2 percentage points lower. The increase in the primary surplus, in turn, has been mostly accounted for by an increase in receipts and, to a much smaller extent, by a reduction in expenditure (Table 4).[24, 25]

While the decline in interest rates has greatly facilitated fiscal consolida-tion, the corrective effort over the past six years has nonetheless been considera-ble. It has included: new direct and indirect taxes and, to a lesser extent, personal social security contributions; cuts in primary expenditure; various other savings, such as reduced interest payments as a result of a more efficient debt manage-ment, and additional revenues reflecting, among other measures, improved tax collection and a clamp-down on fiscal fraud. The importance of the corrective effort is confirmed by an analysis in cyclically-adjusted terms – i.e. allowing for the impact of macroeconomic activity on the budget – which shows a decline of the overall deficit from over 7 per cent of potential GDP in 1992 – when the economy had a positive output gap estimated by the OECD Secretariat at $1/2$ per cent – to less than 1 per cent in 1997 – when the (negative) output gap was around 2 per cent. This analysis also shows a rise of the primary structural balance from $2^3/4$ per cent in 1992 to $6^3/4$ per cent in 1997. Over this period, fiscal consolidation has been

Figure 8. **General-Government public finances**
Per cent of GDP

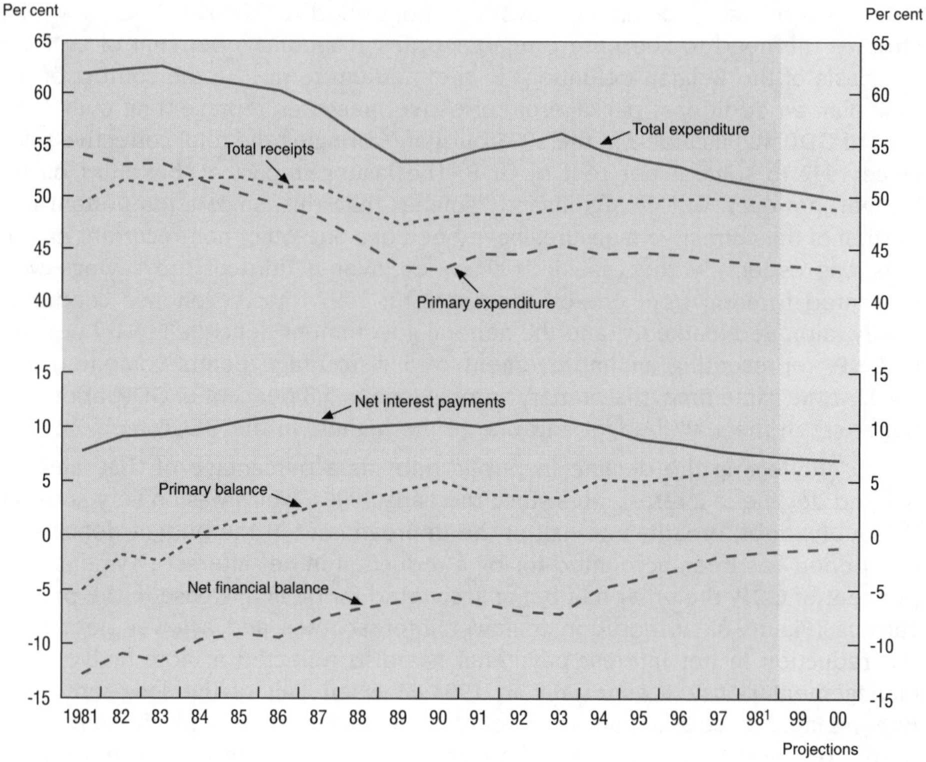

1. Estimates.
Source: OECD Secretariat.

less pronounced in the European Union on average: in 1997, the average budget deficit of EU countries was 2¹/₂ per cent and 1³/₄ per cent on a cyclically-adjusted basis – compared with a deficit of 5¹/₄ per cent on both bases in 1992 (Figure 9, Panels A and B). In sum, from a very poor starting point in the early 1990s, Belgium's performance in fiscal consolidation has been rather impressive, and one of the best in the OECD area, especially on a cyclically-adjusted basis.

Looking at fiscal consolidation in terms of the various subsets of the general government, it is clear that the brunt of the corrective effort has fallen on the Federal government and the social security system (Entité I). Their combined primary surplus has improved by some 1¹/₂ per cent of GDP over the 1992-97 period, with the Federal government accounting for about two-thirds of it,

Table 4. **General government budget**

Per cent of GDP

	1990	1992	1995	1996	1997	1998[1]	1999[2]	2000[2]
Primary receipts	47.3	47.4	49.2	49.4	49.6	49.3	49.1	48.6
Of which:								
Direct taxes	16.8	16.3	18.0	18.0	18.4	18.3	18.2	18.0
Indirect taxes	12.2	12.1	12.3	12.7	12.8	12.6	12.7	12.7
Social security contributions	15.0	15.8	15.4	15.1	15.0	14.9	14.7	14.5
Primary expenditure	43.0	44.5	44.6	44.4	43.9	43.6	43.4	42.9
Of which:								
Government consumption	14.0	14.2	14.6	14.5	14.4	14.2	14.1	14.0
Subsidies	2.8	2.7	2.4	2.4	2.0	2.0	2.0	2.0
Social security outlays	20.5	21.6	21.5	21.6	21.2	21.0	20.8	20.6
Primary balance	4.2	2.9	4.5	5.0	5.7	5.8	5.7	5.7
Interest payments (net)	9.7	9.9	8.5	8.1	7.6	7.3	7.0	6.8
Net financial balance	−5.4	−7.0	−3.9	−3.1	−1.9	−1.5	−1.3	−1.1
Memorandum items:								
Cyclically adjusted:[3]								
Primary balance	3.0	2.8	5.7	6.5	6.7	6.4	6.2	6.0
Net financial balance	−6.7	−7.1	−2.5	−1.3	−0.7	−0.8	−0.7	−0.7
Debt[4]	125.7	129.0	130.8	126.7	121.8	117.3	114.5	111.6

1. Provisional figures.
2. Projections.
3. As a percentage of potential GDP.
4. Maastricht definition.
Source: OECD, *National Accounts* and OECD Secretariat.

and the social security system accounting for the remainder (Table 5). Over the same period, the primary surplus of the *Entité* II (Communities, Regions and local governments) has increased by only ³/₄ of a percentage of GDP (de Callatay, 1998). This distribution of the adjustment – which has followed the suggestions of the *Conseil supérieur des finances* – would seem reasonable since it is broadly proportional to the budget of each *Entité, i.e.* their respective shares in total primary expenditure. However, the improvement recorded by the *Entité* II has been the result of an increase in fiscal resources (personal taxes and VAT taxes) allocated to it in line with the *Loi spéciale de financement*. The growth of the Regions' and Communities' primary expenditure slowed appreciably in 1996 and 1997, but between 1992 and 1997 their primary expenditure rose by 1 per cent of GDP. The improvement in the primary surplus of the public authorities as a whole is thus almost entirely attributable to the *Entité* I.

Figure 9. **Public finances in Belgium and the European Union**

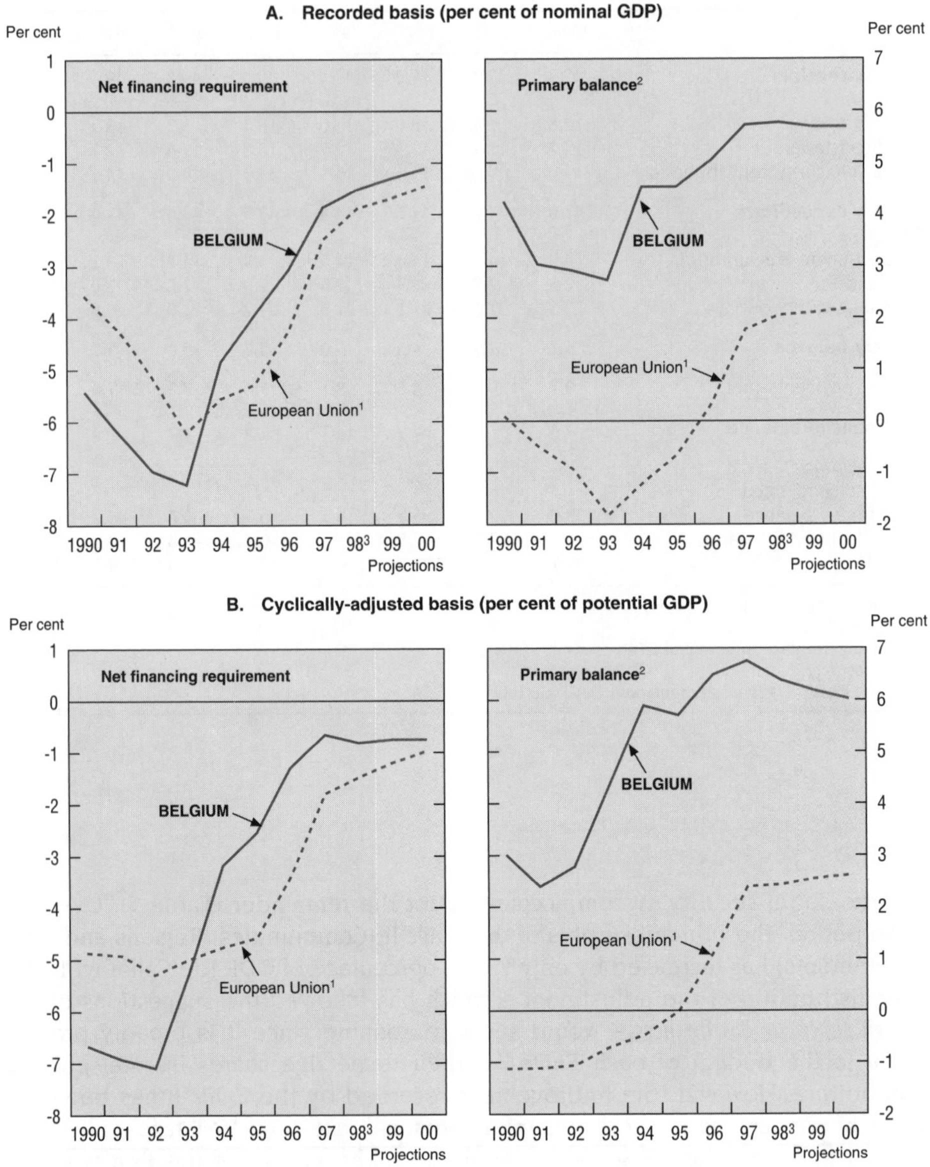

A.   Recorded basis (per cent of nominal GDP)

B.   Cyclically-adjusted basis (per cent of potential GDP)

1.   Excluding Belgium and Luxembourg.
2.   Excluding net interest payments.
3.   Estimates.
Source: OECD, *National Accounts* and OECD Secretariat.

Table 5.   **Fiscal consolidation since 1992[1]**

Per cent of GDP

	1992	1997	Change 1992-97
Entité I			
(Federal government and social security system)			
Total receipts	33.1	33.5	0.5
Primary expenditure	29.3	28.4	−0.9
Primary balance	3.8	5.1	1.4
Entité II			
(Communities, Regions and local governments)			
Total receipts	12.8	14.6	1.7
Primary expenditure	12.8	13.8	1.0
Primary balance	0.0	0.8	0.7

1.   These figures are on a budgetary basis.
Source: Ministry of Finance.

Despite these helpful budgetary developments, the weak point of Belgian public finances has remained the very high public debt as a percentage of GDP. But in this area, too, progress has begun. The authorities have succeeded in setting the debt/GDP ratio on a firmly declining trend – from 135 per cent in 1993 to 122 per cent in 1997. This declining trend has reflected the low level of the government deficit, the narrowing of the differential between the implicit interest rate on the public debt and the GDP growth rate, and the proceeds of privatisation[26] as well as asset management operations which were especially large and reached a total of nearly BF 370 billion in 1996 and 1997. The bulk of this sum (BF 222 billion) represented capital gains recorded by the central bank on previous gold sales which the government was entitled to by law.[27] A further BF 75 billion reduction in government debt resulted from government related agencies investing their excess liquidity in government bonds rather than in bank deposits. All considered, privatisation and asset management operations may have accounted for more than half the reduction in the debt/GDP ratio over the 1993-97 period.

The 1998 budget

The 1998 budget, presented in October 1997, rested, as in previous years, on a cautious macroeconomic scenario from the point of view of both expected growth (2.5 per cent) and the level of short-term interest rates. Because of this and owing to the size of the corrective effort carried out in the past few years and the better-than-expected results for 1997, only a few additional measures were required to offset higher expected spending in a few areas, such as health care and justice. The new measures – entailing both expenditure cuts and additional receipts – totalled BF 17 billion (or 0.2 per cent of GDP) and included: the extension of levies imposed in 1997 on pharmaceutical companies and electricity producers; and one-off initiatives such as the sale of a license for a third mobile phone operator. All considered, with the fiscal decisions embodied in the 1998 budget, the authorities expect Belgium to be one year ahead in the deficit reduction path set out in the new Convergence Plan and nearly two years ahead with respect to the reduction in the debt/GDP ratio.

With an estimated GDP growth rate somewhat higher than that assumed in the 1998 budget and significantly lower short-term interest rates – 3.6 per cent compared with 4.3 per cent in the budget – the OECD Secretariat estimates the general government deficit to have declined to 1.5 per cent of GDP in 1998, with the primary surplus remaining at around 5¾ per cent of GDP (or at around 6 per cent of GDP on the Belgian definition). On a cyclically-adjusted basis, however, both balances may have deteriorated slightly, due to the end of some one-off corrective measures. The debt-to-GDP ratio may have fallen from 122 per cent in 1997 to 117 per cent – with 80 per cent of the decline attributable to a structural improvement in public finances and 20 per cent to capital gains of some BF 90 billion on a new sale of gold by the National Bank of Belgium (9.6 million ounces) credited to the Treasury and used, as in 1997, to retire foreign currency denominated public debt.

The period 1999-2000

The 1999 budget, which was presented in October 1998, included no new major initiatives. Allowing for multi-annual measures announced in previous budgets, and in view of sustained economic growth, persistently low interest rates and the reduction in public debt, the OECD Secretariat expects the general government deficit to continue to decline – to only a little over 1 per cent of GDP in 2000. However, the primary surplus is projected to remain at around 5¾ per cent of GDP (or about 6 per cent of GDP on the Belgian definition) and, on a cyclically-adjusted basis, this balance may deteriorate slightly, reflecting the end of one-off corrective measures introduced in 1998. The debt-to-GDP ratio is expected to remain on a firmly declining trend, falling to less than 112 per cent of GDP in 2000.

Fiscal consolidation beyond 2000

A rapid reduction in the debt-to-GDP ratio is one of Belgium's policy priorities. To this end, the authorities have committed themselves to keeping the primary surplus (on the Belgian definition) at around 6 per cent of GDP in the medium term. As noted in the 1997 Survey (OECD, 1997, pp 46-47), given the high level of public debt and interest payments as a percentage of GDP, under reasonable assumptions concerning growth and interest rates, a large and broadly stable primary surplus will result in a positive interaction in the progressive reduction in the debt and interest payments as a percentage of GDP – the reverse of the so-called "snowball effect" – which will accelerate the reduction of the overall deficit. The Convergence Plan 1997-2000 introduced by the authorities in late 1996 as a follow-up to the Convergence Plan 1992-1996, provides a concrete medium-term framework for a further sizeable reduction of the deficit and debt levels. It shows that, under the macroeconomic assumptions used in the convergence reports of the European Commission and the European Monetary Institute,[28] the debt-to GDP ratio reaches 60 per cent between 2011 and 2015 – the exact date depending on whether the primary surplus is kept at 6 per cent of GDP until the debt reaches 60 per cent of GDP, or whether it is allowed to decline once the overall balance reaches a given level (equilibrium or a surplus of ½ or 1 per cent of GDP). In the first case, the debt/GDP ratio reaches 60 per cent in 2011: in the last three cases, it reaches that level in 2014, 2013 and 2012, respectively. As these scenarios show, the results are relatively insensitive to the exact interpretation of the commitment to keep the primary surplus at 6 per cent of GDP. The option of allowing it to decline progressively to prevent the overall balance from improving beyond a given level – say one-half of a per cent of GDP – would create valuable room for manoeuvre to meet spending pressure associated with population ageing and accommodate further tax cuts. A change in interest rate assumptions also has only a moderate impact on the results: for instance, an increase in the implicit interest rate on the public debt of 2 percentage points, other things being equal, results in the debt/GDP ratio reaching 60 per cent in 2017 rather than in 2011.

Given the already low level of the overall deficit – an estimated 1½ per cent of GDP in 1998 – and barring exceptional shocks, the commitment to a primary surplus of 6 per cent of GDP would seem more binding for Belgium than the EU's Stability and Growth Pact: this commitment can be expected to bring the overall balance into surplus already in a few years time, while in this area the purpose of the Pact is to prevent deficits from exceeding a level considered as excessive – 3 per cent of GDP – except in the case of economic recession and to bring, over the medium term, the budget balance towards equilibrium or into surplus (see Box 1). But, to avoid having to take corrective (*i.e.* restrictive) fiscal measures during an economic downturn, it would seem appropriate to aim for a somewhat higher surplus when the economy is going through a phase of cyclical overheating.

Another major problem in public finance is the lopsided composition of public expenditure. Especially in the early stage of fiscal consolidation in the 1980s, the burden of adjustment fell disproportionately on public investment. As a result, this item has averaged 1½ per cent of GDP over the past decade – nearly half the EU average and one of the lowest in the OECD area (Figure 10, Panel A).

Box 1. The EU's Stability and Growth Pact

The Pact for Stability and Growth, finalised at the Amsterdam Summit in June 1997, consists of two Council regulations. One clarifies the Maastricht Treaty's provisions for an Excessive Deficit Procedure and the other strengthens the surveillance and co-ordination of economic policies. The Pact also calls on participants in the monetary union to commit themselves to aim at a medium-term budgetary balance or at a surplus.

Avoiding excessive government deficits (above 3 per cent of GDP) is considered essential for the success of Economic and Monetary Union. The Maastricht Treaty already included a procedure aimed at discouraging, and reducing when one occurs, excessive deficits. The 3 per cent reference value, however, can be exceeded if: *i)* the origin of the excess lies outside the normal range of situations (exceptionality); *ii)* the excess is limited in time (temporariness); and *iii)* the excess is small enough for the deficit to remain close to the 3 per cent reference value (closeness). These three conditions need to apply simultaneously. The Treaty, however, does specify a precise interpretation of these constraints.

The Stability and Growth Pact gives a more specific interpretation of exceptionality and temporariness. For countries participating in monetary union, the Pact considers a general government deficit above 3 per cent as excessive unless the country is in economic recession. A recession is defined as an annual fall in real output (GDP) of at least 0.75 per cent. Implementation of the Excessive Deficit Procedure depends on the severity of the economic decline. If economic output in a Member State declines by 2 per cent or more, and provided the deficit is temporary, exemption from the Excessive Deficit Procedure is granted. In the event GDP falls by between 0.75 per cent and 2 per cent, exemption can be granted in special circumstances by the Council of Ministers. The country would need to convince the Council that the economic decline was "exceptional" in terms of its abruptness or in relation to past output trends.

Failure to adhere to the Pact could result in the imposition of sanctions. Initially, these would take the form of non-remunerated deposits starting at 0.2 per cent of GDP and a variable component rising in line with the size of the excessive deficit. Such deposits are limited to a maximum of 0.5 per cent of GDP, but would accumulate each year until the excessive deficit is eliminated. Provided the excessive deficit is corrected within two years the deposits are returned to the country. Otherwise, the deposits could ultimately be converted into a fine.

On the other hand, while it is difficult to perform reliable international comparisons of social expenditure, the fact remains that, according to the calculations of the OECD Secretariat, as a percentage of GDP, in Belgium the latter is above the EU and OECD averages (Figure 10, Panel B). To prevent a deterioration of physical infrastructure, and possibly to improve it, it would seem urgent to increase public investment while at the same time curbing social expenditure. There is thus a need to reduce spending on unemployment in all its forms, to step up the

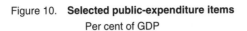

Figure 10.   **Selected public-expenditure items**
Per cent of GDP

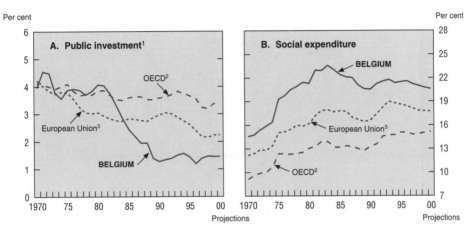

1.   Gross fixed capital formation.
2.   Excluding Belgium, Luxembourg, Hungary, Poland and Czech Republic.
3.   Excluding Belgium and Luxembourg.
Source: OECD, *National Accounts* and OECD Secretariat.

reform of public sector pensions, and to keep health expenditure under control even if it were decided to drop the "norm" limiting its annual growth in real terms to 1.5 per cent (Chapter IV).

III. Implementing structural reform: a review of progress

Introduction

Within the framework set out by the OECD *Jobs Study*, the 1997 OECD *Economic Survey of Belgium/Luxembourg* provided a set of detailed policy recommendations for Belgium (OECD, 1997, Chapter III and Box 1) to boost non-inflationary economic growth and improve the labour market performance – *i.e.* to increase the employment rate and reduce unemployment in all its forms. These recommendations were derived from a review of structural features of the Belgian economy which determine growth and the incidence of non-cyclical unemployment. The analysis emphasised that in Belgium, as in other European countries, the reasons for unsatisfactory labour market outcomes are multiple, deep-rooted and often interacting.

While the unemployment problem can be traced back to the 1970s, the two oil shocks and the economic, social and political conditions of that time, the persistence of high unemployment and its essentially structural character seem to have been due to a different set of factors, some of them peculiar to Belgium. The most important ones may have been the institutional rigidities and features of the labour market, social protection, and the educational system (broadly defined), which have resulted in a rather inflexible wage structure, heavy non-wage labour costs, insufficient incentives to work, and a lack of appropriate skills and qualifications, especially at the lower end of the market.

The 1997 *Survey* noted that over the previous few years the authorities had taken a large number of measures, but that not all of them had followed a sound and coherent blueprint. For instance, the reduction (albeit on a temporary and selective basis) of the age limit for early retirement, and, above all, initiatives encouraging the unemployed – especially those over 50 – to leave the labour force had been inconsistent with the goal of increasing labour force participation and the employment rate. Moreover, the 1996 law on employment and competitiveness had introduced new rigidities and increased the already considerable degree of government involvement in the labour market. The *Survey* argued that the complexity and long-lasting character of the unemployment and non-employment problems pointed to the need for a wide-ranging, multi-year strategy, integrating structural reforms in the labour market and the social security system with initiatives to make the whole economy more dynamic and responsive to change. Such a "package deal" was also desirable to exploit synergies resulting from the mutually reinforcing character of most of the required measures and to minimise the unavoidable cost of adjustment. Among the many specific suggestions, the *Survey* stressed the need to:

- make the wage formation system more flexible, especially at the microeconomic level, with a wider wage structure corresponding to differentials in skill and local conditions;
- reform the unemployment insurance scheme and, more generally, the welfare system to increase incentives to return to the active labour market for unemployed and other inactive persons in unemployment-related programmes;
- strengthen and broaden active labour market policies to provide persons in welfare programmes with the necessary guidance and qualifications – although for some persons in early retirement and for some older unemployed the only realistic alternative to inactivity could be work in special social-job programmes.

The *Survey* also pointed out that, while over the preceding years fiscal consolidation and, more generally, joining EMU from its inception had appropriately been the overriding priority of the Belgian authorities, it now seemed possible to shift progressively the focus of attention to the remaining major problem, namely non-employment. The OECD strategy was to be seen as a comprehensive set of first-best measures – a sort of blueprint for the future which would take time to implement fully. During the transition period, second-best measures would no doubt be adopted.[29] It was also emphasised that the strategy should pay due attention to political and social goals, as well as to country-specific factors – in the case of Belgium, the tradition of social consensus and equitable income distribution. Hence, calls for more wage flexibility, less generous social benefits, and a relaxation of employment protection were combined with suggestions to introduce in-work benefits, step up active labour market policies, and consider special social-job programmes for elderly persons on welfare.

The need for a bold and coherent programme of structural reform aimed at improving the functioning of the labour and product markets has been heightened by recent and prospective developments: due to robust growth, the economy is approaching its estimated potential while unemployment – broadly defined – is still high (Chapter I); and the introduction of EMU, combined with the necessity for Belgium to rapidly reduce the debt-to-GDP ratio (Chapter II), means that fiscal and, above all, monetary policy will largely be unavailable as instruments of economic policy, so that the burden of adjustment to changing economic conditions will primarily fall on the adaptability of the economy, and particularly the labour market. Hence, more than ever, structural reform is the key to higher non-inflationary growth, a sustainable reduction in unemployment, and an economy which can better adjust and adapt to EMU and global requirements.

Progress in structural reform[30]

Since the 1997 *Survey*, the Belgian authorities have pursued their efforts to improve labour market outcomes, operating within the Belgian "mind-frame" which they characterise as emphasising social consensus and the need to prevent the emergence of a class of "working poor" and social exclusion. In this connection, Belgium's poverty rate of 5.5 per cent is amongst the lowest in the OECD (UNDP, 1998). The Belgian authorities acknowledge that technological progress, globalisation, and EMU will require structural reforms in the labour, goods and services and capital markets. More recently, the government has focused its efforts in this area on the preparation of the Belgian National Action Plan for Employment (*Plan d'action belge pour l'emploi*) in connection with the European Employment guidelines. At the special Luxembourg Jobs Summit in November 1997, all EU members agreed to the introduction of 19 employment guidelines with a view to moving towards a more effective and focused European employment strategy. These guidelines are centred around four main themes (or "pillars"): improving employability, developing entrepreneurship, encouraging adaptability of businesses and their employees, and strengthening the policies for equal opportunities. The Belgian government has stated its intention to re-centre its strategy on preventing unemployment, as well as on training and active measures aimed at the reintegration of persons into the active labour force. To prepare the Plan, the government had extensive contacts (*concertation*) with Regions and Communities as well as with the social partners. It was, however, impossible to reach a global agreement with the social partners, and the Plan was finalised by the Belgian authorities. Most of the concrete measures included in the Plan are mentioned below, under the specific sub-headings used in the 1997 *Survey* (Box 2).

Increasing wage and labour cost flexibility

The authorities have made no attempt to revise directly arrangements concerning the administrative extension of sectoral wage agreements which, even when requested by both bargaining partners, force individual employers to set wages that may be at odds with productivity at the firm level, make it more

Box 2.   Implementing the OECD Jobs Strategy – an overview
of progress

Since the previous *Survey*, a number of policy measures in the spirit of the OECD Jobs Strategy have been either implemented or prepared. However, progress has been slow and uneven: a few important measures have not been considered.

Job strategy proposal	Action taken	OECD assessment/ recommendations

1. Increase wage and labour cost flexibility

– Encourage *greater wage differentiation* with respect to skills, sectors and firms.

– Relax arrangements concerning the administrative extension of *sectoral wage agreements and the statutory minimum wage.*

– Increase the use of "opening clauses", *sectoral wage scales at the statutory minimum wage level, and exceptions to the minimum wage for the various target groups.* – Introduce *in-work benefits* – such as a means-tested earned income tax credit – to preserve equity or social goals.	On all these specific points there has been little tangible progress. However, within the framework of the new law on employment and competitiveness, measures have recently been taken to introduce some flexibility, thereby potentially increasing the scope for wage differentiation.	The authorities should consider ways to progress with respect to these specific points, the ultimate goal remaining a phasing-out of the new law on employment and competitiveness and government involvement in the wage determination process in general.

(continued on next page)

OECD 1999

(continued)

Job strategy proposal	Action taken	OECD assessment/recommendations
– Continue to reduce *non-wage labour costs*, with new cuts targeted at the lower end of the labour market or at groups of persons with poor employment prospects (Maribel cuts targeted at the exposed sectors of the economy should be re-targeted at the lower end of the labour market).	Efforts in this direction have continued and, in the framework of the EU Action Plan for Employment, the government has decided on further cuts over the next six years, representing a total reduction in the average labour cost of 3.4 per cent. A large proportion of the existing and future cuts in employers' social security contributions will be consolidated in a unique scheme which will imply a linear, across-the-board reduction in social security contributions and the strengthening of the measures targeted at the lower end of the labour market (the Maribel measures have been reformed).	Fully implement these measures (as announced in the EU Action Plan for Employment).

2. Reform employment and related benefit systems

– Both the duration and level of *benefit entitlements* should be reduced to increase incentives to work.		
– *Job-search* controls and benefit *sanctions* need tightening, which requires better co-ordination between the federal body (ONEM) administering benefits and the regional placement services (VDAB, FOREM, and ORBEM).	No major initiatives have been taken since 1996 to reduce the duration and level of unemployment benefits or to tighten job-search controls and the application of benefit sanctions.	Explore ways to move forwards on all these fronts.

(continued on next page)

(continued)

Job strategy proposal	Action taken	OECD assessment/ recommendations
3. Increase working-time flexibility		
– *Special unemployment-related programmes* – such as *"pré-pensions"* and *"chômeurs âgés"* – should be tightened and progressively phased out. The age limit for early retirement should be raised.	The age limit for early retirement (*"pré-pension"*) has been raised, and now stands at 58 (with only a few exceptions).	Press for further increases in the age limit for early retirement.
– *Programmes which favour work sharing* – such as the part-time pre-retirement programme – can be accepted as a second best and for a transition period only, provided they are voluntary, do not increase labour costs, and support employment (in persons).	Measures have been taken to improve the social security position of part-time workers, and the Action Plan for Employment extends the right to take advantage of the special leave programme (*"interruption de carrière"*). Working time has been "annualised", so that seasonal fluctuations will no longer lead to overtime and additional costs for firms.	Continue and step up these efforts
4. Reform employment security provisions		
– *Employment protection* – which in Belgium is largely decided by the social partners – should be relaxed.	Employment protection has not been significantly relaxed, although restrictions on temporary work (*travail intérimaire*) have been reduced and fixed-term contracts made renewable.	Explore ways to ease further employment protection; for example, by allowing fixed-term contracts to be renewed on an unlimited basis.
– *Notice periods* should be shortened for white-collar workers.	No significant changes.	Shorten notice periods for white-collar workers.

(continued on next page)

(continued)

Job strategy proposal	Action taken	OECD assessment/ recommendations

5. Expand and enhance active labour market policies

– The *"plan d'accompagnement" and other programmes in charge of active policies* should be strengthened and broadened – for instance to include persons aged over 46 – to provide the necessary skills and guidance to persons affected by the suggested tightening of programmes for early retirement and older unemployed.	The Action Plan for Employment indicates that the *"plan d'accompagnement"* is to be strengthened to provide guidance to young unemployed – after six months of unemployment – and to long-term unemployed – after 12 months. A temporary cut in social security contributions will be offered to firms hiring these unemployed. Other measures have been taken: occupational transition programme, strengthening of the part-time work programme provided by local employment agencies, and Smet-jobs.	Broaden the *"plan d'accompagnement"* to include persons aged over 46. To increase the effectiveness of this plan, contact with job seekers should be more frequent and ways should be found to reduce problems arising from the distribution of responsibilities among the federal government, Communities, and Regions.
– Pursue recent efforts to *evaluate active labour market policies*.	Various official bodies, notably the Ministry of Employment and Labour, have continued their efforts to evaluate active labour market policies.	Continue these efforts.

(continued on next page)

(*continued*)

Job strategy proposal	Action taken	OECD assessment/ recommendations

6. Improve labour force skills and competences

– Reduce *failure at the secondary level of education*. – Monitor the *effectiveness of recent reforms* of the elementary and secondary education levels. – Initiate *further reforms* to complement ongoing efforts to simplify and clarify teaching goals; diversify curricula and teaching methods; and strengthen remedial education as an alternative to repeating years.	The Flemish government has recently started a major reform of secondary education, aiming at streamlining study options, enhancing guidance and counselling pupils, and better preparing teachers and school managers. At the primary level of education, the Flemish Community is especially interested in risk groups: it is improving the school admission policy for immigrants, and allocating additional staff to improve the educational opportunities of these pupils. The French Community has undertaken a reform of technical and vocational secondary education and also of general secondary education, in the first case defining skill profiles and developing teaching tools and, in the second, revising all the curricula in order to ensure uniform quality. In primary education, a plan targeting schools at risk has been implemented, with more teachers and more material assistance, while the children of illegal residents are able to attend school in the normal way.	Implement these reforms; monitor and assess their results.

(*continued on next page*)

(*continued*)

Job strategy proposal	Action taken	OECD assessment/ recommendations
– Further expand *apprenticeship training* through reinforced education-industry partnerships.	The system of industrial apprenticeship (offering part-time training and part-time work) has been extended and made less expensive for employers. As a counterpart to further cuts in employers social security contributions (mentioned above), the social partners have committed themselves to increasing expenditure on training. The regions have also taken measures relating to occupational training.	Fully implement these commitments, and consider whether the education-industry partnership concerning apprenticeship training could be further reinforced.

7. Enhance the creation and diffusion of technological know-how

– Improve the *financial infrastructure* which supports the commercialisation of private research, with a view to enhancing R&D and innovation.	The financial infrastructure has not changed substantially, but Flanders has introduced a "Guarantee Fund for Risk Investment" and Wallonia is expected to introduce a loan guarantee scheme to promote the commercialisation of R&D results.	Consider ways to further strengthen the financial infrastructure supporting the commercialisation of private research.
– Nurture an *entrepreneurial climate* by, among other things, cutting red tape at all levels of government, which seems to be especially cumbersome for SMEs.	The government has taken or is preparing a number of measures in this area, including: a legal package in favour of SMEs, and an Agency for Administrative Simplification to streamline existing legislation and assess the likely impact on business of any new proposed legislation.	Fully implement the announced measures and assess recent and future measures in this area.

(*continued on next page*)

(*continued*)

Job strategy proposal	Action taken	OECD assessment/ recommendations
8. Enhance product market competition		
– *Provide the recently established Competition Council and other relevant authorities with sufficient staff* to perform their statutory role in the implementation of the 1993 Competition Act.	The Competition Council has been given additional staff and resources, and the Competition Act has been revised to allow more emphasis to be put on protection against the abuse of economic power rather than on concentration.	Monitor and assess the results of these measures.
– *Entry conditions in the distribution sector should be liberalised*, diminishing the power currently exercised by incumbent shop-owners to limit new entry of outlets.	No significant changes.	Explore ways to move forwards on this front.
– *Rules on shop-opening hours should be relaxed*, to enhance both consumer choice and competition.	"Night shops" have been legalised but legislation in this area remains rather restrictive.	Rules on shop-opening hours should be relaxed further.
– *Reassess the regulatory framework* with a view to streamlining and liberalising existing rules.	As noted in point No. 7, an Agency for Administrative Simplification is to be introduced to streamline existing legislation and assess the likely impact on business of any new proposed legislation.	
– *Privatisation* of companies in which public ownership remains important – *i.e.* in telecommunications and air transport – should be pursued further.	Some progress has been recorded, but in the electricity sector there continue to be serious competition problems.	Continue with privatisation efforts in general, and more particularly explore ways to reduce Electrabel's near monopoly position in both the production and distribution of electricity.

difficult for new firms to break into established markets, and hence may prove detrimental to employment. "Opening clauses" allowing firms, under certain circumstances, to waive given provisions in collective contracts at the branch level, have reportedly been introduced in some manufacturing sectors but their effective use appears to be very marginal. Similarly, there seems to have been no significant relaxation of economy-wide and sector-wide minimum statutory wages[31] and effective wage floors stemming from the welfare system which may price a large number of low-skilled and young workers out of the market – although some new entrants who are less than 30 years old are allowed to start working at 90 per cent of the "normal" wage,[32] and minimum wages are differentiated by age, i.e. are lower for those under 21 years old.

Within the framework of the 1996 law on employment and competitiveness – which aims to limit, on an *ex ante* basis, the maximum increase in labour cost (compensation per employee) in the private sector to the expected weighted average increase in the three reference countries, *i.e.* Germany, France and the Netherlands[33] – three measures have been or are about to be introduced to increase wage differentiation, at least by allowing higher wages, thereby partly responding to the criticism that the new law increased rigidities at the micro level. The measures are:

- a profit-sharing scheme giving firms that have increased employment the right to grant an additional remuneration to their employees, over and above the economy-wide upper limit set for ordinary wage increases;
- a favourable tax and quasi-tax regime for stock options;
- and a favourable tax and quasi-tax regime in respect of the discount granted to employees when there is a new equity issue.

Moreover, in the Action Plan for Employment, the government has pledged to introduce a system of participation of employees in equity capital, and an equivalent system (savings account system) for small businesses.

The suggestion of lowering wages for low-skilled workers to price them back into the market is still regarded as largely unrealistic in Belgium. Hence, there has been little interest in exploring the possibility of combining this approach with the use of employment-conditional or in-work benefits – such as an earned income tax credit – to preserve equity or social goals. Admittedly, as noted in the 1997 *Survey*, for members of specific target groups – such as youngsters with no job experience and lacking the required work attitude or older long-term unemployed – it is probably unrealistic to count on market forces, even combined with active measures, to return most of them to the active labour force. It might be better to encourage some of them to be active, at least on a temporary basis, in special subsidised jobs, performing work of social interest combined, when appropriate, with some training. In this respect, the Belgian authorities have introduced a new programme which uses part of the normal unemployment benefit to subsidise jobs with low productivity (the so-called Smet-jobs). Another form of encouragement is the occupational transition programme in the non-market sector. In addition, the authorities have strengthened the programme allowing local employment agencies (Agences locales pour l'emploi) to offer part-time jobs with limited salaries to long-term unemployed (who retain their unemployment benefits). Other measures have been taken by the Regions and Communities.

The system of automatic wage indexation has not been modified. However, the authorities consider that its effects have been significantly curbed by the "global plan" of 1993, which removed tobacco, alcohol, petrol and diesel fuel from the price index used to calculate wages and social benefits. Moreover, in their view, the relevance of the indexation system has been further reduced by the law on employment and competitiveness which sets maximum rates of growth for labour costs in nominal terms. However, under the law on employment and competitiveness, indexation and the wage drift have "priority", at least in the short term – i.e. they are fully permitted even if they lead to wage increases above the limit set by the law. It remains to be seen how the system would work if, as a result of indexation and the wage drift, labour costs were to increase more than the maximum allowed by the law for a period of several years.[34]

A progressive reduction in non-wage labour costs has been the centrepiece of the government's labour market policy in recent years. These efforts, predating the National Action Plan, have been pursued, with cuts in employers' social security contributions targeted at specific labour market groups – i.e. low-wage workers, youths, and long-term unemployed – and partially compensated by increases in various special contributions on taxable income and indirect taxes (the so-called "alternative financing" of the social security system). Cuts in employers' contributions have reached some BF 60 billion a year, representing a reduction in the average labour cost of about 2 per cent. The Action Plan for Employment includes additional cuts in employers' contributions of BF 18 billion a year, representing a total reduction in the average labour cost of 3.4 per cent over six years (from 1999 to 2004). As a counterpart, the social partners are expected to take appropriate – but as yet not fully specified – measures to improve training and enhance employment. These new cuts will be consolidated with existing ones and extended to all wage-earners.[35] The new consolidated scheme will include: a general per worker cut in employers' social security contributions for all workers in all sectors; and an additional cut for low-wage workers. The temporary cuts targeted at specific groups – such as young unemployed and long-term unemployed – remain in force.

Reforming unemployment and related benefit systems

No major initiatives have been taken since 1996 to reduce the duration and level of unemployment benefits in order to increase incentives to work and enhance the employment of low-skilled workers. As noted in the 1997 Survey, the long duration of unemployment benefits remains a hallmark of the Belgian system[36] and, although benefits are frozen in real terms, the average measure of benefit entitlements is among the highest in the OECD area. Although initial replacement rates are not particularly high compared with other European countries, overall average rates are among the highest in the OECD area, according to standard calculations by the OECD Secretariat (OECD 1997, Belgium, p. 70 and Figure 17). However, these calculations by the OECD Secretariat are for unemployed with a rather long professional career (22 years). Calculations by the Belgian authorities for unemployed with a shorter career show lower levels of replacement rates. Earlier in the decade, the authorities focused their corrective efforts in this area on the use of article 80 which stipulates that, under certain conditions, beneficiaries can be suspended from receiving unemployment benefits if their unemployment spell is "abnormally long". The definition of an "abnormally long" spell was reduced (to 1½ times the average duration of unemployment in the local labour market) and the overall implementation of article 80 was tightened, resulting in the suspension of a significant number of persons from the unemployment scheme. But no further tightening has taken place in the recent period, and suspensions on account of "abnormally long" unemployment have declined. Article 80 still covers only a limited group – unemployed persons aged under 50 who are in a household with a second income earner (*cohabitant*) and have a combined income of more than BF 600 000 – and it allows for several exceptions.

The more effective use of article 80 earlier in the decade also allowed a sort of indirect control on job search with corresponding sanctions. This was an especially valuable aspect given the need for Belgium to strengthen direct surveillance of job search, availability rules, and sanctions through better co-operation and co-ordination between the federal body (ONEM) administering benefits and the regional placement services (VDAB, FOREM and ORBEM) – the long-standing position of the latter being that surveillance of job search is not their priority task.

Increasing working-time flexibility

The age limit for early retirement (*"pré-pension"*), which a few years ago had been reduced to 55 (under certain conditions), has been raised again, and now stands at 58 (with only a few exceptions). Measures have also been taken to improve the social security position of part-time workers, which should enhance both this type of work and part-time pre-retirement. Moreover, the Action Plan for Employment extends the right to take advantage of the special leave programme (*"interruption de carrière"*). These programmes which favour work sharing offer the advantage over other job-related programmes (such as *"pré-pension"* and *"chômeurs âgés"*) of keeping their members in contact with the labour market so that, in case of a sustained economic upturn, these part-time workers could easily resume a full-time status. Hence, although far from ideal, they may be acceptable as a second-best policy and for a transition period – *i.e.* until more appropriate measures can be implemented – provided they are voluntary and do not increase labour costs. Working time has been "annualised", so that seasonal fluctuations will no longer lead to overtime and additional costs for firms, and measures have been taken at Federal and regional level to encourage an overall reduction in working time. Finally, the government has asked the *Conseil supérieur de l'emploi* to consider how to increase the employment impact of measures encouraging worksharing – such as a reduction in working-time and an increased use of part-time jobs – and to review the experience in this area of France, Germany and the Netherlands.

Reforming employment security provisions

Employment protection – which in Belgium is largely decided by the social partners – has not been significantly relaxed, although restrictions on temporary work (*travail intérimaire*) have been reduced and the possibility of having successive contracts of limited duration has, after an experimental period, been made permanent.[37] As noted in Chapter I, temporary work has grown rapidly over the past couple of years. Notice periods for white-collar workers should be shortened.

Expanding and enhancing active labour market policies

As indicated in the Action Plan for Employment, the *plan d'accompagnement des chômeurs*, which is Belgium's main initiative in the area of active labour market policies, is to be strengthened. An agreement has been reached between the federal government, the regional governments, and the social partners on a comprehensive strategy to provide, through this plan, guidance to young unemployed – after six months of unemployment – and to long-term unemployed – after 12 months – directing them either to schooling, training and on-the-job experience programmes or to a job. A temporary cut in social security contributions will be offered to firms hiring these unemployed. Amongst other measures, mention should be made of the occupational transition programme, local employment agencies and Smet-jobs. While these initiatives are welcome, the effectiveness of the *plan d'accompagnement*, as noted by the Ministry of Employment and Labour (1997) in its valuable effort to monitor and evaluate labour market programmes, may continue to be hindered by the distribution of responsibilities among different levels of government which do not necessarily share the same priorities – the federal government and the social security system financing unemployment benefits and the *plan d'accompagnement*, the Communities being responsible for education and training, and the Regions for job search and employment (*i.e. placement des travailleurs*).

Improving labour force skills and competences

Both the French and Flemish Communities have pursued their efforts to correct the shortcomings of the educational system – broadly defined to include vocational education (apprenticeship programmes). The Flemish government has recently started a major reform of secondary education, aiming at streamlining study options, enhancing guidance and counselling of pupils, and better preparing teachers and school managers. Concerning the latter point, model job descriptions have been worked out for 14 different groups of jobs in secondary education. They can be used by individual schools to prepare job descriptions that fit their own educational and professional needs. Moreover, initial and in-service training programmes will be strengthened. As for the curriculum, by bringing together similar options in different fields of study and eliminating outdated and overlapping options it is hoped to achieve greater transparency in secondary education and allow more efficient guidance and counselling of pupils. With regard to guidance and counselling, the centres for psychological and medical counselling will be substantially reformed, integrating educational and career guidance with medical care – with the staff focusing on children at risk at specific points of transition during compulsory schooling. Finally, to meet some of the weaknesses of vocational education, the authorities intend to make this form of education more flexible, allowing pupils – especially those at risk – to proceed at their own pace and choose among various curricula. Concerning repeaters in secondary education in Flanders, a recent partial study covering the first half of the 1990s has shown a generally declining trend of repeaters as a proportion of total pupils.

The French Community has undertaken a comprehensive reform of its technical and vocational secondary education. The reform is based, first, on a definition, which was formulated jointly with representatives of the business community, of skills profiles reflecting the abilities that are expected of young graduates. Based on these profiles, pedagogical tools and banks of evaluation tests are being gradually constituted to ensure uniform quality. Henceforth, within the French Community, the same skills and the same diplomas as in the mainstream secondary system can be obtained through alternating classroom/workplace programmes, whose cost to employers has been cut in line with the learning model for the self-employed ("classes moyennes"). General secondary education is also being extensively reformed, with all curricula being reviewed in order to better ensure a similar level of study in all schools. Based on the new curricula, all programmes are to be reviewed and approved so as to be tailored to the new requirements. Teaching tools are to be pooled for all establishments. Basic education was given priority, with a multi-year reinvestment plan of over BF 4 billion. In co-operation with the Regions, the French Community is equipping all of its secondary schools with cybermedia classrooms as part of a multimedia plan. The underachievement rate, which had been particularly high in the French Community, reversed its downward trend, thanks in particular to the adoption by the lower secondary system of advancement by degree rather than annual promotion.

At the primary level of education, the Flemish Community is especially interested in risk groups: by enhancing local agreements on non-discrimination, the authorities intend to improve the school admission policy for immigrants. Schools with a large number of immigrants are allocated additional staff to improve the educational opportunities of these pupils. Also, more teachers have been hired and trained to enhance the transition of children at risk from nursery school to primary school. The French Community has instituted an aid programme targeting schools considered at risk, which are getting more educators and teachers, along with material assistance for refurbishment and for setting up libraries. The plan required an annual investment of BF 1 billion. Concerning the sensitive issue of children of illegal residents (the *"sans-papiers"*), the French Community has authorised and is providing the funding for such children to attend on an equal footing with its own citizens.

The national system of industrial apprenticeship (offering part-time training and part-time work) has recently been extended and made less expensive for employers. As noted above, in the framework of the Action Plan for Employment and as a counterpart to further cuts in social security contributions, the social partners have committed themselves to increase expenditure on training, and bring it up to the average level of the three major trading partners – Germany, France and the Netherlands.

Enhancing the creation and diffusion of technological know-how

With a view to improving the financial infrastructure which supports the commercialisation of private research, Flanders introduced in July 1997 a "Guarantee Fund for Risk Investment" to protect the capital of investors in future-oriented growth companies. Wallonia is expected shortly to introduce a loan guarantee scheme, endowed with some $25 million, to promote the commercialisation of R&D results. Also, a network has been installed in the four sectoral centres for research to inform enterprises about patent procedures and existing patents.

Several measures have been taken or are being prepared to cut red tape, nurture an entrepreneurial climate and promote small and medium-sized enterprises (SMEs). They include:

  – a legal package in favour of small businesses to relax the access to regulated professions, offer fiscal and financial incentives (also for R&D expenditure), and cut social security contributions for new recruitment;
  – an Agency for Administrative Simplification (under the direct supervision of the Prime Minister's office) to assess the likely administrative impact on business of any new proposed legislation, and streamline existing legislation and regulations;

- a "single administrative window" (*"guichet unique"*) for SMEs;
- a social security identity card to simplify the administration of the social security system and controls in this area;
- social and fiscal ruling, *i.e. ex ante* agreements between enterprises and the administration on social security and fiscal matters;
- a co-ordinating agency for foreign investors (Federal Agency for Foreign Investment), combined with streamlined procedures for foreign investors, and advice in this area at major diplomatic posts abroad;
- an *ex ante* tax treatment of stock options;
- non-taxable discounts – up to 20 per cent – for employees buying shares in their own company;
- and the introduction of a single identification number so that the information required can be put together in all the administrative data banks in such a way as to reduce the number and content of the forms to be filled in by companies.

Increasing product market competition

Increased competition in product markets is an essential component of the job strategy. This is especially true for Belgium, where reform in this area could enhance the movement of labour away from declining industries and firms and towards the most dynamic segments of the economy, thereby facilitating the easing of many restrictive labour market arrangements. Since April 1993, Belgium has had a strict and comprehensive competition legislation, on an equal footing with European Union law and the national law of most other Member countries. However, a lack of resources – among other things – seems to have prevented the Competition Council (*Conseil de la concurrence*) and the other relevant bodies to perform fully their statutory role in the implementation and supervision of the 1993 Competition Act. The Competition Council has taken relatively few decisions on practices that restrict competition, and has not always given its decisions within a reasonable period of time. Recently, the authorities have taken measures to correct this situation, providing the Competition Council and Competition Service with additional staff and resources. Also, the Competition Act has been revised to allow more emphasis to be put on protection against the abuse of economic power and other restrictive practices rather than on concentrations: to limit the potential number of concentration cases to be examined, the thresholds determining potentially unlawful concentration have been changed and will be applied only to activity in the Belgian market.

Little seems to have been done to liberalise entry conditions in distribution. As regards rules on shop-opening hours, they have been somewhat relaxed: "night shops" have been legalised and Sunday shop-opening has been allowed under certain conditions. But in this area too, the legislation remains rather restrictive. For instance, "night shops" cannot be open during the day.

Concerning privatisation, 25 per cent of the financial company ASLK/ CGER has been sold to Fortis and legislation has been introduced to sell the remaining 25 per cent public holding. Legal and regulatory decisions have been taken to allow the public sector airport operator (RVA/RLW) to merge with a private company – Brussels Airport Terminal Company (BATC) – and list the new company (BIAC) on the stock exchange. In the electricity sector there are serious competition problems since Electrabel has a near monopoly position and dominates all aspects of the industry, notably the production of electricity and its distribution. The authorities have recently taken measures transposing the European Directive on liberalisation of the electricity sector. A period of perhaps as much as ten years has been scheduled to allow for a progressive transition and adjustment to competitive conditions.

Assessment and scope for further action

The past year and a half has seen a number of developments which can be expected to improve the functioning of the labour and goods markets. On the whole, however, progress has been slow and rather uneven. This is not entirely surprising: OECD's job strategy was presented as a sort of blueprint for the future to get the discussion started, but which would take time to implement. Also, the approach adopted by the Belgian authorities has fitted into the European framework which, for the time being, does not cover, among other points, the wage determination process and incentives to work, and can thus largely be seen as a subset of the jobs strategy.[38] Within this EU framework, the Belgian authorities have continued to emphasise cuts in employers' social security contributions, appropriately focused on low-wage workers, combined with "active" measures – such as training and guidance. The cuts planned over the next six years are expected to bring employers' social security contributions fully in line with those of Germany, France and the Netherlands, on average – the target of the Belgian authorities. Given the continuing need for fiscal consolidation to reduce the debt-to-GDP ratio, the scope for further cuts seems rather limited, especially when compared with the size of the problem in the labour market.

It is true that recent macroeconomic outcomes in this area have been encouraging. Compensation per employee in the private sector has increased broadly in line with that in the three reference countries – Germany, France and the Netherlands – and the standardised unemployment rate has declined significantly and is below the EU average. But these results should not lead to complacency. The decline in unemployment has largely reflected cyclical developments, even if structural measures – such as cuts in non-wage labour costs – may have increased the labour content of growth; and the standardised unemployment rate, while below the EU average, is well above the OECD average and still high by historical standards. Moreover, the decline in the claimant-based unemploy-ment rate (national definition) has partly been the result of administrative deci-sions leading to the withdrawal of many old unemployed from the labour force – and hence from unemployment as commonly defined (see Chapter I). With persons in the early retirement programme and in other unemployment-related programmes, these old unemployed partly account for the low rate of employ-ment in Belgium. As for the modest increase in wage costs, this is not surprising given the law on employment and competitiveness. The 1997 Survey noted that the new law "should be much more binding than the previous one" (OECD, 1997, p. 86), i.e. the 1989 Law on Competitiveness.[39] But this macroeconomic wage moderation may come at a price – that is, the long-term danger of potentially large harmful effects arising from rigidities introduced by the law at the microeconomic level. Even if the profit-sharing scheme discussed above succeeds in introducing some upside flexibility, downside rigidity will remain unchecked. In addition to a misallocation of resources, this situation will progressively lead to pent-up tensions, with the risk of an excessive correction at a later stage. Hence, the law on employment and competitiveness should be progressively phased out before the slow-building and difficult-to-detect harmful microeconomic effects seriously threaten the working of the economy and undermine potential growth.

To prepare for a phasing out of the law on employment and competitive-ness without jeopardising wage moderation at the macroeconomic level, the focus of attention of employment policy should include, in addition to reducing non-wage labour costs, also freeing the wage formation process, especially at the low-wage end of the labour market. Virtually all the specific recommendations in this area presented in the 1997 Survey are still relevant. For instance, it was noted that several provisional measures could facilitate the transition to a more flexible wage formation process, allowing downward wage adjustments at the microeconomic level and thereby increasing the employment prospects for young people and other low-skilled workers: the social partners when negotiating collec-tive agreements should lower the minimum sectoral wage to the minimum statu-tory wage level; greater use could be made of "opening clauses"; and existing exemptions from the statutory minimum wage could be generalised to employers hiring various target groups – such as older persons, youngsters, or long-term unemployed. More generally, easing job protection rules and discontinuing the practice of administrative extension of collective agreements would help in reducing the power of insiders – i.e. persons with a job – in the wage determina-tion process and allow for more flexibility.

It was also stressed in the 1997 Survey that, to preserve social and equity objectives and avoid creating "working poor" while also strengthening work incen-tives, these job-creating measures should be accompanied by a reform of social protection. A combination of a wider wage distribution and in-work benefits – such as an earned income tax credit – could help to create employment opportunities for low-skilled workers and people who have prematurely withdrawn from the labour force, enhance incentives to work, and assure a minimum standard of living. The implications for public finance of a shift of persons from a passive benefit situation to low-paying jobs complemented by in-work benefits are difficult to calculate but, all considered, might well be positive in the medium term; and, anyway, returning these people to the active labour force is a priority, lest they become permanently unemployable because of age, obsolete qualifications, or a general loss of attitude to work. Nonetheless, given that virtually no OECD countries have yet experimented on a large scale with increased wage flexibility combined with in-work benefits, this approach should be followed in a pragmatic and flexible way; and since even earned income tax credits would raise effective marginal tax rates over a range of the income distribution, care should be taken to minimise the risk of "poverty traps" – i.e. circumstances in which workers earning low pay have little or no incentives to raise their earnings.

Current efforts to step up active labour market policies should be pursued. With a view to facilitating the return of some of the older persons currently in special unemployment-related programmes to the active labour force, the obligation to participate in the *plan d'accompagnement* should be extended to persons aged over 46; and to enhance the effectiveness of this plan, contact with job seekers should be more frequent and ways should be found to reduce problems arising from the specific Belgian administrative set-up, which requires a distribution of responsibilities among the federal government, Communities, and Regions. Moreover, as many older inactive persons with obsolete skills may be largely "unemployable" – i.e. it may be difficult to return them to the active labour force, regardless of their wage level – it might be appropriate to offer to some of them special subsidised jobs, performing work of social interest. For other target groups of persons who would otherwise also be "unemployable", such as youngsters with no job experience and lacking the required work attitude, the authorities have already introduced similar programmes on a rather limited scale. These could be extended progressively, and the jobs offered ought normally to be temporary and combined with training programmes.

As little progress has been recorded in reforming unemployment and related benefit systems, most of the recommendations presented in this area in the 1997 *Survey* remain valid. Efforts should be pursued to curb the duration of earnings-related unemployment benefits, if not through the use of article 80 – revised anew to widen its scope and speed up its application – then through other initiatives: co-operation and co-ordination between the federal body administering benefits (ONEM) and the regional placement services (VDAB, FOREM and ORBEM) have been strengthened with respect to active employment policy and may also be with respect to checks on availability; above all, however, job-search controls and the application of benefit sanctions should be stricter. Although sanctions in Belgium are severe compared with many other OECD countries, their application, for example in the case of refusal of suitable work, is ineffective for legal as well as institutional reasons. Moreover, the age limit for early retirement should be increased further and, more generally, ways should be explored to tighten or phase out special unemployment-related programmes, such as *"pré-pensions"* and *"chômeurs âgés"* – with the help of active policies and subsidised jobs.

For social and political reasons, increasing wage flexibility and redressing incentives to work has proved a difficult and slow process. It might thus be appropriate to concentrate policy efforts also on improving competition in product markets. For instance, the current licensing procedure for the establishment of shops acts as an excessive barrier to entry, favouring incumbent shop owners without necessarily advancing societal objectives in such areas as urban planning. Hence, entry conditions in the distribution sector should be liberalised; and rules on shop-opening hours should be relaxed further. These are two areas where the scope for improvement seems especially large, and where deregulation holds the promise not only of improving consumer choice and competition, but also of enhancing private sector job creation. This would facilitate the task of making the labour market more flexible which, in turn, is a crucial condition for reaping the full benefits of product market reform. Experience in other Member countries has shown that product market reform is likely to cause shocks to employment – positive in certain sectors and negative in others.[40]

In the electricity sector, EU directives will impose a certain amount of competition in 1999, but more will be required to put this sector on a solid competitive foundation. As a first step, the Committee for the Control of Electricity and Gas should be turned into an effective supervisory agency with a clear mandate to protect the interests of all consumers. The implementation of the decisions taken recently concerning the liberalisation of the electricity sector should have the effect of breaking up Electrabel's dominance in the areas of production and distribution – or, at the very least, making access to the transmission grid open and fair.

IV. The health care system

Introduction

The Belgian health care system has never been considered in depth by the EDRC. In 1992, a study by the Directorate for Education, Employment, Labour and Social Affairs (OECD, 1992) noted that the Belgian health system demonstrated many strengths: it provided comprehensive health insurance cover to the entire population, ensuring high levels of quality and equity; patients were free to choose both their insurer and their service provider; and, in comparison with neighbouring countries, Belgium seemed to achieve a similar performance in terms of health outcomes while spending a slightly lower share of its GDP. However, as in many other OECD countries, it is in the health sector that public spending has risen most rapidly in the 1980s and in the first half of the 1990s. The Belgian government has repeatedly taken measures to restrain the growth of expenditure in this sector, but the cost of health care and its financing has remained a major policy issue, and questions have increasingly been raised about the long-term viability of the system in its present form, especially in view of the expected impact of population ageing and the rapid introduction of new and more expensive medical technology. It may thus be appropriate to review in some detail the Belgian health care system, and consider how it could be reformed to strike a better balance between, on the one hand, the need to slow the rate of increase in expenditure and make the system more efficient and, on the other, the objective of preserving its characteristics of quality and equity, which are strongly supported by a large majority of Belgian society.

This chapter is divided into four sections. After presenting, in the first section, a brief overview of the historical evolution of the Belgian health system, its main features – in terms of institutional aspects and outcomes – are identified in the second section. The third section considers recent reform efforts and developments; and the final section discusses current and prospective problems, some major policy issues, and recommendations for further policy initiatives.

Historical overview

The key features of the Belgian health care system largely reflect decisions which were progressively taken in the period following the Second World War: the Law of 1963 completed the introduction of a compulsory public health insurance combined with a private system of delivery of health care based on independent medical practice, free choice of doctor and hospital, and (reimbursed) fee-for-service payment. The management and administration of health insurance was essentially entrusted to non-government non-profit organisations, *i.e.* mutual sickness funds or *mutualités*, with a large role for *concertation* – for instance between *mutualités* and doctors to determine fees and reimbursements. The role of government was limited to the regulation and partial funding of the system and to the pricing of drugs and the setting of hospital rules and budgets. The Law of 1963 was the result of a broad social consensus on the desirability of providing quality medical care to everybody on an equal basis, and ensuring a high degree of freedom of choice to both patients (in choosing their doctors) and providers (in deciding on the appropriate therapy).

In the hospital sector, the authorities took steps to curb the growth of expenditure as early as the mid-1980s. The continuing rapid increase in health costs, combined with the pressing need for fiscal consolidation, obliged the authorities to undertake a number of reforms – notably in 1992-93 – to curb the growth of public health spending, while preserving as much as possible the underlying principles of equity, freedom of choice, and quality of care. Hence, as discussed below, corrective efforts have focused on eliminating abuse and waste, and raising the efficiency of the system by increasing the cost-consciousness (*responsabilisation*) of all major players and modifying their behaviour. But corrective measures have also included a stringent "norm" limiting the annual growth of health care expenditure in real terms to 1.5 per cent, as well as the introduction of a few significant exceptions to the principle of fee-for-service and selective increases in the co-payment or cost-sharing of patients (*ticket modérateur*).

The process of federalisation of the country – which has taken place over the past two decades or so – has not greatly affected the compulsory health insurance system: being part of the social security system, it has remained the responsibility of the federal government. On the other hand, the responsibility for some other aspects of health care has been shifted to the Communities and Regions. These aspects include: preventive care, health education, and the implementation of various decisions initiated at the federal level – such as initiatives concerning the number and size of hospitals.

Main features of the system

Institutional aspects

Overview

A distinguishing characteristic of the Belgian health care system is that it combines compulsory, comprehensive, and universal public health insurance with patients' free choice and independent medical practice (*médecine libérale*). It rests on the solidarity principle, since, as a rule, contributions are proportional to participants' revenues – with no reference to the health risk – while reimbursements are equal for everyone – except for especially vulnerable social groups.[41] The compulsory health insurance scheme is an integral part of the Belgian social security system. It covers major risks for the whole population and minor risks for nearly 90 per cent of the population.[42] It is administrated by five *mutualités*,[43] a fund for the railways and one public fund, which are entrusted with the role of providing compulsory insurance, reimbursing fee-for-service payments, and other functions (see below). Patients pay for most ambulatory care and are reimbursed, in the proportion stipulated by law: for most consultations and most patients this proportion is 75 per cent, the remaining 25 per cent representing the co-payment. On the other hand, the bulk of hospital costs is paid directly by the *mutualités*, with only a token co-payment by patients.[44] There is free choice of doctors, and patients do not need to see a general practitioner before consulting a specialist – *i.e.* there is no "gatekeeper". The system is subject to extensive regulation by both the authorities (federal and regional) and the *mutualités* and provider organisations themselves (through self-regulation). The central government has the final responsibility for the level of contributions and reimbursement rates, as well as for the rules governing the relationship between the *mutualités* and the providers. Moreover, it has veto power over the level of fees, and plays a central role in negotiating drug prices. It is also responsible for the accreditation of doctors and nurses, and regulates the hospital sector (see below).

Since co-payment by patients represents only around 15 per cent of total costs, the main source of financing health care covered by compulsory insurance is public revenues, with social security contributions and general taxation accounting each for a little over 40 per cent, and some other minor sources – such as contributions from old-age pensions and taxes on car insurance – accounting for the remainder. With effect from 1995, however, the *"gestion globale"* (global management) of the social security system abolished the distinction between contributions and tax revenues for each branch of the social security taken separately. There are no longer, therefore, any specific contributions for health insurance, since this scheme is an integral part of the social security system.

In addition to compulsory health insurance, the *mutualités* offer voluntary health insurance for minor risks (out-patient care, etc.) for the self-employed, about 75 per cent of whom have such an insurance. The *mutualités* also offer complementary insurance to cover additional services for all of their affiliated members. This last segment of the insurance market has grown steadily over the past few years – from BF 8.3 billion in 1993 to BF 10.7 billion in 1996. Risk-based private health insurance offered by private for-profit companies is still very small compared with public health insurance but, like complementary insurance offered by the *mutualités*, it has grown steadily, especially for hospital costs, apparently reflecting some reduction in coverage and reimbursement in the compulsory scheme. Unlike *mutualités*, which are prevented by law from doing so, private insurance companies can offer cover for the proportion of medical expenses which the individual must pay under the compulsory insurance.[45] But apart from special situations or market niches, the possibility for private for-profit insurance companies to compete with *mutualités* on the market for complementary health insurance seems limited, given the tax-exempted status of the *mutualités* and their possibility of relying on economies of scale; and private for-profit insurance companies are excluded by law from the compulsory health insurance market. The turnover of private for-profit insurance companies has grown from BF 4.3 billion in 1993 to BF 6.2 billion in 1996. By comparison, outlays of the compulsory and voluntary public insurance schemes on account of current health expenditures amounted to over BF 440 billion in 1996.

The mutualités

The *mutualités* are organised mainly according to religious or political affiliations – a situation reflecting historical circumstances.[46] Membership in a *mutualité* is compulsory for most employees, self-employed and retired people, but the choice of *mutualité* is free. However, with the compulsory insurance cover offered and the contribution rates levied being determined by law – and hence identical – the *mutualités* have essentially a captive and non-contestable market in this segment of health insurance, and competition for new members centres on supplementary programmes, on geographical convenience, and on the quality of service delivery, such as the speed of settling claims. Nonetheless, competition is strong, partly because revenue to cover administrative costs depends on the size of the membership. As for the financing of the insurance cost (as distinct from the administrative cost) of the *mutualités*, to preserve solidarity, surpluses and deficits are effectively pooled by a special government agency responsible for health and disability insurance (*Institut national d'assurance maladie-invalidité* or INAMI).[47] In fact, reflecting different revenue and risk levels of their respective memberships, *mutualités* have significantly different capacities to earn contributions as well as different claim burdens. Deficits usually exceed surpluses and, by *ad hoc* government decisions, the net position is generally financed through subsidies. Over the years, cumulated deficits have become much larger than cumulated surpluses. While this approach provides little incentive for the *mutualités* to reduce overall costs, it explains why overt "cream skimming" – *i.e.* the selection of low-risk and high-income members by the *mutualités* – is largely non-existent. In addition to receiving their funds from it, the *mutualités* are also supervised by INAMI, which is itself administered by a general board composed of representatives of employers, employees, *mutualités*, and the government – with the latter having a power of veto over decisions. Health service providers are represented in an advisory capacity.

The fee schedule – the so-called "nomenclature" – on which reimbursement to patients is based, is negotiated each year in a system of medical *concertation* between representatives of the *mutualités* and the medical profession (*Commission médico-mutualiste*). In this case, as when bargaining with drug companies on pharmaceutical prices, the *mutualités* see themselves as representing the consumers. Since agreements must be approved by the government, this arrangement amounts to a bilateral monopoly supervised by the government. If more than 40 per cent of practitioners reject it, an agreement is not implemented, in which case the government has three possibilities:

- submit an alternative draft agreement to the practitioners;
- fix the fee levels for some or all of the services;
- fix the reimbursement levels, leaving the practitioners free to fix their own fees.

Reimbursement is generally 75 per cent of the negotiated fee,[48] except for the poor, the elderly and certain other social groups for which, as noted, above a certain yearly ceiling it is 100 per cent. Costs of hospital stay are fully covered by the compulsory national insurance (apart from a fixed and relatively modest daily co-payment for the part covered by insurance), with no distinction between private and public hospitals. However, costs of hospital stay and nursing care are strictly separated from costs of medical services (including laboratory and radiology services) which are covered by the negotiated fee schedule, with patients paying the co-insurance contributions.

Health care providers

Most physicians are independent and, with a few exceptions, paid on a fee-for-service basis. However, as noted, reimbursable fees are largely controlled by the government and set at the national level ("nomenclature"). Hence, competition among physicians is mainly of a non-price character. The "nomenclature" sets an effective price floor. The Order of Physicians considers pricing below the negotiated level unethical practice, and may even temporarily suspend non-abiding physicians from medical practice. On the other hand, there are no legal or "ethical" impediments to charging fees above the reimbursable level ("nomenclature"), and this is not unusual, especially for specialists and specialist hospital services (Nonneman and van Doorslaer, 1994), although it may not always be done in an entirely transparent way.

About 60 per cent of all Belgian hospitals are non-profit private institutions, and the remainder are public institutions.[49] Most of the private hospitals are owned by non-profit associations (ASBL – *Association Sans But Lucratif*) which originally had links with religious charitable orders, some 5 per cent are owned by the *mutualités*, and a small number by doctors (specialists). Entry into the market for hospital services is restricted by government regulation. To be reimbursed by the *mutualités* and subsidised by the Department of Public Health, a hospital must obtain a license to operate a certain number of beds in each specific category (intensive care, surgery, maternity, etc.). For the financing of their activities, hospitals rely on two major sources: first a prospective budget based on a standard cost per day[50] set annually for each hospital by the Department of Public Health; and second, fee-splitting arrangements with staff physicians. The standard cost per day is also the price per patient-day; it is paid directly to the hospital by the patient's *mutualité* which is itself 75 per cent financed by the INAMI and 25 per cent by the Department of Public Health. In addition, the patient pays to the hospital a fixed sum per day as a co-insurance contribution. The budget system is designed to contain hospitals' overall costs and promote efficiency (mainly through the calculation of the standard cost per day which, as noted above, is partly based on average costs of a representative sample of hospitals). Measures have been taken over the last few years to ensure a better division of resources between hospitals.

In addition to the licensing system, the government – in co-operation with Regional and Local authorities – controls overall hospital capacity through the financing of investment in this sector. The rules applying to the financing of investment are broadly the same for private and public hospitals.[51] In both cases, construction and renovation work has to be agreed by the Regional Ministry of Health, in which case the regional government, through a public subsidy, funds 60 per cent of the investment cost of public and private hospitals, with the remainder being funded by government-guaranteed loans.[52] Over the years, the government has used its control over the hospital sector, among other goals, to try and reduce the number of hospital beds, transforming some of them into less expensive nursing home beds.

As for the provision of longer-term medical care, the *mutualités* cover the cost of nursing care and help with daily activities in rest and nursing homes. They also cover the cost of care for persons who have been declared eligible for admission into homes for the elderly. In both cases, there are five categories of daily rates, depending on the degree of dependency. However, daily rates are somewhat lower for homes for the elderly.

Pharmaceuticals

Rules and regulations concerning the distribution of pharmaceuticals and the pharmaceutical industry are the responsibility of the federal government.

Hence, before their introduction on the Belgian market, the price of all drugs is set by the Ministry of Economic Affairs after consulting the Price Commission, on which are represented the social partners. Belgium is one of the last countries in Europe, with Luxembourg, with such an itemised price fixing. In addition, for drugs approved for reimbursement – *i.e.* meeting specific social and medical criteria – the price is also reviewed by a technical committee of the INAMI and made known to the pharmaceutical firm. When agreement has been reached on the price, the latter becomes a legal provision. For reimbursement purposes, drugs are divided into six categories. Drugs for the most serious pathologies are fully reimbursed: others have reimbursement rates of 75, 50, 40, 20 and 0 per cent.

Performance and costs

Health care spending[53]

Health care spending in Belgium is closely in line with that of other Member countries on average. Total health spending (around BF 660 billion) accounted for 7.6 per cent of GDP in 1997, exactly the same as the (unweighted) OECD average and very close to the EU average (7.9 per cent of GDP) (Figure 11). At around $1 700 (measured at purchasing power parity) per capita health expenditure was only marginally above the OECD average, and was close to the

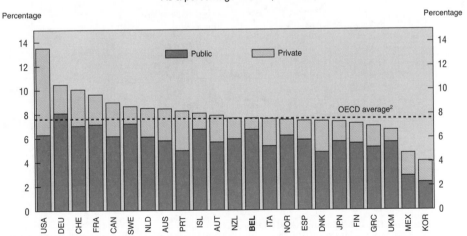

Figure 11. **Health expenditures in OECD countries**
As a percentage of GDP, 1997[1]

1. Total expenditure.
2. Unweighted average, 1996 for Turkey.
Source: OECD Health Data 98.

"expected" level, given Belgium's per capita income (Figure 12). On the other hand, Belgium has the smallest proportion of private health expenditure, which in 1997 represented only a little over 12 per cent of total health expenditure (or about 1 per cent of GDP).

Over the past few decades, nominal health spending (including investment) has grown very rapidly in Belgium, generally exceeding GDP growth by a significant margin. But this margin has varied considerably from decade to decade: after being rather narrow in the 1960s, especially compared with the OECD average, it widened sharply in the 1970s, before shrinking again in the 1980s and in 1990-97, when – at 0.3 percentage point – it was well below the OECD and EU averages (Table 6). Excluding investment, it is mainly expenditure for hospital

Figure 12. **Health expenditures and GDP per capita**
1997,[1] US$[2]

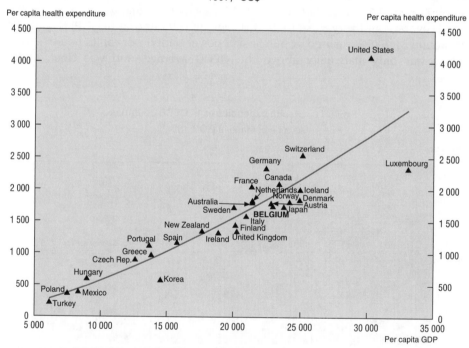

1. 1996 for Czech Republic, Hungary, Poland and Turkey.
2. Total expenditure on health care and GDP figures converted into US dollars at purchasing power parity exchange rates. The equation of the regression line is the following:
   LN (health expenditure per capita) = -7.17 + 1.47*LN (GDP per capita)
   R squared = 0.92   T: (-8.75) (17.54)
Source: OECD Health Data 98.

Table 6. **The growth of nominal health spending**[1]

	Annual average growth in excess of GDP				As a percentage of GDP	
	1960-70[2]	1970-80[2]	1980-90[2]	1990-97[2]	1960[2]	1997[2]
Belgium	**1.9**	**5.4**	**1.5**	**0.3**	**3.4**	**7.6**
United States	3.6	2.5	3.5	1.6	5.1	13.6
Japan	5.0	4.1	−0.8	2.8	3.0	7.3
Germany	2.9	3.8	−0.1	2.7	4.8	10.5
France	3.6	3.0	1.8	1.6	4.2	9.9
Italy	4.0	3.7	1.7	−1.0	3.6	7.6
United Kingdom	1.5	2.6	0.7	1.6	3.9	6.7
Canada	2.8	0.3	2.6	−0.1	5.4	9.0
Australia	1.9	3.0	0.8	0.3	5.0	8.5
Austria	2.3	4.2	−0.7	1.4	4.3	7.9
Czech Republic	..	..	..	6.5	5.0	7.0
Denmark	5.6	4.2	−0.7	−1.1	3.6	7.4
Finland	4.2	1.5	2.3	−1.5	3.9	7.2
Greece	3.8	0.9	2.0	8.7	2.4	7.0
Hungary	..	..	..	−0.2	6.6	6.5
Iceland	4.9	3.2	3.5	0.2	3.3	8.1
Ireland	3.8	6.0	−2.9	0.1	3.8	6.8
Korea	..	4.4	3.4	0.6	2.1	4.0
Luxembourg	..	5.8	0.6	1.0	3.7	7.0
Mexico	..	..	..	5.4	3.5	4.7
Netherlands	4.9	3.3	0.5	0.4	3.8	8.5
New Zealand	2.2	1.8	1.2	1.3	4.4	7.6
Norway	4.6	5.2	1.2	−0.6	2.9	7.5
Poland	..	..	..	3.2	4.4	5.2
Portugal	..	9.4	1.5	3.6	2.8	8.3
Spain	10.5	5.1	2.3	1.1	1.6	7.4
Sweden	4.8	3.0	−0.7	−0.3	4.7	8.6
Switzerland	5.1	3.5	2.0	3.0	3.2	10.1
Turkey	..	4.5	1.3	1.1	2.4	3.8
EU[3]	4.1	4.1	0.6	1.2	3.6	7.9
OECD[3]	4.0	3.8	1.1	1.5	3.8	7.6

1.   Including investment.
2.   Or nearest year available.
3.   Unweighted average.
Source: OECD *Health Data* 98.

and ambulatory care which has accounted for the rapid long-term growth of total health expenditure. Expenditure for pharmaceuticals, on average, has grown at a more moderate pace, and as a proportion of GDP has recorded little net change since 1970 (Figure 13). Restricting the analysis to the last 15 years and to current health expenditure of the public sector,[54] the share of hospital fees has declined

Figure 13. **Growth in health spending by category**[1]
Change in ratio to trend GDP (percentage points) 1970-97[2]

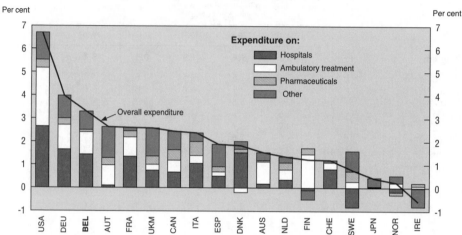

1. Current expenditure. For Ireland, Sweden and United Kingdom, public expenditure is used.
2. Or closest year available.
Source: OECD Health Data 98.

somewhat – from 28½ per cent of total expenditure in 1980 to 25½ per cent in 1995 – and the share of practitioners' fees (including clinical biology) has fallen more markedly – from 43 per cent to 33 per cent, with half the decline accounted for by a fall in the expenditure share of clinical biology. Over the same period, the share of expenditure for pharmaceuticals has first declined and then risen, showing virtually no net change (16½ per cent of the total); and the share of all other current health expenditure has risen from 12 to 25 per cent, partly reflecting rapidly growing expenditure for advanced medical technologies. As in several other OECD countries, these expenditure trends seem to reflect, at least in part, a substitution towards less costly components of health care in response to spending controls or constraints imposed on hospitals and certain medical acts, such as clinical biology. Indeed, in line with tendencies in other OECD countries, the average length of hospital stay has dropped – from nearly 21 days in 1977 to 11 days in 1996 – and both the number of hospital beds per inhabitant and their average occupancy rate have declined (Table 7).

The rapid growth in health care expenditure since 1970 has reflected many factors. Some of them – such as the progressive ageing of the population, the increase in the standard of living combined with the desire for better health care, the continuing development of expensive new medical techniques, and a more qualified and better paid medical staff – have been common to several

Table 7. **Hospital capacity and utilisation**

	Beds for 1 000 inhabitants		Average bed occupancy (per cent)		Average length of hospital stay (days)		Admission rate of population (per cent)	
	1970[1]	1996[1]	1970[1]	1996[1]	1970[1]	1996[1]	1970[1]	1996[1]
Belgium	**8.3**	**7.2**	**85.7**	**83.6**	**20.7**	**11.3**	**9.3**	**20.0**
United States	7.9	4.1	80.3	66.0	14.9	7.8	15.5	12.4
Japan	12.7	16.2	81.6	83.6	55.3	43.7	5.4	9.3
Germany	8.8	9.6	88.6	80.9	23.7	14.3	15.4	20.9
France	9.2	8.7	83.2	81.1	18.3	11.2	7.4	22.7
Italy	10.5	6.0	77.9	72.0	19.1	9.8	15.7	16.2
United Kingdom	9.4	4.5	82.1	80.6	25.7	9.8	10.9	23.1
Canada	7.0	5.1	80.4	84.2	11.5	12.0	16.5	12.5
Australia	11.4	8.7	83.0	82.9	..	15.5	..	16.9
Austria	10.8	9.2	86.4	78.8	22.2	10.5	15.5	25.1
Czech Republic	11.4	9.5	79.3	77.6	16.3	12.8	20.2	21.0
Denmark	8.1	4.9	80.6	81.3	18.1	7.3	14.4	19.8
Finland	15.1	9.2	91.0	87.7	24.4	11.6	18.2	25.7
Greece	6.2	5.0	76.0	69.4	15.0	8.2	10.5	15.0
Hungary	8.1	9.3	89.8	76.5	15.4	10.8	16.6	23.4
Iceland	13.0	14.8	98.3	84.0	28.3	16.8	16.4	28.0
Ireland	5.5	3.7	80.1	83.2	13.3	7.2	12.4	15.5
Korea	1.6	4.6	56.6	69.6	14.0	13.0	0.8	6.3
Luxembourg	12.6	10.7	82.6	75.0	27.0	15.3	13.4	19.4
Mexico	0.9	1.1	52.9	68.6	..	4.1	..	5.8
Netherlands	11.4	11.2	90.9	88.7	38.2	32.5	10.0	11.1
New Zealand	10.8	6.8	..	57.3	15.8	6.5	9.3	13.8
Norway	15.7	15.0	83.1	82.2	21.0	9.9	13.2	15.3
Poland	5.2	5.5	..	..	..	11.0	10.1	11.6
Portugal	6.3	4.1	74.1	73.9	23.8	9.8	6.9	11.4
Spain	4.7	4.0	69.0	76.7	18.0	11.0	7.1	10.0
Sweden	15.3	5.6	83.6	81.9	27.2	7.5	16.6	18.1
Switzerland	..	20.6	84.6	82.6	26.0	25.2	13.1	15.0
Turkey	2.0	2.5	52.0	57.4	9.0	6.3	4.2	6.3
EU[2]	9.5	6.9	82.1	79.7	22.3	11.8	12.2	18.3
OECD[2]	8.9	7.8	79.8	77.4	21.6	12.9	12.0	16.3

1. Or nearest year available. For Belgium, data refer to, respectively: 1970 and 1996; 1977 and 1995; 1977 and 1996; and 1970 and 1996.
2. Unweighted average.
Source: OECD *Health Data* 98.

OECD countries; but some other factors have been more specific to the Belgian health care system. In fact, especially until a few years ago, distorted incentives insufficiently countered by regulations seem to have encouraged excess supply conditions and over-consumption in various segments of the health care market. Even today, despite an increase in the co-payment for ambulatory care, patients may still have insufficient incentive to limit their demand; and since providers, with only a few albeit significant exceptions, are paid on a fee-for-service basis, they have strong incentives to expand service and induce demand. At the same time, the *mutualités* and the government have been rather successful in keeping medical fees and pharmaceutical prices relatively low by international standards. Hence, it has been said that Belgium has a "low price-high volume health system" (Nonneman and van Doorslaer, *op. cit.*, p. 1487).

Regional differences in medical consumption and expenditures per capita seem to be large in Belgium, even compared with a theoretical norm, *i.e.* after allowing for differences in patient characteristics such as age, income, labour market status, education and environmental factors (Schokkaert, Van Dongen and Dhaene, 1991). However, the latest report of the *Conseil général* of the INAMI (INAMI, 1996), notes that over the recent period there has been a convergence in the evolution of the average health cost per beneficiary in Flanders and Wallonia as compared with the national average. More importantly perhaps, the report stresses that differences in per capita medical consumption within regions are also very large and often larger than averages between regions.[55]

Performance

The relationship between spending on health care and the health status of the population is complex, being affected by many factors, some of them difficult to define and measure – *e.g.* life style. Moreover, the concept of health status is itself multi-dimensional and hard to quantify. Nonetheless, on the basis of various objective indicators, it would seem that the overall health status of the Belgian population has improved significantly over the past decade, although it remains about average compared with that of other Member countries.

Life expectancy at birth – which was 70 years for men and 77 years for women in 1982 – rose to 74 and 80 years, respectively, in 1997, ranking among the highest in the OECD area. Moreover, life expectancy is still increasing, and the differential between males and females has narrowed. On the other hand, while infant mortality has declined from 1.6 per 100 live births in 1975 to 0.8 in 1992, it remains above that of most other OECD countries; and perinatal mortality – at 0.8 per cent of total births in 1992 – is only about average by international standards (Figure 14, Panel A). The same is true for the Belgian performance in terms of the number of avoidable years of life lost under age 70 per 100 000 persons – around 6 700 for males and 3 800 for females in 1992 (Figure 14, Panel B). This is a useful indicator of health status and of outcomes of the health system since it represents the shortening of life expectancy due to avoidable or curable diseases. Measures have been taken in this area, but it is still too soon to assess

Figure 14. International comparison of health outcomes

A. Child mortality rates, 1992

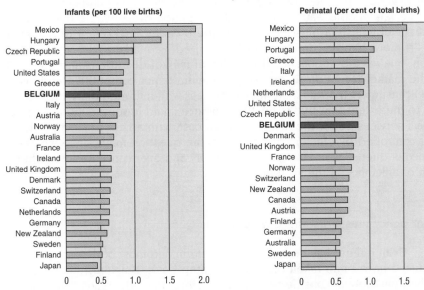

Infants (per 100 live births)

Mexico, Hungary, Czech Republic, Portugal, United States, Greece, **BELGIUM**, Italy, Austria, Norway, Australia, France, Ireland, United Kingdom, Denmark, Switzerland, Canada, Netherlands, Germany, New Zealand, Sweden, Finland, Japan

0   0.5   1.0   1.5   2.0

Perinatal (per cent of total births)

Mexico, Hungary, Portugal, Greece, Italy, Ireland, Netherlands, United States, Czech Republic, **BELGIUM**, Denmark, United Kingdom, France, Norway, Switzerland, New Zealand, Canada, Austria, Finland, Germany, Australia, Sweden, Japan

0   0.5   1.0   1.5   2.0

B. Potential years of lives lost, 1992 (per 100 000 persons aged under 70)

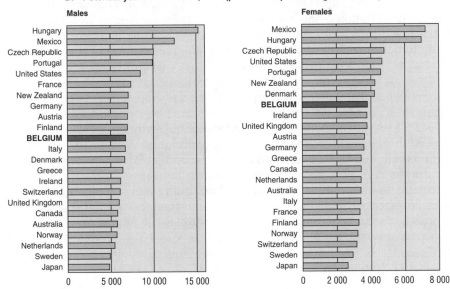

Males

Hungary, Mexico, Czech Republic, Portugal, United States, France, New Zealand, Germany, Austria, Finland, **BELGIUM**, Italy, Denmark, Greece, Ireland, Switzerland, United Kingdom, Canada, Australia, Norway, Netherlands, Sweden, Japan

0   5 000   10 000   15 000

Females

Mexico, Hungary, Czech Republic, United States, Portugal, New Zealand, Denmark, **BELGIUM**, Ireland, United Kingdom, Austria, Germany, Greece, Canada, Netherlands, Australia, Italy, France, Finland, Norway, Switzerland, Sweden, Japan

0   2 000   4 000   6 000   8 000

Source: OECD Health Data 98.

their effects. Finally, according to the authorities, broadly speaking, Belgium is not confronted with a problem of waiting lines for patients in the health sector: access to general practitioners seems to be particularly quick and convenient, and there are few people waiting for hospital in-patien care.[56] While the absence of queues is obviously a plus for patients, the broader assessment of this state of affairs is more complex. In a world with competitive markets and complete information, queues are unquestionably a sign of market distortions and inefficiency. But the market for medical services in Belgium is not competitive and, as elsewhere, consumers (patients) are inevitably less well-informed than doctors. Moreover, to the extent that public health insurance could lower the marginal price of medical services below the marginal social cost, with access to such services not being controlled by efficient mechanisms, the question might arise whether the absence of queues is not a sign of oversupply and over-consumption, rather than a sign of efficiency of the system.

Recent policy measures and developments

Even if there has been no overall reform and most of the many measures introduced have been taken on a step-by-step basis, Belgium's health care system has undergone considerable change since the mid-1980s. The first such changes concerned the hospital sector, with services reserved for acute and chronic cases and psychiatric beds being reorganised or rationalised, while the method of allocation of the hospital budget was fundamentally overhauled. Other specific measures were also taken. For instance, starting in 1985, attempts were made to better control what seemed to be an excessive use of diagnosis testing (clinical biology). A national budget for this item was introduced, combined with a data management system to identify high prescribers. In 1989, the fee-for-service system for hospital patients was replaced by a daily rate and a fee per admission; and in 1992, a new system for out-patient tests was introduced, with sharply reduced fees, strict monitoring of individual prescription behaviour, and the request that heavy prescribers provide an explanation. Also, in 1990, the government was allowed by Parliament to fix a global budget for health care expenditure with, in the case of target overruns, obligatory corrective mechanisms – such as automatic downward fee adjustment and obligatory refunding by high-cost providers. In practice, however, the automatic adjustments were not respected. This approach consisting of direct government control in the form of fixed budgets and sanctions brought expenditure in this area reasonably under control: gross inefficiencies by over-prescribing for certain special cases were curbed, if not eliminated (Nonneman and van Doorslaer, *op. cit.*, p. 1490).

The economic environment deteriorated seriously around 1993 and, with Belgium wanting to meet the criteria for membership of the European Monetary Union, the government introduced a "global plan" for employment, competitiveness and the social security system. In this last area, confronted, on the one hand, with a new acceleration in the growth of spending and, on the other, with the imperative need to resume fiscal consolidation after an increase in the budget deficit during the economic downturn of 1993, the plan aimed at cutting social security expenditure and increasing revenues. As regards health care, corrective measures centred on the introduction of a "growth norm", limiting the annual increase in expenditure to 1.5 per cent in real terms, starting in 1995.[57] The "norm" determines a global budget for health care expenditure as well as budgets or targets for sub-sectors ("enveloppes budgétaires"). Its implementation is monitored closely – i.e. on a quarterly basis – with the automatic activation of corrective measures – such as the adjustment of fees and rates of reimbursement – in the case of target overruns. The "norm", however, allows a certain degree of flexibility: for instance, it excludes some exceptional or specific expenditures – such as increases in salaries granted to health care personnel, and epidemics – and the triggering of automatic corrective measures is not, in principle, aimed at ensuring the respect of the "norm" within the year itself, but generally for the following year, except in certain sectors.

In addition, the 1993 reform aimed at increasing the cost-consciousness and cost-participation (responsabilisation) as well as the supervision of all major players in order to modify their behaviour and reduce unnecessary consumption of medical acts and pharmaceuticals. In the case of service providers, this was to be achieved through the so-called "medical profiles" (profils médicaux) about services and prescriptions by individual doctors, so as to detect obvious abuse, and a more extensive use of the budget technique for clinical biology. Patients' behaviour was to be affected mainly through a selective increase in co-payments, and health funds (mutualités) were to be made more financially responsible for health expenditure. After long negotiations, in mid-1994 it was decided that starting in 1995, mutualités would be progressively more responsible for their budget shortfalls, in line with the following time schedule:[58]

    1995-96   15 per cent of the shortfalls;
    1997-98   20 per cent of the shortfalls;
    from 1999   25 per cent of the shortfalls.

However, mutualités would not be responsible for shortfalls caused by "exogenous factors", such as lower income received from the social security sector, increases in health expenditure due to wage increases granted to nursing staff and epidemics. The mutualités were left free to decide how they would finance their share of any shortfalls, with an increase in contributions being considered as the most likely solution. As a result of these arrangements, mutualités were expected, in their bilateral negotiations, to press health providers to contain expenditure, thereby reducing the risk of budget shortfalls. That said, the cost participation of the mutualités is both partial and asymmetric.[59]

To mitigate the impact of the increase in co-payments and preserve as much as possible the principle of free access to health care to everyone, the government took a number of accompanying measures, including:

- a widening of the definition of especially vulnerable social groups – originally widows, invalids, pensioners and orphans (VIPO) whose incomes do not exceed a certain amount – enjoying special treatment concerning co-payments;
- the introduction of yearly co-payment ceilings for especially vulnerable social groups (*franchise sociale et fiscale*) above which patients pay no co-payments (see note 41).

Despite these corrective efforts, expenditure for public health increased rapidly in 1996, exceeding the "norm" by a large margin, partly as a result of accounting factors – a shift of some expenditure from 1995 to 1996 – and a flu epidemic. A number of new measures – some of them of a structural character – were thus taken in September and December 1996, as well as in March 1997 and in the 1998 budget. Most of these measures represented selective cuts in medical fees, tariffs and *forfaits* but they also included levies on pharmaceutical companies. Provisional figures show that the "norm" was respected in 1997, but a new overrun is expected in 1998 (with a deficit in the health insurance scheme of nearly BF 8 billion).

In early 1998, reacting to an initiative of the authorities to limit doctors' fee supplements in hospital wards with two or more beds, the medical profession, through one of its unions (Absym), declared the 1998 fee schedule no longer in force, thereby ending the so-called *Pax medica*. The fee schedule ("nomenclature") had been negotiated, as every year, by representatives of the medical profession and the *mutualités* (*Commission médico-mutualiste*). This decision of the medical profession gave practitioners the possibility of setting their fees on an entirely free basis – albeit with an unchanged level of reimbursements. For the time being, however, the majority of members of the medical profession have not taken advantage of this possibility. While discussions and initiatives aiming at restoring the *Pax medica* have continued, the government has formed several working groups to examine the supply structure and interrelations within that structure in the health system.

The task ahead

Current and expected problems

The Belgian health care system, as already noted, has many positive features which make it especially attractive for patients. Patients are provided with a comprehensive solidarity-based insurance coverage, receive good service, and are subject to only modest co-payments; they are also free to choose their doctors, as well as their insurer; and, under a largely fee-for-service system, they can demand almost any treatment. But these very features, combined with independent medical practice (*médecine libérale*), create a weak or distorted pattern of incentives which are not sufficiently countered by government control and self-regulation by the medical profession. This makes the system vulnerable to abuse and inefficiency, resulting in over-consumption and unnecessary expenditure.

According to the authorities, there is an over-supply of hospital beds, doctors, dentists, physiotherapists and pharmacists – a situation which may contribute to unnecessary medical acts and an over-consumption of pharmaceuticals. Available evidence largely confirms this assessment. At 3.4 per 1 000 inhabitants, the number of physicians in Belgium in 1995 was above the EU and OECD averages – 3.1 and 2.8, respectively – and the fifth highest in the OECD area (Table 8). Moreover, in the ambulatory sector, the number of contacts with physicians, at 8.0 (per capita and per year), was also high by international standards. As for the consumption of pharmaceuticals, expenditure per capita was among the highest in the OECD area in 1996, although prescriptions per capita were below the EU and OECD averages in 1993, and average hospital bed occupancy was above these averages in 1995. Finally, both the number of hospital beds per inhabitant and the average length of hospital stay were broadly in line with international standards (Table 7).

The structural shortcomings discussed above may help explain the difficulty encountered by the authorities in their efforts to restrain the growth of health spending. Combined with other factors, they make the outlook of the health care system especially uncertain. In fact, in coming years, health expenditure can be expected to continue to be buoyed by several factors, including: the desire for better health care partly related to a rising standard of living;[60] the cost of more highly qualified medical personnel; and the introduction of new expensive medical technology. Moreover, the impact of population ageing is projected to increase, accentuating the demand for medical care (Lambrecht, 1997; Fasquelle and Weemaes, 1997).

At the same time, the authorities see little likelihood of revenue rising more than as a result of the positive effects deriving from economic growth and higher employment: on the one hand, there is a pressing need to pursue fiscal consolidation and rapidly reduce the debt-to-GDP ratio (see Chapter II); on the other, the government wants to cut social security contributions further to reduce labour costs and promote employment of low-skilled workers. Since "alternative financing" – *i.e.* taxes and other revenues which do not directly affect the cost of labour – can hardly be expected to provide sufficient additional revenues, the equilibrium of the social security system could mean either allocating the savings made in other social security sectors or in interest payments to the health care

Table 8. **Indicators of resource use in the health sector**

	Average growth (number of physicians)		Physicians per 1 000 inhabitants	Proportion of specialists	Ambulatory sector		
					Contacts with physicians, per capita per year	Prescriptions per capita	Total expenditure on pharmaceuticals per capita[2]
	1970-80[1]	1980-96[1]	1996[1]	1996[1]	1996[1]	1996[1]	1996[1]
Belgium	**4.8**	**2.8**	**3.4**	**46.9**	**8.0**	**10.4**	**306**
United States	3.6	2.8	2.6	50.0	6.0	6.5	344
Japan	2.8	2.9	1.8	..	15.8	..	349
Germany	3.4	4.4	3.4	62.6	6.4	13.5	289
France	5.2	3.1	2.9	50.2	6.3	52.0	337
Italy	9.8	4.8	5.5	..	11.0	21.1	284
United Kingdom	2.7	1.7	1.6	..	5.9	9.3	218
Canada	3.6	2.2	2.1	42.4	6.8	16.1	258
Australia	4.9	3.5	2.5	36.4	6.6	9.6	202
Austria	2.0	3.8	2.8	54.4	6.3	17.2	247
Czech Republic	2.7	1.5	2.9	74.4	..	32.1	234
Denmark	4.9	2.2	2.9	..	5.3	7.4	165
Finland	6.8	3.6	2.9	56.3	4.3	6.3	209
Greece	5.1	3.8	3.9	55.7	5.3	9.0	236
Hungary	4.0	2.2	4.2	64.4	14.8	28.6	172
Iceland	5.3	3.6	3.0	..	4.8	16.4	312
Ireland	2.5	3.4	2.1	..	6.6	13.5	126
Korea	..	7.0	1.2	63.2	9.5	..	..
Luxembourg	4.9	2.6	2.2	64.4	..	14.5	250
Mexico	..	5.5	1.5	45.8	2.2	..	32
Netherlands	5.2	3.4	2.6	35.8	5.4	8.0	193
New Zealand	5.3	2.8	2.1	30.4	3.8	8.8	214
Norway	4.2	2.8	2.8	62.9	3.8	6.9	174
Poland	3.2	2.3	2.4	..	5.4	..	..
Portugal	9.0	2.8	3.0	68.6	3.2	19.8	282
Spain	6.6	4.2	4.2	..	6.2	26.5	223
Sweden	5.7	2.5	3.1	71.1	2.9	6.4	218
Switzerland	5.4	2.6	3.2	35.7	11.0	19.0	190
Turkey	7.0	6.5	1.1	42.1	1.0	..	60
EU[3]	5.2	3.3	3.1	56.6	5.9	15.7	239
OECD[3]	4.8	3.3	2.8	53.0	6.5	15.8	227

1.   Or nearest year available. For Belgium, date refer to, respectively: 1971-80; 1980-95; 1995; 1995; 1993; 1993 and
     1996.
2.   Figures converted into US dollars at purchasing power parity exchange rates.
3.   Unweighted average.
Source: OECD *Health Data* 98.

sector, or reducing expenditure. Raising patients' co-payments could reduce
health expenditure or, at least the financing need of the compulsory health
insurance scheme. But here too the authorities believe that the room for

manoeuvre is very limited: international evidence shows that the demand for medical acts is generally rather price inelastic; and, for equity reasons, an increase in co-payments would, no doubt, be combined with extensive exceptions for vulnerable social groups.

Finally, the "growth norm" cannot be a permanent instrument of health care cost control since it has little if any relation to any notion of efficiency or optimality. It was introduced as a temporary measure to curb health expenditure and ensure further fiscal consolidation. It needs to be replaced by measures based more on cost benefit analysis or appropriate incentives.

The need for further initiatives

Without the "norm" and with the spontaneous trend growth of expenditure likely to exceed that of revenues, the health care system in its present form may not be sustainable over the longer term. But the degree of uncertainty is very high. In addition to the variables already mentioned, the outcome will also depend on a number of more general considerations, including: the overall economic context and particularly the rate of growth of real GDP; progress in correcting the employment/unemployment problem which could have a major impact on the financial position of the social security system; and socio-political decisions concerning the share of social security expenditure or even total public expenditure to be allocated to the health sector. Without taking a firm view on any of these points or on any specific scenarios, it would seem prudent to prepare for a progressive squeeze of resources in the health sector, and take appropriate structural measures to curb expenditure, especially in view of the desirability of dropping the "growth norm".

The authorities broadly agree on the need for reforming the health system but, given the special characteristics of health care – notably the difficulty that consumers have in making informed choices – and country-specific considerations, they strongly favour remaining within the existing framework of largely non-market arrangements, continuing to rely on *concertation* among major players, under the supervision and ultimate management of the government. The stated aim is to ensure that the Belgian health care system will continue to reconcile the principles of solidarity, quality of care, and freedom of choice at a reasonable cost (compared with other OECD countries). For the time being, the authorities envisage continuing with the recent approach, implementing gradual changes by expanding or complementing initiatives which have already been introduced. This approach largely relies on: the *responsabilisation* of all the major players with respect to the cost of health care; "peer pressure" on doctors and other care providers; and a large number of rules and regulations to curb expenditure – including stricter controls on the supply of hospital beds, doctors, dentists and certain other care providers, and a wider use of *forfaits* (*i.e.* fixed amounts) for medical institutions, single patients and specific medical acts. To foster progress in all these directions, the authorities count on closer collaboration between various relevant institutions – notably between the Public Health Administration (*Administration de la santé publique*) and the INAMI – as well as on better information and statistical data – hence their commitment to develop PHARMANET and other medical data banks, and to introduce a *"dossier médical centralisé"* (central medical file).

Through rules and regulations, the focus is on limiting as much as possible inefficiencies resulting from the distorted pattern of incentives implicit in the basic institutional structure of the system; relatively little is planned to modify these incentives and the structure of the system through the injection of more competition or other market forces – such as a further increase in co-payments. The authorities and apparently also a large majority of the Belgian "establishment", if not of the population at large, consider managed care – especially in the form implemented in the United States by for-profit health-maintenance organisations (HMOs) – to be alien to Belgian aspirations and inconsistent with the existing institutional framework. Yet, over the past few years, the Belgian health care system has arguably moved in the direction of a form of managed care, albeit an opaque one, based on solidarity, with a national pooling of risk and under the ultimate management of the government. In fact, as noted, the aim of the norm is to determine the total amount to be spent by the public sector on health care *ex ante* on the basis of resources available, rather than *ex post* on the basis of perceived need and actual expenditure; and the allocation of this pre-determined total amount is done using techniques such as budgets for specific health institutions (*e.g.* hospitals and nursing homes), *forfaits* for special diseases or medical acts, and the requirement that to be sure of reimbursement patients obtain the permission (from their *mutualité*) before undergoing an expensive operation or treatment.[61]

Some of the corrective measures currently considered by the authorities – notably a wider use of *forfaits*, reliance on "peer reviews", and the introduction of a *"dossier médical centralisé"*[62] – seem promising or, at least, may be worth exploring. Through a reduction of unnecessary medical acts, they could lead to significant savings. Other measures – such as better information and the *responsabilisation* of all parties – may also be tried but, unless they are translated into concrete guidelines or cost/price incentives, can hardly be seen as more than ancillary initiatives. Considering the current approach as a whole, it remains to be seen whether, over the longer term, it will be sufficient to broadly equate expenditure and revenue. The outcome will depend, among other factors, on difficult-to-quantify technical and medical considerations – such as the scope for a wider use of *"forfaits"* for specific pathologies or medical acts, and the related potential savings. It is also uncertain whether the Belgian system of *concertation*, which worked reasonably well in the past when health expenditure was allowed to grow rapidly, can be relied upon to strongly curb expenditure and allocate it among competing claims. While recent friction between doctors and *mutualités* and the end of the *Pax medica* may be just a temporary aberration, they may also be an indication of things to come.

Unfortunately, there is no theoretical reference model in the realm of health care, in part because one feature of the market is that consumers (patients) are imperfectly informed. In practice, models are fairly different from one country to another, and it would be dangerous to conclude that techniques that seem to work relatively well in one country could be used just as successfully in others. Market-oriented measures are no panacea in this area; admittedly, they are often used to curb the growth of health care expenditure, but they may conflict with the principle of equity or equality of treatment, and even their effectiveness is not always proven. However, the Belgian authorities might envisage taking market-oriented measures on a strictly limited basis, and only as a complement to their administrative system, taking care that this does not unduly weaken the principle of equity or equality of treatment in the public health care system. Of course, decisions on the efficiency/equity trade-off require value judgements which ultimately belong to the socio-political realm, rather than to economics. Nonetheless, if the sustainability of the Belgian health care system is in doubt and difficult decisions need to be taken, a more appropriate pattern of incentives could significantly facilitate the adjustment by reducing waste and inefficiency. Moreover, insofar as risk-based private insurance and *forfaits* already exist in the Belgian health care system, a further modest reduction of the set of medical services covered by the compulsory health insurance scheme – with greater latitude for additional coverage by *mutualités* or risk-based private insurance – combined with the introduction of capitation payments to curb the growth of spending under the existing fee-for-service system, would be more a question of degree than of principle.

To allow private for-profit insurers to provide an efficient complement to public compulsory insurance would require a level playing field in the provision of health care insurance, a situation which currently does not exist since the *mutualités*, which also offer supplementary health insurance, are not subject to various taxes paid by private insurance companies. Moreover, with regard to the provision of compulsory public insurance, it might be useful to consider whether *mutualités* should be allowed to compete on the basis of contribution rates – possibly with no right to reject applicants, in order to avoid "cream skimming". This approach may be more conducive to efficiency in the provision of medical care than the current system where, with the service package as well as contributions and reimbursement rates fixed and identical for all *mutualités*, the latter compete merely in terms of peripheral services for their members – such as holiday camps, etc. Moreover, to clarify their role, avoid conflicts of interest, and enhance competition, *mutualités* should no longer be allowed to act, directly or indirectly, as providers of medical care through their ownership or control of hospitals and pharmacies, even though such activities may give them a better understanding of the area they are dealing with.

A limitation of patient's "free choice" – defined not just as the ability to choose their practitioner, but also to ask for virtually any kind of treatment – may be necessary to minimise excessive use of what appears to consumers to be a nearly free health service. This "moral hazard" issue is particularly important for a health insurance scheme relying on solidarity finance; and since the health care market is characterised by imperfect knowledge on the side of the customers (the patients), a limitation of freedom of choice may not necessarily entail a reduction in effectiveness and quality of treatment, or in welfare. To keep a balanced approach, such a limitation of choice may best be achieved by experimenting with a combination of new regulations and techniques, including: a more extensive use of *forfaits* (as also envisaged by the authorities); capitation fees; and, possibly, the "gatekeeper" technique. With respect to the latter, however, there are pros and cons, and the net effect may be small. On the one hand, the "gatekeeper" system may enhance efficiency by preventing patients from seeing the wrong specialist or from seeing a specialist unnecessarily; on the other hand, it may increase the number of overall contacts with doctors as well as expenditure, since to see a specialist a patient in this case has to see a generalist first.

A more extensive use of *forfaits* may require an increase in resources – in terms of staff and expertise – of relevant public bodies to allow them to provide the necessary guidelines and monitor their implementation. This is likely to be a demanding task since technological progress will probably require guidelines to be constantly reassessed and often modified. Moreover, a reliable and extensive medical data base is an essential precondition for the successful introduction of many non-market based initiatives to contain expenditure: for instance, by allowing the identification of best or worst practice doctors and hospitals in an objective and quantified way, it would make "peer pressure" a significantly more effective tool; in the case of the capitation fee, it would minimise the risk that a patient's health profile and service needs might not be taken fully into account; and linking PHARMANET with a data bank of the prescription record of individual physicians should allow the system to reap the benefits of "best-practice" standards. The authorities feel that Belgian health data may soon be very detailed and comprehensive. But completing work on various data banks and linking them up in an operational system will require stepped-up co-operation between public institutions, hospitals and doctors. It might also raise questions concerning the threat to privacy and the risk of simplistic interpretations. While these concerns are legitimate and should be taken duly into account, they should not be allowed to prevent the introduction of these promising statistical tools. More generally, efforts should be stepped up to make an optimum use of information technology to process data about patients in order to establish which treatments work best and which are the most cost-effective.

A further significant restriction of the fee-for-service rule combined with "peer reviews" and other measures to limit consumption can be expected to lower the income of physicians, reduce their number over the long-term, and contribute to the correction of the current situation of excessive supply in this segment of the health care market. This would seem a more efficient way of tackling the problem, at least over the longer term, than rationing the number of doctors "allowed" to graduate from medical schools or limiting the number of physiotherapists to be *agréés* (certified) by the INAMI. This is the method introduced by the authorities who have, however, added a periodic assessment of the results achieved. If, as a temporary measure, a form of quantity control were deemed necessary, it might be preferable to impose a quota on access to medical schools (*numerus clausus*), rather than on graduation.

The consumption of generic drugs currently represents a very small proportion – less than 1 per cent – of total drug consumption. But the price gap between brand name drugs (protected by copyright) and generic drugs is also rather small – some 15-20 per cent – and concerns only about 40 products. It is, however, expected to widen significantly in a few years' time as a number of important and expensive brand name drugs will move to the generic category. Hence, although the narrowness of the Belgian market may make it less attractive to the producers of generic drugs, it might be appropriate to start encouraging the use of generic as opposed to brand name drugs – perhaps through different reimbursement rates and incentives for pharmacies to substitute generic for brand name drugs.

Finally, the authorities should consider stepping up preventive medicine, especially in the light of the findings of health surveys which ought to be conducted at regular intervals, and better co-ordinating it among the various levels of government concerned – even though results and payoffs in this area cannot be expected before several years. A recent study[63] has noted with concern the increased consumption of cigarettes and alcoholic beverages among the young (15-19 year olds) in Belgium. These are just two of the most obvious examples where additional and more effective preventive measures would be desirable: they could include raising, so far as is possible, taxation on tobacco and alcohol so as to make their prices more of a disincentive. But preventive policies should be reconsidered more generally, for instance with respect to vaccination, the screening of diseases, health education of the population and, last but not least, the use of car seat-belts.

In sum, the authorities agree that the health care system needs further reforming: first, to eliminate over-consumption and inefficiency; and second, over the longer term, to curb the growth of expenditure which would otherwise tend to outrun the growth of resources. They also acknowledge that the "norm" should be phased out. But rather than turning to market mechanisms, they envisage pursuing the current approach, which includes: making patients more cost-conscious, relying on "peer pressure" on practitioners, and extending the use of various forms of *forfaits*, all in a framework of *concertation* among the major players and under the ultimate supervision of the government. In other words, rather than allowing the – perhaps in the long term inevitable – reduction in patient free choice and fee-for-service rule to be brought about by market forces, Belgium hopes to develop an administrative mechanism which will allow it to ration and allocate medical services, while better preserving equity and solidarity than would be the case with market forces.

Notes

1. The rate of capacity utilisation in manufacturing reached the record level of 83.4 per cent in the first quarter of 1998.

2. To improve the investment climate, at end-1997, the government decided to apply the principle of "fiscal ruling" to investments of both domestic and foreign origin. A "fiscal ruling" is a prior agreement between the tax authorities and enterprises concerning the tax liabilities generated by their investments.

3. The VAT rate for houses and flats of less than 190 m^2 and 100 m^2, respectively, was reduced from 21 per cent to 12 per cent.

4. The fairly big swings in the inflation rate during the course of 1998 were partly due to a revision of the consumer price index at the beginning of 1998.

5. For a discussion of this law and its implications see Chapter III.

6. Number of hours per day. Source: *Union professionnelle des entreprises de travail intérimaire.*

7. So far, only two enterprises have concluded a collective labour agreement with their personnel which includes a 32 hour working week for some of them. Because of improvements scheduled to be made to this scheme, the number of enterprises concerned can be expected to increase.

8. Based on the end-June figures.

9. Unemployed aged 50 years or over.

10. From 514 000 at end-September 1995 to 438 000 at end-September 1998.

11. From 73 000 at end-September 1995 to 133 000 at end-September 1998.

12. While itself not entirely satisfactory, this concept may provide useful additional information on the degree of under-utilisation of labour resources in the Belgian labour market. In fact, since the mid-1970s, a large number of people have joined a variety of government programmes which allow them to become inactive (and leave the labour force), to acquire the status of partially unemployed, or to be hired in special partly-subsidised jobs. In some respects, even broad unemployment may understate the true degree of under-utilisation of labour resources in Belgium, since it does not include people on social assistance not seeking a job and discouraged workers with no social benefits – *i.e.* workers who either leave the labour force in the face of poor job prospects or decide not to enter it. The number of people on social assistance (MINIMEX) has increased sharply since 1990 and represented some 1¾ per cent of the narrowly-defined labour force in 1997. Only about one-third of them are registered as job seekers and hence included in unemployment figures. As for discouraged workers, according to data compiled by the OECD Secretariat, they represented around 1½ per cent of the narrowly-defined labour force in 1993. Unfortunately, there are no accepted standard calculations of "broad unemployment" that would serve as a basis for international comparison.

13. The European Employment Observatory has recently developed its own version of "broad unemployment" (or "extended unemployment"), applying it to all EU countries (European Commission, 1998).

14. Reflecting the growing importance of part-time work, on a full-time basis "broad unemployment" actually edged up in 1997, before falling in 1998.

15. Defined as total employment in persons, as a per cent of the working-age population. The problem with this indicator is that it does not show the extent to which low employment is due to individual choices – that is, the preference between working and not working (or working only part-time) – or to market imperfections.

16. The current-account surplus of the Belgian-Luxembourg Economic Union was 5.6 per cent of GDP in 1997 and may have been of the same order of magnitude in 1998.

17. The impact of interest rate changes also depends on the reaction function of the public sector, by far the most important debtor in Belgian financial markets. For all these reasons, in the case of Belgium, the calculation of a formal "financial conditions indicator", as the OECD Secretariat has done for a few other Member countries, does not seem to be warranted.

18. In view of the introduction of EMU, the National Bank of Belgium has taken a number of steps concerning the instruments of monetary policy. For instance, since the European Central Bank plans to use reserve requirements, which is a completely new instrument for Belgian money market participants, the National Bank of Belgium has proposed to domestic credit institutions to participate in the last four months of 1998 in a transitional system of reserve requirements to prepare for the new monetary environment.

19. That is, without any increase in nominal terms in the annual transfer received from the Treasury.

20. The saving was 1 per cent of GDP in 1992, $2\frac{1}{2}$ per cent in 1993, 1 per cent in 1994, $\frac{1}{4}$ per cent in 1995 and $1\frac{1}{2}$ per cent in 1996.

21. The Belgian definition of "primary surplus" is slightly different from the one used by the OECD Secretariat in that, while it does exclude interest paid, it does not exclude interest and other revenues received, with the result that the primary surplus thus calculated is normally bigger than when calculated by the OECD Secretariat.

22. Since the measures taken in the framework of the Convergence Plan 1997-2000 were largely structural, their positive impact on the budget is expected to decline only moderately in the next few years – from BF 100.2 billion in 1997 to BF 87.5 billion in 2000 (for the Entité I).

23. As a result of better-than-expected macroeconomic conditions and budget outcomes, some one-off corrective measures included in the 1997 budget – such as sales of public buildings – were not carried out.

24. For a more detailed analysis of the increase in the primary surplus since the early 1990s, see the 1997 Survey, pp. 41-43.

25. The increase in receipts has not, however, entirely offset the loss noted in earlier years.

26. The proceeds of privatisation approached 1 per cent of GDP in 1997. They included: BF 30 billion resulting from the disposal of 24.7 per cent of the capital of the ASLK/CGER; BF 54 billion resulting from the disposal of 50 per cent of the shares of

the holding *Crédit communal*/Dexia; and BF 6.7 billion resulting from the listing on the stock market of 14.8 per cent of the capital of the holding GIMV (*Société régionale d'investissement de Flandre*).

27. The proceeds were used, with the consent of the European Monetary Institute, to reduce foreign currency denominated government debt.

28. These assumptions include: an estimated underlying growth rate of the Belgian economy of 2.3 per cent; an inflation rate of 2 per cent; and an implicit interest rate on the public debt of 6 per cent.

29. These included: certain forms of voluntary work-sharing – such as part-time pre-retirement; "opening clauses" allowing firms to negotiate with their work force to pay below the wage minima set in collective contracts at the branch level; and the generalisation of exceptions for the statutory minimum wage.

30. An overview of progress in structural reform in a summary form is presented in Box 2.

31. In 1975, the social partners decided to introduce a guaranteed minimum monthly income (*Revenu minimum mensuel moyen garanti* or RMMMG) which is binding and in many respects equivalent to a legal minimum wage.

32. For instance, in the case of *le stage des jeunes, le contrat de première expérience professionnelle* and *l'emploi-tremplin*.

33. The law was introduced to simultaneously support employment and preserve international competitiveness – especially in the period following the end of the 1995-96 real wage freeze and leading to the introduction of EMU.

34. The law states that if, as a result of the automatic wage indexation (based on the "health index") plus the autonomous wage drift, labour costs were to increase more than the maximum allowed, the disposable margin for wage increases in the following years would be correspondingly reduced.

35. The *Maribel* measures were amended with effect from 1 July 1997, this resulting in the abolition of the *Maribel-bis* and *Maribel-ter* measures which were targeted at firms exposed to international competition (mainly in manufacturing).

36. The difference with other European countries should not be overstated. As noted in the 1997 *Survey*, while in Belgium most jobless persons may remain in the unemployment schemes for an indefinite period, in many other countries after a certain period they are moved either to social assistance or to other social security schemes.

37. It is now possible to run together four contracts, each of a maximum duration of six months.

38. However, the "equal opportunity aspect" is not explicitly covered in the OECD job strategy, while it is one of the four pillars of the EU approach.

39. This Law required the social partners (*Conseil central de l'économie*) to assess at regular intervals the international competitive position of the Belgian economy on the basis of specific criteria – notably the evolution of the export performance and labour costs – and make recommendations to the government which, if competitiveness was threatened, could take a number of measures.

40. For example, airline deregulation in the United States led to a large employment creation in this sector, while electricity deregulation in the United Kingdom led to the opposite result.

41. As a result of the *"franchise sociale"* and the *"franchise fiscale"*, for certain persons, co-payments (excluding for pharmaceuticals and care provided in psychiatric establishments) are waived above specific yearly levels. The *"franchise sociale"* covers widows,

disabled, pensioners and orphans (or VIPO) as well as some other groups with specific social benefits – such as old persons with a minimum social assistance benefit. The *"franchise fiscale"* covers taxpayers with especially low revenues.

42. Compulsory public health insurance is provided by two, financially separate, schemes: the general scheme (*"régime général"*) covers both major and minor risks and applies to employees and civil servants, retired, disabled and their dependants (representing nearly 90 per cent of the population); the scheme for the self-employed and their dependants (*"régime des indépendants"*) – representing around 10 per cent of the population – covers only major risks. Major risks mainly represent in-patient (hospital) care and special (expensive) technical services. Minor risks include out-patient care, medicine, dental care, etc. The compulsory scheme includes both health insurance cover and income support in the event of illness.

43. More precisely, there are currently 87 *mutualités* consolidated in five national unions.

44. According to the authorities, co-payments represented some 8 per cent of the cost of ambulatory and hospital care in 1995. Since pharmaceuticals are not covered by the *"franchise sociale"* and the *"franchise fiscale"*, their effective co-payment rate is higher, which brings the overall co-payment rate to around 15 per cent of medical expenditure covered by the compulsory insurance.

45. Also, both the *mutualités* and private insurance companies are forbidden by law from reinsuring the co-payment.

46. Before the Belgian health care system acquired its present institutional structure, to gain financial stability and political protection, *mutualités* used to associate with various fractions of the labour movement, which were largely organised on the basis of philosophical or religious tendencies – *i.e.* catholic, socialist and liberal.

47. Since 1995, however, this pooling approach has been modified somewhat, and in the coming years the *mutualités* will be responsible for a growing proportion of their financial shortfalls (see below).

48. For some care, reimbursement may be less, not exceeding 60 per cent. For some activities, on the other hand, the fee is restricted to the amount reimbursed under the sickness insurance cover.

49. There are also a few for-profit hospitals; these hospitals are not entitled to public subsidies for construction and equipment.

50. The standard cost per day is based on several factors, including historical costs, average costs of a sample of hospitals with similar characteristics, case mix and work load.

51. This is true for private non-profit hospitals but not for private for-profit hospitals which, as noted above, are not entitled to public subsidies.

52. To assure the service of these loans, appropriate interest and repayment charges are included in the budget of hospitals and hence in the daily price of hospital stays paid by the *mutualités*.

53. Throughout this chapter, figures on health care spending are from OECD Health Data 98. They include health spending by the public sector (federal government and regional governments) for current and investment purposes, as well as spending by the private sector (including household spending on over-the-counter drugs). It has nonetheless been claimed that these data may underestimate the true expenditure on health since they omit a number of expenditures, notably by regional authorities.

See Wouters, Spinnewyn and Pacolet (1988). In order, above all, to make comparative studies between countries possible, it would seem that the quality and coverage of health statistics need to be improved and standardised.

54. More precisely, current health expenditure covered by the *Institut national d'assurance maladie-invalidité* (*Régime général* and *Régime des indépendants*).

55. In an appendix to this report, experts from two universities (*Université libre de Bruxelles* and Catholic University of Louvain) show that, on the basis of a theoretical norm like the one mentioned above, medical expenditure is somewhat greater in Flanders than in Wallonia.

56. The only major exceptions are: for examination on a Magnetic Nuclear Resonance apparatus (MNI), since Belgium has the lowest number of MNIs per capita in Western Europe (3.1 per 1 million inhabitants); and, as in most European countries, for transplants, mainly due to a shortage of donors. Steps have been taken to increase the number of MNIs, as part of a multi-year plan.

57. The "norm" uses as the price deflator the so-called "health index" which excludes the price of tobacco, alcohol, and petrol and diesel fuel.

58. Although this responsibility had already existed since 1963, it was only "theoretical", and cumulated surpluses (*vis-à-vis* the government) and deficits were wiped out in 1974, 1980 and 1988. As part of the new arrangement, cumulated surpluses and deficits since 1980 were frozen, but the deficits would be reinstated if the *mutualité* which recorded them were to return into the red.

59. In the event of the norm being exceeded, the overrun percentage subject to cost participation is capped; if the norm is under-utilised, the percentage is not capped. This can result in a biennial cycle of overruns.

60. Health care is generally regarded as a "superior good". Hence, it is normal, over the long term, for health expenditure to increase faster than GDP.

61. For many people in Belgium, a fundamental difference between the Belgian health system and a co-ordinated care system could lie in the fact that, under the Belgian compulsory insurance scheme, the decision to give a patient expensive treatment is taken by experts working for public bodies or non-profit organisations (*mutualités*), whose concern is to prevent abuses and reduce needless consumption of medical care, whereas under a co-ordinated care system, that decision is taken by employees of commercial insurance companies who could be suspected of seeking to restrict costs by refusing care that is justified.

62. Efforts should be made to computerise medical data systems, not only to make them more efficient from an administrative point of view, but also to facilitate the use of the information generated for relevant research.

63. The study, which was commissioned by the nine ministers with responsibilities in the health area in Belgium, was carried out in 1997 by the *Institut scientifique de la santé publique Louis Pasteur* in co-operation with the *Institut national de statistique* and the *Centre universitaire de Limbourg*.

List of acronyms

ASLK/CGER	Financial company
BATC	Brussels Airport Terminal Company
CPI	Consumer Price Index
EMU	European Monetary Union
EU	European Union
FOREM	Regional placement service
GIMF	*Société régionale d'investissement de Flandre*
HMO	Health Maintenance Organisation
INAMI	*Institut national d'assurance maladie-invalidité*
MINIMEX	Minimum social assistance scheme
MNI	Magnetic nuclear resonance apparatus
NAWRU	Non-Accelerating Wage Rate of Unemployment
ONEM	Federal body administering unemployment benefits
ORBEM	Regional placement service
PHARMANET	Medical data base
R&D	Research and Development
RMMMG	*Revenu minimum mensuel moyen garanti*
RVA/RLW	Public sector airport operator
SMEs	Small and Medium-sized Enterprises
VAT	Value Added Tax
VDAB	Regional placement service
VIPO	*Veuves, invalides, pensionnés et orphelins*

Bibliography

de Callatay, E. (1998)
"Les finances des Régions et des Communautés en Belgique", *Reflets et perspectives de la vie économique*, No. 2.

European Commission (1998)
Employment Observatory, SYSDEM, *Trends* No. 30, summer.

Fasquelle, N. and S. Weemaes (1997)
"Perspectives financières de la sécurité sociale à l'horizon 2050", *Planning Paper* No. 83, Bureau fédéral du Plan, Brussels.

INAMI (1996)
Conseil général, "Troisième rapport".

Lambrecht, M. (1997)
"Le vieillissement démographique", *Planning Paper* No. 81, Bureau fédéral du Plan, Brussels.

Ministry of Employment and Labour (1997)
La Politique fédérale de l'emploi, Brussels, pp. 76-77.

Nonneman, W and E. van Doorslaer (1994)
"The role of the sickness funds in the Belgian health care market", *Social Science & Medicine*, Vol. 39, No. 10, pp. 1483-1495.

OECD (1997)
Economic Surveys, Belgium/Luxembourg, Paris.

OECD (1998)
Employment Outlook, Statistical Annex, Table B.

OECD (1992)
"The reform of health care: a comparison of seven OECD countries", *Health Policy Studies* No. 2, Paris.

Schokkaert E, H. Van Dongen and G. Dhaene (1991)
Investigation into the Differences in Medical Consumption in Belgium, Report to the INAMI/RIZIV, Catholic University of Louvain (in Dutch).

UNDP (1998)
Human Development Report.

Wouters, R., H. Spinnewyn and J. Pacolet (1988)
Het Profijt van de Non-Profijt, Koning Boudewijnstichting and Hoger Instituut voor de Arbeid, Brussels (in Dutch).

Annex

Calendar of main economic events

1996

December

Under the law on promoting employment and the preventive safeguarding of competitiveness, the government, on account of the failure of the trade unions and employers' organisations to conclude an inter-professional agreement, sets the maximum nominal increase in per capita wage costs at 6.1 per cent for 1997 and 1998.

1997

February

The European Commission gives its agreement to a new Maribel regulation applicable to all industrial sectors as from 1 July.

April

A Royal Decree gives a legal status to the activity of collective investment undertakings specialising in the acquisition of stakes in companies with high growth potential, listed on the recently created EASDAQ (European Association of Securities Dealers Automated Quotation) and EuroNM (Euro Nouveau Marché) markets.

May

New legislation on public procurement, *i.e.* state orders, to bring it into line with European regulations.

The government decides to liberalise telecommunications markets completely from 1 January 1998.

June

Partial privatisation of Distrigaz.

August

Completion of the privatisation of the Crédit Agricole: the Banque Bacob acquires the last block of shares of the former public credit institution.

September

The federal government approves the contract specifications for a third mobile telephone (GSM) network.

Creation of Telenet-Flandres, a telecommunications network which will compete with the federal telephone company Belgacom.

October

The federal government presents its 1998 budget. The overall budget deficit will be cut from 2.8 per cent of GDP to 2.3 per cent in 1998. At the federal level, fiscal strategy consists in stabilising, as a percentage of GDP, the primary surplus at the 1996 level, *i.e.* 5.3 per cent of GDP (on the basis of the Belgian definition). As regards the budgets of the Regions and Communities, they comply with the recommendations of the Conseil Supérieur des Finances: their net borrowing requirement must fall to 0.4 per cent of GDP.

The National Bank raises its central rate and most of its other rates by 30 basis points. The central rate rises from 3 to 3.3 per cent.

November

The BBL is taken over by the Dutch Banking and Insurance group ING.

1998

January

Merger of the financial institutions KB and CERA, the Assurances Boerenbond Belge (ABB) and the holding company Almanij, to form a Banking and Insurance group.

February

The *Conseil de la concurrence* approves three opinions concerning: the notification of concentrations, the obligation to inform workers about competition matters, and the modification of the framework for the protection of competition.

March

Further to the budget control, the government announces its new public finance targets for 1998: a primary surplus of 6 per cent of GDP, a public deficit of 1.7 per cent (compared with 2.3 per cent in the previous budget), and a total debt down to 118.5 per cent of GDP (compared with 122.3 per cent projected initially).

May

The European Council decides that Belgium (as well as ten other candidate countries) meets the requirements for the adoption of the single currency and will thus join the euro-zone on 1 January 1999.

June

The European Commission gives its go-ahead to the take-over of the Générale de Banque by the Belgian-Dutch group Fortis.

September

A transitional system of compulsory reserves placed with the National Bank comes into force for a period of four months. The rate on end-of-day advances is cut by 5 basis points to 4.5 per cent.

October

The federal government presents its 1999 budget. The overall budget deficit will be cut from 1.6 per cent of GDP in 1998 to 1.3 per cent. Debt will fall from 118 per cent of GDP at end-1998 to 115 per cent at end-1999. The federal primary surplus will be stabilised at 5.3 per cent of GDP. In line with the recommendations of the *Conseil supérieur des finances*, the Communities and Regions will present a balanced budget for 1999. The overall primary surplus will be 6 per cent of GDP.

November

The social partners conclude a preliminary agreement binding the entire private sector for 1999 and 2000. For 1999-2000, wage increases (indexation and seniority included) may not exceed 5.9 per cent. This figure is a benchmark which may be exceeded when a company makes a special effort on the jobs and training front.

LUXEMBOURG

Assessment and recommendations

Growth has remained robust...

The Luxembourg economy has continued to perform well, with GDP growth picking up to around 4³/₄ per cent in 1997, and probably also in 1998. Exports have been a major driving force, underpinned by buoyant export markets and a strong export performance of the financial and communication sectors. Private consumption has strengthened due to higher wage increases and robust employment growth. Investment has also been buoyant, partly due to special factors such as the purchase of some aircraft.

... with strong job creation, declining unemployment...

Despite 15 years of strong job creation, tensions in the labour market have largely been absent due to the growing presence of foreign workers. Unemployment has been declining in 1998, and although remaining around a historically high level for Luxembourg, it is one of the lowest in the OECD area. The employment rate is relatively low as many older workers – by moving to early-retirement or disability schemes – have left the labour force. Hence, a broader concept of labour under-utilisation ("broad unemployment"), which adds people of working-age in benefit schemes and labour market programmes to registered unemployment, shows a less favourable development, with broad unemployment exceeding 13 per cent of the broad labour force in 1997 – compared with less than 12 per cent in 1995.

... and virtually no inflationary pressures

Inflationary pressures have been largely absent, and consumer price inflation has followed developments in neighbouring countries. Wage rises edged up to nearly 3 per cent in 1997, but this was mainly due to the institutional wage indexation which resulted in a 2.5 per cent general wage increase at the beginning of the year. In general, recently-concluded collective labour agreements provide little or no signs of strong wage rises, with contractual real wage increases merely picking up to slightly over 1 per cent. As a result, compensation per employee is expected to decelerate to 1.6 per cent in 1998. Given moderate wage developments, unit labour costs in the manufacturing sector have developed favourably compared with those of Luxembourg's trading partners. But international price competitiveness has been virtually unchanged, as export prices typically move in tandem with those of foreign producers.

The outlook is favourable

Real GDP is projected to grow at around 3½ per cent in both 1999 and 2000. A further increase in the number of cross-border workers should prevent the economy from overheating but will also keep unemployment at around current levels, despite robust employment growth and the implementation of a national employment plan. Consumer price inflation is projected to stay low – in line with developments in neighbouring countries. The risk and uncertainties concern primarily the external sector and, on balance, are on the downside. Apart from the international financial crisis, a major uncertainty concerns the impact of European Economic and Monetary Union on the financial sector, and the degree to which the loss in revenues from foreign exchange dealings is compensated by increased cross-border activities, facilitated by the single currency. In a more distant future, the possible imposition of an EU-wide withholding tax on savings could reduce the attractiveness of Luxembourg for foreign depositors.

Monetary conditions have remained easy...

Within the Belgium-Luxembourg Economic Union (BLEU), monetary conditions have remained relatively easy over the past year and a half. The contractionary impact of the small increase in short-term rates has been more than outweighed by the expansionary effects of a steady decline in long-term rates even though, due to a possible decrease in inflationary expectations, the decline in real terms may have been smaller and the Luxembourg (and the Belgian) franc, in effective terms, has recently appreciated somewhat. As all the Maastricht criteria had been fulfilled, Luxembourg easily qualified to participate in monetary union from its inception. Hence, monetary policy arrangements have to be adapted. The Central Bank of Luxembourg – as successor of the Luxembourg Monetary Institute – is actively setting up an operational framework to carry out the policies of the European Central Bank from January 1999. Furthermore, new instruments will be introduced, such as remunerated minimum reserves with the European Central Bank, but these changes are unlikely to greatly affect the position of Luxembourg as a financial centre.

... and fiscal policy has become more expansionary, as taxes have come down...

Fiscal policy has become more expansionary, as the government reduced taxes and increased spending on infrastructure projects and social security. According to government projections, the general government surplus could decline from 2.9 per cent of GDP in 1997 to 1.4 per cent in 1998, despite the strong performance of the economy. Income taxes and business taxes have been reduced, in order to preserve the competitiveness of the Luxembourg economy in an international environment characterised by a widespread reduction in tax rates. The normal tax rate for companies came down to 37.45 per cent in 1998 – compared with 40.3 per cent in 1996.

... and central government and social security spending has been growing rapidly

Central government spending is expected to rise by almost 6 per cent in nominal terms in 1998, mainly because of earlier commitments such as the multi-annual wage agreement for the public sector, and new investment projects on infrastructure and school buildings. Social security spending has also been growing rapidly, due partly to policy decisions but – as in the case of health care – also to rapid cost increases and growing demand. New legislation concerning the disability scheme and the introduction of a long-term nursing care scheme may further add to underlying pressure on expenditure. Social security reform – the implementation of which is largely within the confines of the social partners – has been very slow. To prevent a further expansion of the social security sector, it would be useful if the authorities could explore mechanisms for containing expenditure growth, as is already the case for central government spending. Such moves would need to be underpinned by structural reform of the various schemes.

Longer-term concerns centre on the pension schemes

Longer-term concerns centre on the pension schemes in the public and private sector. Although the Luxembourg pension schemes are in a more favourable position than those of many other countries, pension liabilities are building up. Pension reform plans have mainly focused on curbing expenditure in the public sector scheme by bringing it more in line with the less favourable private sector scheme. Recently, parliament approved the government's plans in this area. However, more reforms seem to be called for, such as a better management of the financial reserves of the pension funds and the creation of a funded complementary pension system.

Favourable tax regimes have come under closer scrutiny

The government has pursued an active policy to enhance the attractiveness of Luxembourg as a site for financial and industrial activity. Tax advantages in comparison with neighbouring countries, strict bank secrecy rules, a liberal regulatory environment, and the rapid implementation of EU directives in Luxembourg law, combined with a favourable geographical location at the heart of Europe and a qualified and multilingual labour force have been central in creating competitive advantages in financial services. Globalisation and technical innovation have enabled companies to exploit differences in tax regimes between countries. Tax competition *per se* is welcome as it focuses on delivering public services in a cost-effective way. Moreover, differences in tax regimes between countries also reflect preferences in public provisions as opposed to private provisions of goods and services. However, concerns have been raised about possible harmful aspects of tax competition. At the end of 1997, the EU council chaired by Luxembourg, agreed to a package of measures to tackle harmful tax competition in order to help to reduce tax distortions in the Single European Market. To counter possible negative effects of tax competition in the financial and other service sectors, the OECD has adopted a set of Guidelines to deal with harmful preferential tax regimes in the OECD area. The Luxembourg authorities, specifically objecting to the Guidelines' reference to the removal of impediments to the access of banking information by the tax authorities, have abstained from approving these Guidelines, and are therefore not bound by them.

Diversification policy should yield to structural reform as EU regulations tighten

Another important aspect of the government's industrial policy is the implementation of incentives to attract new industries as part of the diversification policy, within the framework of EU directives. This policy has been successful in creating jobs in the manufacturing sector – most of which have been taken by cross-border workers – although it may also have distorted the allocation of resources and delayed the adjustment process in the regions affected by the restructuring of the steel industry. The tightening of restrictions on state aid by the European Commission will restrain the scope of the diversification policy in future. Hence, the authorities should focus their policies more on structural reform to enhance competitiveness by removing rigidities in the labour market and further pursue regulatory reform.

Structural reform efforts should be stepped up

Given the favourable economic environment, the need for structural reform has been less apparent than in many other countries, and this may have slowed its pace. The National Action Plan for the Promotion of Employment seems more directed at preventing a further deterioration of labour market performance than at improving it. The proposed measures to upgrade skills should be pursued but may show results only in the medium term. On the other hand, the Plan puts great emphasis on training programmes, subsidised employment programmes, and the promotion of entrepreneurship. Relatively little attention is paid to elements aimed at improving the functioning of the labour market by enhancing incentives to work and by creating more flexibility in the economy in general.

More should be done to reduce labour costs...

A number of recommendations in the 1997 *Survey* still require action. The role of the social minimum wage as an instrument to achieve equity goals should be reassessed with regard to its effects on the labour market. For example, a lower minimum wage could be considered for certain groups, such as for young people above the age of 17 and long-term unemployed, to bring wages better in line with productivity if it turns out that low-skilled or inexperienced workers are being priced out of employment. Indeed, if the level of wages required to price low-skilled workers back into the market were unacceptable, due to equity considerations, wages could be complemented by in-work benefits

– while respecting fiscal constraints and paying attention to avoid excessively high marginal effective tax rates. Alternatively, possible negative effects of the social minimum wage on employment creation could be mitigated by relying more on subsidies for employers. In addition, reductions in social security contributions could be targeted more at low-skilled workers. Finally, given the high replacement rate, incentives to encourage people to actively seek a job or a place in a training scheme could be strengthened further, if not by reducing the generosity of the social security system, at least by intensifying the surveillance on availability for work and job search, and by applying even more strictly benefit sanctions for refusing suitable work or training. According to the Luxembourg government, high net replacement rates do not have a significant effect on the length of unemployment spells. Therefore, it prefers to maintain the generosity of the system and improve placement and counselling services. Moreover, sanctions have been applied more often to those unwilling to take up work. Concerning a more degressive age-dependent social minimum wage, the Luxembourg government refers explicitly to engagements undertaken in other international fora, in particular the Council of Europe, whose social charter allows a maximum differential of 25 per cent between the social minimum wage for young persons and adults.

... relax working hour restrictions, and improve labour participation

The authorities should act more forcefully in relaxing working-time restrictions, especially for part-time workers. Given that part-time work is almost exclusively done by women, such measures may be more effective in stimulating female participation than additional wage subsidies for this group. The government's decision to subsidise collective agreements to reduce working hours and at the same time hire unemployed may prove to be costly and inefficient and should be reconsidered. However, concerning labour market flexibility it should be noted that in specific cases, the application of the strict legislation in this area is often relaxed to suit the requirements of individual firms. In addition, more recently, the government has introduced a law in Parliament, widening the possibilities for derogation of collective agreements and making the strict working time legislation more flexible. With a view to raising labour force participation, recently introduced tighter controls on access to the disability scheme should be maintained.

Good public
health care, but
at high costs

The public health sector has been an area where expenditure has risen very rapidly. The Luxembourg health care system provides universal and comprehensive health care, in combination with a private health care provision. Rationing of health services, for instance hospital waiting lists, has been avoided. The health status of the population is high by international comparison. These positive results have been achieved at relatively high costs, even though the average age of the population is lower than in most other countries. Health care indicators point to an over-consumption in the hospital sector and of pharmaceuticals. A major problem is that the health system does not have the possibility to regulate the supply of doctors, as every physician practising in Luxembourg is by law accredited to the Luxembourg health system. Remuneration of health professionals, which is largely based on a fee-for-service system, provides little incentive to minimise costs. In addition, the administration of the public health fund (U*nion des* *caisses de maladie*, UCM) and health-care providers face a soft budget constraint and investment decisions in the hospital sector are often influenced by socio-political considerations rather than based on a cost-benefit analysis.

Measures to
address
inefficiencies
seem
insufficient...

To curb health expenditure growth, the UCM has set up data banks to monitor health expenditure in the ambulatory sector and has started to challenge claims in cases of abuse. Such pressures may have resulted initially in a marked slow-down in treatment, but its effectiveness has faded in the meantime. Moreover, recent rulings by the European Court have undermined these control mechanisms, by giving Luxembourg residents more freedom to buy health care in neighbouring countries. In the hospital sector, the system of financing has been changed through the introduction of prospective budgets. Although the new budget system has provided more transparency, it has hardly been used to increase cost effectiveness in the hospital sector. Moreover, a reduction in the number of hospital beds has proved to be difficult to achieve.

*... and more
needs to be done*

Given expected future expenditure pressures, due to technical progress and population ageing, more changes will probably be required to keep the system affordable. The authorities should strengthen the role of general practitioners, making them gatekeepers of the system. A combination of capitation and fee-for-service systems might help in reducing the number of visits. Efficiency in the hospital sector could be improved by benchmarking hospital services and their costs; using lump-sum payments for certain specific medical acts could help in this respect. In addition, the oversupply of hospital beds should be reduced more swiftly, and co-operation intensified with medical establishments in neighbouring regions. Finally, it would be recommendable to revise the tripartite structure of public health care by reducing the influence of the social partners on public health insurance.

Summing up

Overall, the Luxembourg economy has performed very well over the past 15 years, fuelled by buoyant growth of financial and other business services. Since the beginning of 1997, the manufacturing sector has again started to contribute to growth, underpinned by the start-up of new activities, the completion of the steel industry's restructuring, and the recovery in neighbouring countries. Although monetary and fiscal policies, on balance, are unlikely to provide much restraint over the coming years, the chances of overheating are small as the economy can continue to rely on an influx of cross-border workers. However, some imbalances have become apparent, especially in the labour market where, despite strong employment growth, labour force participation has remained low. The emphasis should be on increasing labour force participation. Hence, the pace of structural reform should be stepped up, and focused on improving the qualifications of low-skilled workers in order to promote their integration, on increasing incentives to work and on lifting restrictions on working hours, which have proven to have a detrimental effect in terms of jobs and unemployment.

I.   Recent trends and prospects

The Luxembourg economy has continued to perform well. Economic activity has strengthened as production in the manufacturing sector has picked up, and the service sector has continued to expand rapidly. After growing by around 4³/₄ in 1998, real GDP is projected to grow around 3¹/₂ per cent both in 1999 and 2000 (Table 1). Employment creation is expected to remain among the highest in the OECD, but as cross-border workers take most of the new jobs, unemployment may hardly change. Despite the long expansion, the economy has not shown signs of overheating, and inflation has remained subdued.

Output growth has been buoyant...

Activity in the manufacturing sector has picked up strongly since the third quarter of 1996, and production increased by around 7 per cent in 1997 and in the first half of 1998, but is likely to have slowed down in the second half of the year. The turnaround has been most noticeable in the steel sector, where demand has been boosted by the recovery of the European economies and the rebuilding of stocks. However, order books have started to weaken since April, pointing to slower, production growth in the second half of 1998. The improvement in the steel market coincided with the replacement of the last blast furnace by an electrical one in May 1997, which completed a LF 24 billion conversion programme in the steel industry which had started in 1993. Production in the other manufacturing sectors also progressed strongly, partly because of non-recurrent factors such as the expansion of a wood processing plant. Furthermore, production in the construction sector has strengthened significantly since the first quarter of 1998, partly due to a substantial increase in public investment.

The service sector has continued its remarkable expansion and output growth was 6 per cent in 1997 (in current prices), only slightly lower than a year earlier. The financial sector remains one of the main pillars of the Luxembourg economy, contributing 17 per cent of GDP (national version)[1] and 9 per cent of employment. However, growing competition in international banking has led to rationalisation in the banking sector and interest margins have come down

Table 1. **Demand and output: recent trends and projections**

Annual percentage change, 1990 prices

	1995 current prices		1997[1]	1998[1]	1999[2]	2000[2]
	LF billion	Per cent of GDP				
A. Demand and output						
Private consumption	278.8	53.9	2.5	2.6	2.4	2.5
Government consumption	67.2	13.0	1.7	2.8	2.8	2.8
Gross fixed investment	111.4	21.6	14.1	6.5	4.7	5.0
Final domestic demand	457.3	88.5	5.5	3.8	3.1	3.3
Stockbuilding[3]	11.7	2.3	−0.6	0.2	0.2	0.2
Total domestic demand	469.1	90.8	4.8	4.0	3.3	3.5
Exports of goods and services	467.5	90.5	6.0	7.5	5.0	5.3
Imports of goods and services	419.8	81.2	6.1	7.0	5.1	5.5
Foreign balance[3]	47.7	9.2	0.5	1.2	0.4	0.4
GDP at constant prices	..	..	4.8	4.7	3.4	3.5
GDP price deflator	..	..	2.4	1.5	1.4	1.6
GDP at current prices	516.8	100.0	7.3	6.3	4.9	5.1
B. Memorandum items:						
Private consumption deflator	..	..	1.1	1.1	1.3	1.5
Industrial production	..	..	7.1	5.1	2.5	2.6
Total employment	..	..	3.2	3.0	2.5	2.5
Unemployment rate (per cent)	..	..	3.6	3.1	3.2	3.3

1.   Provisional figures.
2.   Projections.
3.   Contribution to growth of GDP.
Source: OECD Secretariat.

steadily to 0.65 per cent in 1997, compared with 1.2 per cent in 1983.[2] Nevertheless, fee-earning activities have substantially increased, and are now making up about 30 per cent of gross earnings.[3] Although the exposure of the banking sector to the Asian and Russian markets is limited, the sector has reacted prudently to recent international developments by substantially increasing its bad debt provisions. Among other remarkable developments in the service sector is the steady expansion of the satellite network. Currently there are eight satellites in operation and the service can be received by around 70 million European households.

... underpinned by strong export growth...

On the demand side, exports have been the main force behind the current buoyancy of the economy as exports of goods, and in particular steel products, have rebounded sharply. Other manufacturing branches, such as the chemical industry (plastic, tyres and man-made fibres) and machinery have also performed well. Moreover, the start-up of some new industries, such as wood processing has provided an additional boost. Export growth of services, mainly those of the financial and the communication sectors, has also been buoyant. However, as imports accelerated sharply due to the buoyancy of investment, and in particular the purchase of some aircraft, the contribution of net exports to GDP growth was limited to around ½ percentage point in 1997, though it could have exceeded 1 percentage point in 1998.

... booming investment...

The favourable cyclical environment has played an important role in the current investment boom: business investment outside the steel industry has bounced back sharply, thus more than offsetting the scaling down of investment in the steel industry. Moreover, investment has been sustained by the steady expansion of the satellite network, as each year since 1993 one satellite has been launched.

The improvement in the investment climate is reflected by the pick-up of new investment projects, through the mediation by the Board of Development (*Comité de développement économique*). In 1997, 10 new projects were pledged, for a total amount of LF 8 billion (or 6 per cent of total investment), running over several years. Also, investment projects under the industrial diversification law increased sharply to LF 23.5 billion spread out over several years, and supported by LF 3.7 billion of government subsidies, mainly in the form of capital transfers.[4] Nevertheless, the authorities have found it difficult to attract new investors. The small industrial base of the country is a clear disadvantage, as foreign investors make more and more use of mergers and acquisitions to gain a foothold. Moreover, the lack of available industrial buildings for leasing has been a handicap, as new firms often prefer to limit their initial financial commitment.

Residential investment accelerated by 3 per cent in 1997, sustained by low mortgage interest rates and a favourable economic climate. Given the growth in mortgage lending and building permission, the expansion in this sector is likely to have strengthened in 1998. In addition, government investment has grown substantially, owing to an increase in the school building programme and the commencement of the construction of two motorways in 1998.

... and buoyant household demand

Household disposable income has considerably strengthened over the past two years. At their biennial adjustment in January 1997, the social minimum wage and related benefits were raised by 3.2 per cent. Moreover, in the following month all wages and benefits were adjusted by 2.5 per cent, in conformity with the institutionalised wage indexation (*échelle mobile*). Disposable income was further boosted by a LF 7 billion (1.2 per cent of GDP) income tax reduction in the 1998 Budget. At the same time, national employment has been growing steadily by around 1¼ per cent, and real wage settlements by around 1 per cent. As a result, private consumption seems to have been picking up rapidly and is expected to have grown by 2½ to 2¾ per cent in 1997 and 1998. Government consumption strengthened, also as Luxembourg assumed the Presidency of the European Union during the second half of 1997.

Unemployment has been declining

Total employment growth has remained at around 3 per cent. In 1997, employment in the steel sector declined further by almost 500 persons (8 per cent of the work force in the sector) following the closure of the last blast furnace. However, these losses were more than compensated by further employment creation in the service sector, thus underlining the widening gap between a buoyant service industry and – at least in employment terms – a sluggish manufacturing sector, notwithstanding a substantial increase in manufacturing employment, outside the steel industry (Figure 1, Panel C).

Despite fifteen years of strong job creation, tensions in the labour market have largely been avoided due to a growing presence of foreign workers. The availability of cross-border workers has been stimulated by the relatively high net wages in Luxembourg[5] and the large supply of labour from the surrounding regions. Currently, around 75 per cent of the net increase in jobs is taken by these cross-border workers, whose share in domestic employment has steadily increased to over 30 per cent. Moreover, more than 30 per cent of the population are foreign nationals, and their share in employment is around 25 per cent. Thus the majority of the active labour force does not have Luxembourg nationality (Figure 1, Panel D).

Unemployment has been declining since the beginning of 1998 and, at just below 3 per cent in August, it was 0.5 percentage point lower than a year earlier. But this decline has partly reflected a change in definition, which has entailed the removal of all participants in labour market policy measures from the national unemployment definition.[6] Taken together, the number of registered unemployed and participants in labour market programmes was almost unchanged in August 1998, compared with a year earlier. A broader concept of labour market under-utilisation ("broad unemployment") which adds working-age people in all kinds of benefit schemes and labour market programmes to unemployment, shows that labour market conditions are less favourable than

Figure 1. **Overview of the labour market**

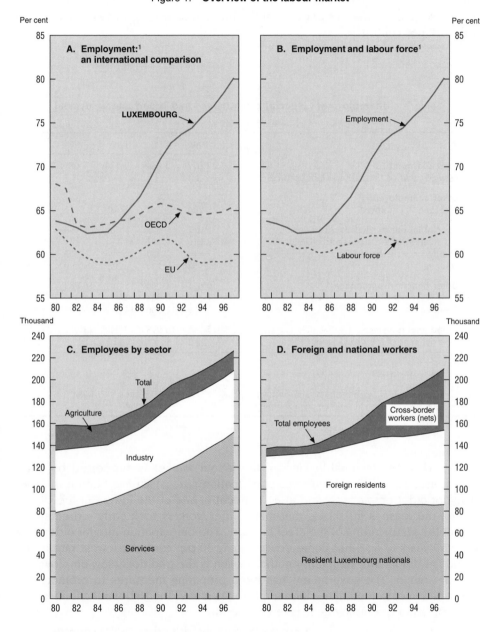

1.   As a per cent of the working age population.
Source: STATEC, *Statistical yearbooks* and OECD Secretariat.

suggested by traditional unemployment measures (Table 2). Broad unemployment rose to more than 13 per cent of the broad labour force in 1997 – compared with 11.7 per cent in 1995.[7]

Table 2.   **Unemployment, special programmes and broad unemployment**

Annual averages

	1980-85	1990	1995	1996	1997[1]
I. Unemployment	2 077	2 060	5 130	5 680	6 354
As a per cent of the national labour force	1.4	1.3	3.0	3.3	3.6
II. Other unemployed					
Part-time unemployed	126	42	39	113	203
III. Special labour market programmes	2 412	627	1 082	1 396	2 421
Job creation in the steel sector (DAC)	2 216	101	171	144	1 499
Youth work scheme (DAT)	114	380	558	762	714
Training	82	146	353	490	208
IV. Other benefit programmes	10 621	14 244	15 791	16 483	16 888
Early retirement[2]	1 362	2 378	1 421	1 352	1 400
Disability[3, 4]	9 259	11 866	14 370	15 131	15 488
V. Broad unemployment (I + II + III + IV)	15 235	16 973	22 042	23 672	25 866
As a per cent of the broad labour force	9.2	9.5	11.7	12.3	13.2

1.   Provisional or estimated data.
2.   *Préretraite ajustement* or for shift workers.
3.   End of year.
4.   Disabled resident in Luxembourg. Data for 1980-90 have been estimated by the OECD Secretariat.
Source: Statec and Inspection générale de la Sécurité sociale.

This less favourable view of the labour market is supported by other indicators, such as the labour force participation rate, which has been low, especially for older employees, and at 61 per cent is one of the lowest in the OECD. One of the reasons for this is that many older workers took early retirement as part of the restructuring of the steel industry. The participation rate for older men (over 50 years of age) has come down to only 30 per cent, the lowest rate in the European Union after Belgium. Another reason is the traditional low employment rate of women. The government has been preparing measures to promote the participation of women in the labour market as part of the National Action Plan for the Promotion of Employment (see Chapter III).

Unemployment still compares favourably with other OECD countries. The contrast is even more striking compared with the surrounding regions: in 1997, the number of unemployed in Luxembourg was only 6 400 (3.6 per cent of the labour force) compared with almost 200 000 (above 9 per cent of the labour force) in the surrounding regions (Statec, 1998).[8] According to the authorities, the severe unemployment problem in the surrounding regions is one of the reasons for the absence of any improvement in domestic labour market conditions. Other important factors are not only the lack of qualifications – 60 per cent of registered unemployed in Luxembourg have less than nine years of education – but also insufficient incentives to look for work (OECD, 1997a). However, since the last *Survey*, counselling and placement services have been improved, and sanctions for those unwilling to take a job have been imposed more often. A particular problem is the growing number of older unemployed (older than 50 years), of which more than a third has been registered with the Public Employment Service for more than a year. Youth unemployment, although almost twice the overall unemployment rate, does not seem to pose a serious problem as only around 10 per cent are registered for longer periods of time.

Moderate wages and low inflation

Wage rises have accelerated to close to 3 per cent in 1997, mainly due to the above-mentioned biennial revision of the social minimum wage and institutionalised wage indexation (Table 3). Taking these two factors into account, there

Table 3. **Compensation per employee**

Percentage changes

	1991	1992	1993	1994	1995	1996[1]	1997[1]
Compensation per employee	6.4	5.3	5.0	4.0	2.2	1.8	2.7
Of which:							
Mining and manufacturing	7.8	4.1	7.7	5.2	6.8	0.6	2.8
Construction	17.9	–3.8	–2.9	1.5	2.6	–0.3	2.8
Market services	5.7	7.1	5.2	4.4	0.3	2.0	2.4
Banking and insurance	7.9	10.2	9.9	11.6	–1.1	2.8	3.0
Non-market services	3.0	7.1	5.7	2.3	3.0	2.4	3.4
Employer's contribution	–0.4	–0.1	0.2	–0.5	–1.5	0.4	..
Gross wage	6.7	5.4	4.8	4.5	3.7	1.4	..
Wage indexation (*échelle mobile*)	2.9	3.2	1.8	3.0	1.9	1.0	2.3
Real wage (including wage drift)	3.8	2.2	3.0	1.5	1.8	0.4	..
Memorandum item:							
Minimum wage[2]	9.6	5.0	7.1	3.5	2.1-7.3	0.8	5.6

1. Estimates.
2. The distinction between workers with and without dependent family members was abolished in 1995.
Source: Statec, Inspection générale de la Sécurité sociale and OECD Secretariat.

are only faint signs that wage inflation will pick up: new collective agreements in the banking sector and steel industry provide for annual real pay rises of around 1 per cent for 1998 and 1999. Moreover, the growing presence of cross-border workers in Luxembourg has avoided tensions in the labour market and limited upward pressures on wages, as their wages are substantially lower than those of residents.[9] Hence, compensation per employee is projected to decelerate to 1.6 per cent in 1998. Overall, wage developments in the 1990s do not seem to be very different from those in neighbouring countries, despite generally tighter domestic labour market conditions – even allowing for broad unemployment (Figure 2).

Figure 2. **Compensation per employee: an international comparison**
Growth rate, per cent

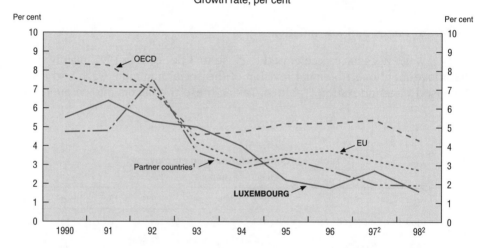

1. Belgium, France and Germany.
2. Estimations.
Source: STATEC and OECD Secretariat.

Consumer price inflation has followed more or less the declining trend in neighbouring countries (Figure 3). After rising for most of 1997, inflation has been coming down, reaching 0.5 per cent in October. In particular, energy prices have contributed to a slowing of inflation, being around 5 per cent lower than a year earlier. These price movements have not been significantly divergent from those in the surrounding countries.

Figure 3. **Consumer prices**

Per cent change over previous year

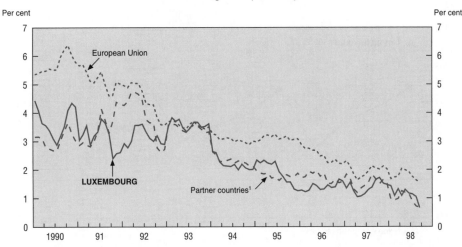

1. Belgium, France and Germany.
Source: OECD, *Main Economic Indicators.*

High current-account surplus

After a sharp improvement during the second half of 1996, international competitiveness in the manufacturing sector – as measured by a competitiveness indicator based on unit labour costs in a common currency – has remained fairly stable (Figure 4, Panel A).[10] Only the indicator for the steel sector saw a further improvement in the first half of 1997 but fell back in the second half of that year. Producers do not seem to have used their improved position to reduce prices as output prices have moved almost in parallel to those of foreign producers (Figure 4, Panel B), as Luxembourg's manufacturing sector is to a large extent characterised by "price taking", particularly in the steel industry.[11] Although unit labour costs have lagged behind producer prices (Figure 4, Panel C), profit margins have not necessarily been increased. Prices for other inputs, such as scrap iron, have risen sharply because of the depreciation of the Luxembourg franc *vis-à-vis* the dollar, and increased demand for raw materials by the steel sector.

Exports of goods (in value) were 10.5 per cent higher in 1997 than a year earlier, largely attributable to a pick up in steel shipments and higher prices for (long) steel products, which cover around 25 per cent of exports. The switch-over to electric steel-making processes, although hardly affecting the overall trade balance, has changed the composition of trade: electricity imports have replaced

Figure 4.   **Competitiveness of the manufacturing sector**
Index 1995 Q1 = 100

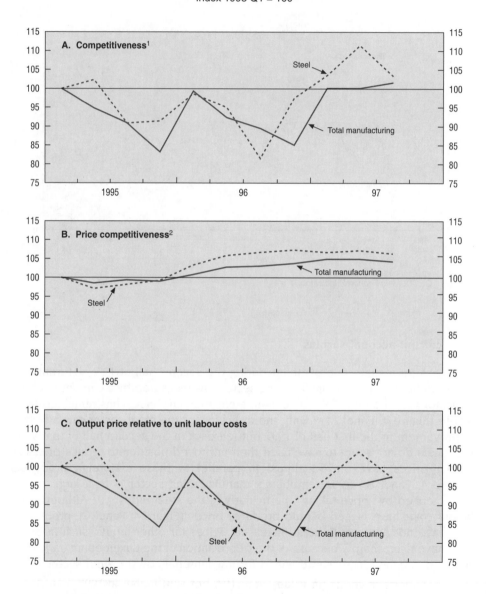

1.   Foreign output prices (in common currency) relative to Luxembourg unit labour costs, (see Krecké and Pierretti [1997]). An improvement in competitiveness is indicated by an increase in the index.
2.   Foreign output prices (in common currency)/Luxembourg output price
Source: STATEC.

coke and oil imports since the closure of the last blast furnace, and imports of scrap iron have replaced imports of iron ore as raw materials in the industry. But the trade balance deteriorated sharply, mainly because of exceptional factors such as the purchase of two aircraft in the second half of 1997. The deterioration in the trade balance was only partly offset by an improvement in the service balance, of which more than 50 per cent is generated by the financial sector. Also the exports of communication services strongly increased, owing to the expansion of the satellite network. However, the surplus on the income account deteriorated due to the growing number of cross-border workers. Overall, the current account surplus fell to around LF 70 billion (13 per cent of GDP) (Table 4).[12]

Table 4. **Current balance of payments**

LF billion

	Average 1990-93	1994	1995	1996	1997[1]	1997 S 1[1]	1998 S 1[1]
Current balance of payments	95.0	90.8	84.8	87.0	74.1	33.9	32.3
As a per cent of GDP	23.7	18.2	16.3	15.9	12.6		
Goods and services							
Goods	−55.7	−58.7	−46.9	−51.9	−66.3	−32.4	−29.0
Exports	209.1	216.6	272.4	259.9	308.5	143.1	167.0
Imports	264.8	275.3	319.3	311.8	374.8	175.5	196.0
Services	39.7	46.1	69.2	76.6	82.8	46.3	42.0
Exports	95.7	121.7	246.1	283.5	334.9	160.3	183.1
Imports	56.0	75.6	176.9	206.9	252.1	114.0	141.1
Income (net)	119.3	115.4	80.9	77.7	74.5	29.3	27.3
Compensation of employees	−22.4	−37.5	−43.1	−48.8	−56.0	−26.3	−30.2
Investment income[2]	141.7	152.9	124.0	126.5	130.5	55.6	57.5
Current transfers (net)	−8.3	−12.0	−18.4	−15.4	−16.9	−9.3	−8.0
General government	−4.5	−8.0	−3.9	−0.8	−1.5	−2.1	−2.0
Other sectors	−3.8	−4.0	−14.5	−14.6	−15.4	−7.2	−6.0

1. Provisional figures.
2. Without reinvested earnings.
Source: Statec.

Exports of goods strengthened further in the first half of 1998, and were 20 per cent higher in value terms than a year earlier. As imports were 13.5 per cent higher, the deficit on the trade balance improved only slightly. The current-account surplus remained almost unchanged for the same period, as an improvement in investment income was offset by a further increase in compensation of cross-border workers.

Favourable short-term outlook

Short-term prospects for the economy remain favourable, with the service industry being the main driving force. Already one of Europe's investment fund leaders, Luxembourg looks well positioned to take advantage of the creation of a single European pension market. The government has already prepared legislation to be implemented, once EU legislation has cleared the way for cross-border pension products. In addition, the communications sector is expected to gain further momentum, following the steady expansion of the satellite network. However, growth in the banking sector is likely to slow as a result of the introduction of EMU, as foreign exchange earnings – which are currently 4 per cent of the banking sector gross revenues – will be reduced. The manufacturing sector is projected to slow due to the deceleration of activity in Europe, but also as some of the current dynamism is due to exceptional factors such as the start-up of new activities and the pick-up in steel production after the termination of a substantial investment programme.

The employment situation is unlikely to change much, despite the implementation of a LF 2.6 billion employment plan (see Chapter III). Although employment growth should remain robust, unemployment is expected to stay around current levels, as the high influx of cross-border workers is projected to continue, thus preventing skill shortages and mitigating wage claims. The economy is unlikely to overheat and consumer price inflation could remain in line with that in neighbouring countries.

As far as the risk are concerned, a small economy as Luxembourg depends largely on developments in neighbouring countries, especially for the manufacturing sector, and the current international financial crises could have an important negative impact. In addition, the service sector, and more specifically the banking and insurance industry, depends heavily on European Union legislation, and the removal of non-tariff barriers in the European market, in particular for cross-border pensions. Apart from the international financial crisis, a major uncertainty for the projections is the impact of European Economic and Monetary Union. As mentioned earlier, the banking sector is likely to lose part of its foreign exchange earnings, but the impact may be limited as large part of foreign exchange dealings involves currencies outside the euro area. Moreover, the sector is likely to benefit from increased cross-border activities, facilitated by the introduction of a single European currency. In a more distant future, the possible imposition of a Europe-wide withholding tax on savings, as proposed by the European Commission, could reduce the attractiveness of Luxembourg for foreign depositors and might have negative consequences for the Luxembourg banking industry.

II. Economic policies

The Luxembourg authorities have been operating in a favourable economic environment: general government finances have been in surplus for over a decade and the debt-to-GDP ratio – at around 7 per cent – has been well below the criterion of the Maastricht Treaty. On the monetary side, long-term interest rates have continued to trend down, reaching historically low levels, at least in nominal terms. On the fiscal side, policy has become more expansionary, as government investment has increased sharply, in particular for schools and motorways, and taxes have come down. Future challenges centre on the affordability of the social security system, and in particular the pension system. Furthermore, the process of globablisation has increased the need for international co-operation on taxation, and tax incentives have come under closer scrutiny by the European Union and the OECD.

Monetary policy

Owing to economic union with Belgium, Luxembourg does not have an independent monetary policy and interest rates are closely linked to Belgian rates. Hence, as in Belgium, money market rates have edged up while long-term rates have continued to trend down, reaching historically low levels, at least in nominal terms. Due to the convergence of long-term interest rates with German rates, Luxembourg franc issues dropped sharply in 1997 as investors favoured other EU currencies with higher interest rates, such as the Italian lira or the Spanish peseta. Also currencies outside the prospective monetary union area were in favour, such as the Danish krone or currencies with potential exchange-rate gains such as the US or Australian dollar. The market for Luxembourg franc issues, as well as for issues in all other national currencies of the euro area, will disappear with the start of European Economic and Monetary Union from the beginning of 1999.

The Luxembourg economy fulfils all the Maastricht criteria and the European Commission decided in the middle of 1997 that the economy had achieved sufficient convergence to join monetary union. Membership has led to a number of changes in domestic monetary policy arrangements and the functioning of the Luxembourg Monetary Institute (IML). The IML became the Central Bank of Luxembourg (*Banque centrale du Luxembourg*) on joining the European System of Central Banks (ESCB) in June 1998. The primary objective of the Central Bank is to maintain domestic price stability, while its basic tasks are to implement the monetary policy of the European Central Bank; to conduct foreign exchange operations; to hold and manage the official reserves of Luxembourg; to promote the smooth operation of payment systems; and to issue currency and manage its circulation. The Bank shall continue the supervision of that part of the financial sector for which it has competence (banks, investment funds, other financial institutions, except insurance undertakings). In accordance with the Maastricht Treaty, the Bank is independent insofar as ESCB-related tasks are concerned. Currently, the government is preparing a bill to split competences: the Central Bank of Luxembourg will carry out central bank activities in the strict sense; and the *Commission de surveillance du secteur financier* the prudential supervisory tasks.

The new central bank is setting up the infrastructure to carry out monetary operations. The European Central Bank has announced that remunerated minimum reserves will become one of the monetary instruments. As minimum reserves were not imposed in the past in Luxembourg, the authorities initially feared that their introduction might weaken competitiveness and could result in a relocation of financial activities. But, as the reserves will be remunerated by the prevailing repo rate, the possible negative effects have been minimised. Other monetary instruments will be standing facilities and open market operations.

Fiscal policy

Overview

Luxembourg's fiscal performance compares favourably with that of other OECD countries, with the general government account having been in surplus for over a decade. Generally, the social security sector – in particular the pension scheme – has been in surplus, and the accounts for central government and local authorities have been in surplus or close to balance. Although no formal medium-term target for the general government balance is set, a budget norm exist for central government and balance requirements for the different social security schemes. Central government spending is subject to an expenditure norm, based on a medium-term real GDP growth rate and the institutionalised wage indexation mechanism (*échelle mobile*). In practice, the norm is applied in a flexible way to allow for exceptional expenditures. Moreover, due to the lack of historical data, the medium-term growth rate is based on estimated GDP growth in recent years, and varies from year to year: in the 1997 budget proposal, the medium-term growth rate was set at 3 per cent, while in the 1998 budget proposal it was set at 3.6 per cent. In addition, large investment projects are not subject to the budget norm and are financed outside the central government budget by special investment funds, though government funding of these funds is subject to the norm. Hence, in recent years, current expenditure has exceeded the budget norm without capital spending being squeezed.[13] According to the authorities, the part of central government spending that is subject to the budget norm has edged down, from around 31 per cent of GDP in the early 1990s to around 29 per cent in 1998. However, once special funds are taken into account, central government spending has slightly increased from 29 per cent in 1994 to 30 per cent in 1998 (Table 5).[14]

Balance requirements exist in the social security sector, where the different schemes are legally required to maintain minimum reserves. However, social security spending is not subject to a norm, and has steadily increased as

Table 5. **Central government budget**[1]

LF billion

	1994 Final	1995 Final	1996 Final	1997 Provisional	1998 Estimate
Primary receipts	148.7	156.0	171.1	185.2	186.7
as a per cent of GDP	29.8	30.1	31.3	31.6	30.1
Of which:					
Indirect taxes	62.0	65.2	72.7	77.0	77.3
Direct taxes	75.0	77.7	85.7	92.1	93.5
Primary expenditure	144.0	156.1	164.3	176.3	186.7
as a per cent of GDP	28.9	30.1	30.1	30.0	30.1
Of which:					
Consumption	42.0	47.8	49.4	54.2	54.4
Transfers to other sectors	29.0	24.3	26.1	28.3	29.2
Transfers to local government and social					
security	49.7	59.2	63.1	67.4	69.2
Investment and capital transfers	21.7	23.1	23.5	23.9	31.0
Primary surplus	4.7	−0.1	6.8	8.9	0.1
Net interest payments	−0.7	−0.6	−1.0	−1.4	−1.8
Financial balance	5.4	0.5	7.8	10.3	1.9
as a per cent of GDP	1.1	0.1	1.4	1.8	0.3
Memorandum items:					
Budget growth norm	4.7	4.9	3.8	5.9	5.1
Expenditure growth					
(excluding special funds)	8.7	3.6	11.0	2.2	0.9

1. National definition. This table is not comparable with Table 6 which is on an SNA basis. The accounts of special state funds have been consolidated with the central government account.
Source: Inspection générale des finances and OECD Secretariat.

a per cent of GDP, sometimes due to policy decisions but – as in the case of health care – also due to rapid cost increases and growing demand in the existing schemes (see also Chapter IV). If surpluses in the social sector fall short of their legal requirements, statutory benefits have to be reduced, contributions have to be raised, or central government has to increase transfers to the social security sector. It should be noted that such transfers are subject to the budget norm of the central government.

Recent budgetary outcomes for 1997 and the 1998 budget

According to provisional estimates, the 1997 budget outcome was substantially better than projected and the surplus in the general government account edged up to 2.9 per cent of GDP in 1997 (Table 6). Tax revenues were expected to have slowed, following tax reductions for enterprises. However, as a result of tax windfalls, in particular in the financial sector, tax receipts were 6 per cent higher than a year earlier. Government investment surged owing to the start of some large school projects. The general government debt was – at only 6.4 per cent of GDP – very low compared with other OECD countries.

Table 6.   **General government budget and debt**

SNA basis, LF billion

	1994	1995	1996[1]	1997[1]	1998[2]
General government net lending	13.6	9.5	15.3	17.1	8.4
As a per cent of GDP	2.7	1.8	2.8	2.9	1.4
Central government	4.8	–0.1	6.9	8.9	0.1
Local government	1.0	1.7	2.7	1.9	0.1
Social security	7.8	7.9	5.7	6.3	8.2
General government gross debt	27.6	30.0	34.7	37.8	42.3
As a per cent of GDP	5.5	5.8	6.3	6.4	6.8

1.   Provisional.
2.   Estimates.
Source: Inspection générale des finances and OECD Secretariat.

Assuming medium-term GDP growth at 3.6 per cent, the government fixed the budget norm for 1998 at 4.25 per cent. According to the government, almost 90 per cent of the budgetary expansion was already earmarked for increases in salaries and pensions for civil servants and an increase in child benefits by LF 1 000 for each child per month. The budgetary impact of the latter was offset by a similar reduction in the dependency exemption for each child in the income tax, as part of the restructuring of child support. This change will be especially beneficial for low-income families, who will profit little from the reduction in income tax, as also proposed in the budget. Hardly any room was left for new spending initiatives within the central government budget, and expenditure restraint was budgeted to fall on government employment and capital expenditure. However, many of the new spending initiatives, especially for infrastructure, would be financed outside the budgetary framework by special funds. Thus, total government investment was projected to increase by more than 25 per cent – reaching more than 3 per cent of GDP – as a start was made with the construction of two new motorways.

In response to intensified international tax competition, the government continued to reduce company taxes, to match more favourable tax regimes elsewhere. The corporate tax rate was again reduced in 1998 to 30 per cent and – under certain conditions – the wealth tax became deductible from the corporation tax. Moreover, the system of tax provision in the financial sector was broadened and enterprises were allowed to make special provisions for the costs associated with the introduction of the euro in 1999. As a result, the normal tax rate for companies came down to 37.45 per cent in 1998 compared with 40.3 per cent in 1996. The budget also contained measures to reduce income taxes by LF 7 billion (1.2 per cent of GDP), partly to neutralise the effects of inflation on tax brackets. Despite these measures, tax receipts were again projected to increase. However, total central government receipts may have fallen as transfers from local authorities dropped sharply, due to changes in the financing of nursery and primary education. On this basis, the surplus of the central government budget may have almost completely disappeared. In addition, the surplus in the local authority sector is also expected to have been lower. However, the overall surplus of the social security sector may have improved, owing to a temporary rise in the contributions for health insurance to bolster the reserves of the health fund to the legally required level. Overall the authorities expect the general government finances to have remained in surplus in 1998. The public sector debt is expected to have increased to 6.8 per cent of GDP, as the government has taken over the debts of the national railway company.

The 1999 budget and beyond

In the 1999 budget, central government expenditure is projected to rise by 5.9 per cent, well below the 1999 expenditure growth norm (6.6 per cent). Central in the budget is the National Action Plan to Promote Employment, with total costs of LF 2.6 billion (0.4 per cent of GDP), mainly financed by the Employment Fund (see Chapter III). The Plan foresees the introduction of a parental leave scheme (LF 1.5 billion), half of which is financed by the budget. The government also participates for 45 per cent in the financing of a long-term nursing scheme (initial total costs LF 6.2 billion), which will be introduced in 1999. As in 1998, child benefits will be increased by LF 1 000 for each child, as part of the restructuring of child support. Government investment remains at a relatively high level (3 per cent of GDP), due to the continuing construction of two motor-ways and some school building projects. Furthermore, the government's multi-annual investment plan includes the construction of a new light railway, the so-called "Bus-Tram-Bahn". The government expects that the central government budget (excluding the special funds) will show only a slight surplus.

The current fiscal position of Luxembourg is healthy and budgetary problems are not expected in the near future. However, a potential problem is the rapid expansion of government expenditure, especially in the social security sector. The introduction of a long-term nursing care scheme and the widening of the disability scheme may further add to underlying pressures on expenditure. Currently population-ageing problems are less serious in Luxembourg than in most other countries, because of the relatively young population and the heavy reliance on cross-border workers, who currently contribute more to the system than they receive in benefits. However, these workers are building up substantial claims on the social security system and the number of pensions has already been growing faster than the number of contributors to the pension scheme. Nevertheless the reserves of the general pension scheme are still beyond the legal limits.

At the end of 1995, the government commissioned an actuarial study of all existing pension schemes in Luxembourg. The study showed that – with zero employment growth in the public sector – there will be two civil servants for each retired civil servant by the year 2030, compared with a ratio of three civil servants per retiree in 1994. Following this report, the government prepared legislation for a new pension bill in the public sector, bringing it more in line with the less favourable scheme in the private sector. It entails the continuation of the current system for retired employees; a transitional phase for current civil servants; and the setting up of a scheme for future civil servants, comparable to the one in the private sector. Public sector pensions will be reduced from 83.3 per cent of final income to a minimum of 72 per cent. Even under the new system, public sector workers still wanting to receive their so-called 5/6 pension can do so by working until they are 65. The pension reform bill was recently adopted by parliament.

Further measures may be necessary to preserve the long-term sus-tainability of the pension system. The financial position of the pension fund could be further improved by a better management of the fund's reserves. Currently, the reserves are exclusively invested in Luxembourg, partly in real estate and other long-term assets and partly in short-term assets. The tripartite Social Eco-nomic Council has recommended that social funds' management of reserves should be improved, by broadening the range of investment products and giving the funds the legal possibility to invest in stocks. Furthermore, the authorities could consider to create a funded complementary pension system for the private and public sector.

Tax policies to promote financial and industrial activities

The government has pursued an active policy to enhance the attractiveness of Luxembourg as a site for financial and industrial activity. The absence of monetary reserve requirements for banks, tax advantages over neighbouring countries,[15] a liberal regulatory environment, and the rapid implementation of EU directives in Luxembourg law, combined with a favourable geographical location at the heart of Europe and a qualified and multilingual labour force have been central in creating competitive advantages in financial services. Luxembourg's traditional insistence on protecting the confidentiality of banking information, (except in clearly defined circumstances, such as money laundering) has also contributed to its success as a centre for financial activity.[16] Today, more than 200 banks have been established in the country, accounting for 17 per cent of GDP (national version, cf. footnote 1), 20 per cent of central government revenues and 9 per cent of employment.

Recent years have brought increasing attention to the international aspects of taxation and of the need for tax co-ordination, particularly within the European Union. Various factors have contributed to this interest such as the process of globalisation and the development of global strategies by multinational enterprises. Technological innovation has affected the way in which multinational enterprises are managed, making a physical location of management and other service activities much less important. International financial markets continue to expand. The OECD has long recognised that fair competition in this new environment encourages government to deliver public services in a cost-effective way. Moreover, differences in tax levels and structures between countries reflect preferences in public versus private provisions of goods and services. However, these developments, as noted in the recent OECD Report on Harmful Tax Competition (OECD, 1998a), opened up the danger that governments may develop tax schemes as well as non-tax measures to attract geographically highly mobile activities. Globablisation also opens up new ways for individuals and companies to minimise their tax liabilities by exploiting differences in tax systems between countries. Thus the spread of preferential tax schemes may encourage activities, which are primarily aimed at promoting profit-shifting without corresponding shifts in real activities. This form of tax competition is regarded as harmful as it carries the risk of distorting trade and investment and could lead to the erosion of national tax bases.[17]

To counter the negative effects of tax competition on international welfare, the EU and the OECD recently issued reports on this subject. At the end of 1997, the EU council, chaired by Luxembourg, agreed to a package of measures to tackle harmful tax competition in order to help to reduce tax distortions in the Single European Market. The package includes a Code of Conduct on business taxation. The OECD has adopted a Report including a set of Guidelines, limited to financial and other service activities (OECD, 1998a). Although recognising the need to combat harmful preferential tax regimes, the Luxembourg authorities find the approach of the OECD Report and Recommendations to counteract harmful tax competition partial and unbalanced. In particular, they object to the assessment that bank secrecy is a criterion to identify such regimes. Thus, the authorities have abstained from approving the OECD Report or its Recommendations and are not bound by them.[18]

Another aspect of the government's policy to improve the economic structure is the implementation of financial aid and other incentives to attract new industries as part of the diversification policy. The policy aims at improving the economic and regional structure and is especially targeted at regions confronted with severe job losses due to the restructuring of the steel industry. As EU regulations restrict this type of industrial policy and general investment grants are no longer permitted with the exception of small and medium sized enterprises, a new industrial diversification law came into force in 1993, restricting investment grants to regional aid, and introducing three subsidy schemes for small business investment, R&D, energy-saving and environment-protecting investment. During the period 1976-1995, more than 120 projects profited from these measures and created more than 10 000 new jobs in the business sector. However, the effects on national employment were limited as resident and non-resident foreign workers have taken 75 per cent of these jobs (Statec, 1997b). The projects approved in 1997 are expected to create 1 000 new jobs, almost 50 per cent more than a year earlier.

The diversification policy has been successful in creating jobs in the manufacturing sector, although it may have resulted in a sub-optimal allocation of resources by substituting administrative judgement for market judgement as to the most promising industries or growth areas for the economy. The authorities feel that this risk is minimal, as given the size of the economy, they are in much closer contact with industry than authorities in other countries. Another objection to the policy is that these tax incentives (or subsidies) do not seem to address a clearly identified market failure but are mainly motivated by social or political objectives such as maintaining employment in the steel producing regions. In the present context of almost full employment, subsidies may be especially harmful because they may have delayed the adjustment process. The tightening of restrictions on state aid by the European Commission will restrain the scope of the diversification policy in future. Hence, the authorities should focus their policies more on structural reforms to enhance competitiveness by removing rigidities in the labour market and further pursue regulatory reform (see Chapter III).

To preserve international competitiveness, the government has aimed at reducing the tax wedge, and notably employers' social security contributions, by increasing transfers to the social security funds. Currently, social security contributions constitute only 50 per cent of the receipts of the social security sector.[19] In 1996, the total tax wedge (including social security contributions) of the average production worker in Luxembourg was 34.5 per cent, compared with 56.4 per cent in Belgium (OECD, 1997b). Recent actions in this area include the successive increases in government transfers to the child benefit system (*allocation familiales*) to replace the employers' contributions to the system in 1994 and to finance the increases in child benefits in 1998 and 1999. The Social Economic Council (*Conseil économique et social*, 1998) has warned against the growing share of government funding of the social security budget, as it may reduce the role of the social partners in this sector. Furthermore the Council expressed concern that this policy might cause imbalances in the long term: with pension liabilities rapidly building up, additional tax receipts – generated by new jobs – could become inadequate to finance the increase in social security spending.

III. Implementing structural reform: a review of progress

Introduction

Within the framework set out by the OECD Jobs Study, the 1997 OECD *Economic Survey of Luxembourg* (OECD, 1997a) provided a set of detailed policy recommendations to improve the functioning of the labour market (Box). These recommendations were derived from a review of structural features of the Luxembourg economy, which determine employment possibilities and the level of structural unemployment. The analysis emphasised that Luxembourg's unemployment problems were minor in comparison with those in other European countries, but that unemployment was on a rising trend. Moreover, labour force participation is relatively low, partly reflecting that a large number of people of working age were in other benefit schemes, such as disability and early retirement, and had effectively left the labour market. In addition, female participation has been low, as many women prefer to stay at home to look after their children, which is facilitated by high family incomes, generous child benefits and income tax deductions for children.

The increase in unemployment over the past two decades may to some extent reflect an increasing mismatch between supply of and demand for labour, against a background of a lack of sufficient skills and wage adjustment. Due to the restructuring of the steel industry and automation in the banking sector, job opportunities for low skilled workers have largely disappeared, and the demand for higher skilled and qualified jobs has risen. The authorities also attribute the slow rise in unemployment to the poor labour market conditions in regions within commuting distance from Luxembourg, where unemployment has remained at around 9 per cent, compared with only 3 per cent in Luxembourg. During the past 20 years, an increasing number of people from these areas have found work in Luxembourg, attracted by good job prospects and relatively high (net) wages. Currently, these cross-border workers take around 75 per cent of jobs created in Luxembourg.

Box. Implementing the OECD Jobs Strategy – an overview of progress

Since the previous *Survey*, a number of policy measures in the spirit of the OECD Jobs Strategy have been either implemented or prepared. However progress has been slow and uneven and a few important measures have not been considered.

Job strategy proposal	Action taken	OECD assessment/ recommendations
1. Increase wage and labour cost flexibility		
– Reform the wage bargaining system, phase out wage indexation and consider relaxing the administrative extension of sectoral wage agreements.	The government has submitted a new law on collective agreements to Parliament, giving more possibilities for derogation of collective agreements.	Improve flexibility in wage bargaining and remove wage indexation.
– Reduce the minimum wage and its indexation.	The minimum wage was twice increased in 1997, due to the biannual revision and the statutory wage indexation, and will be increased again in 1999.	Reduce the impact of the minimum wage by either reducing the minimum wage for certain groups, such as young people above the age of 17, in combination with in-work benefits or by subsidies to employers.
– If for political or social reasons wage flexibility cannot be increased sufficiently, further reduce taxes and employers' social security contributions for low-skilled workers.	Social security contributions for blue-collar workers were temporarily increased in 1998.	Reduce social security contributions for low-wage earners or at least for blue-collar workers.
2. Reform unemployment and related benefit schemes		
– Reduce the generosity of the social security system and especially the unemployment benefit scheme.	The generosity of the system has been maintained but placement and counselling services have improved and sanctions have been applied more often.	Assess whether this is sufficient and strengthen incentives to look for work or a place in a training scheme at least by intensifying the surveillance on being available for work and job search, and an even stricter application of sanctions for non-compliance.

(continued on next page)

(*continued*)

Job strategy proposal	Action taken	OECD assessment/ recommendations
– Reduce the withdrawal rate of benefits of additional earnings in the general assistance scheme (RMG).	No action has been taken in this area.	Improve incentives to look for work for people in the RMG.
– De-couple the housing assistance from the RMG.	Housing assistance rules will be changed in the revised RMG scheme.	Assess whether this has been sufficient.
– Tighten access to early retirement and disability schemes.	Access to some early retirement schemes has been relaxed. A new law has been introduced in parliament broadening the scope of the disability scheme. Medical criteria for disability have been tightened.	Tighten access to the early retirement schemes. Re-examine beneficiaries at regular intervals and promote their integration in the labour market.

3. Expand and enhance active labour market policies

– Apply more strictly the working requirement in the RMG scheme.	The Public Employment Service has intensified the individual support of the young and long-term unemployed. Benefits will be withdrawn from those who refuse to participate in training programmes. The Public Employment Service will be reinforced and remodelled.	Assess whether recent steps have been sufficient.

4. Increase employment flexibility

– Relax employment protection legislation and ease restrictions on fixed-term contracts.	The strict working hours legislation for part-time workers will be relaxed on a temporary basis. The government has submitted a new law to Parliament, allowing for a relaxation of the working hours regulations.	Continue to reform the strict working hours legislation and remove obstacles for part-time work and temporary work contracts.

Luxembourg's strict labour market regulations are similar to those in surrounding countries, although the social and economic context of Luxembourg has often allowed pragmatic and flexible solutions. An additional important element of labour market flexibility is provided by the continuous increase in cross-border workers. However, some impediments to (national) employment growth could be identified, such as restrictions on fixed-term contracts or strict employment protection rules, which may have an adverse effect on the hiring of long-term unemployed. Other major impediments stem from a lack of incentives to look for work, reflecting generous social welfare benefits and high marginal effective tax rates. The authorities have taken measures especially to promote employment for the young and long-term unemployed. Among the many specific suggestions, the *Survey* stressed the need to:

- reform the wage bargaining system, abolish wage indexation and reduce minimum wages;
- reduce the generosity of the social security system and, more generally, increase incentives to return to the active labour market;
- apply more strictly the working requirement in the social assistance scheme (*revenu minimum garanti*, RMG);
- relax employment protection legislation and restrictions on fixed-term contracts.

Recently, the government presented a National Action Plan to Promote Employment (*Plan d'action national en faveur de l'emploi*) in connection with EU guidelines, and prepared by a tripartite commission (*Comité de coordination tripartite*) chaired by the Prime Minister. Reflecting the priorities established by the European Council, the Plan is centred around four pillars: the improvement of employability, the development of entrepreneurial skills, the encouragement of adaptability in businesses, and the strengthening of equal opportunity policies. The measures proposed by the National Action Plan are a compromise between government and social partners. Its purpose is not only to combat unemployment but also to preserve existing employment, to increase the participation of the resident population, and particularly of women, and to target young people and long-term and older unemployed or those that risk becoming long-term unemployed. Special attention is given to education, training and lifelong learning programmes. The authorities estimate the costs of the Plan to be around LF 2.6 billion, partly to be financed by an increase of 1 franc on the social security charge on petrol. This increase will not spill over into the institutionalised wage indexation mechanism.

Increase wage and labour cost flexibility

No progress has been made in improving wage flexibility but the government recently submitted a new law on collective agreements to Parliament, which gives enterprises more possibilities for derogation of collective agreements. The authorities are not in favour of abolishing the institutionalised wage indexation, as it is in their view a guarantee for social peace. The indexation will only be suspended during periods of serious economic crises as laid down in the 1975 wage indexation law.[20] Concerning wage negotiations, the 1994 agreement between the government and the social partners (employers and employees) to moderate wages is still in force, stating that real wage increases should lag behind productivity growth. The biennial revision of the social minimum wage has not been changed and the social minimum wage was increased by 3.2 per cent in January 1997, following the real wage increase in the total economy. Moreover, the Prime-Minister announced during his State of the Nation address that social minimum wages will be adjusted again in January 1999 for past real wage increases, underlining the government's policy that all residents should share in the rising overall prosperity.

Another way to promote employment for low-skilled people would be to lower non-wage labour costs for workers at the lower end of the wage scale. The government has not introduced new measures to reduce non-wage labour costs, given the lack of response from employers to existing programmes for long-term and older unemployed. On the contrary, non-wage labour costs for blue-collar workers were increased by 0.8 percentage point in 1998, in order to restore the reserves of the health funds. This increase is temporary and health insurance contributions are set to come down again in 1999.

Reform unemployment and related benefit schemes

Access to the disability scheme should have been tightened, following several court rulings stating that disability in the current legislation is incompatible with the possibility of exercising a full-time job. However, strong growth of new disability pensions continued unabated at least until recently, as well as the decline in the average age of the disabled. Hence, the authorities have concluded that the actual practice of granting disability pensions is likely to differ considerably from the legal provisions. To end ambiguities, the government is preparing a new disability act. In the new act, a distinction will be made between general disability and occupational disability, similar to legislation in France and Germany. A person will be declared generally disabled if his potential earnings are less than a third of the social minimum wage. If the earning capacity is reduced by more than 50 per cent, a person can receive an occupational disability pension, which is 50 per cent of the general pension benefit but can be cumulated with income from other professional activities up to a certain ceiling.[21] Recently, medical criteria for disability were tightened, resulting in a lower inflow into the disability scheme.

The 1997 *Survey* recommended tightening access to early retirement schemes. The National Action Plan, however, includes some measures to facilitate access to these schemes. The government has announced that it will reduce some constraints, that have limited the use of the part-time early retirement scheme (*préretraite progressive*).[22] Also, in the solidarity early retirement scheme (*préretraite-solidarité*) rules for replacing an older worker by an unemployed person will be relaxed. However, it should be noted that the extensive use of the early retirement schemes is set to end, now that the restructuring of the steel industry is complete. Furthermore, no changes have been made to the unemployment benefit scheme, which was judged in the previous *Survey* to be too generous, in particular in terms of net replacement rates. According to the authorities, the high net replacement rations do not have a significant effect on the length of unemployment spells. Only 20 per cent of unemployed stay for the full period of one year in the unemployment scheme.[23] Therefore, they have preferred to maintain the generosity of the system and have improved placement and counselling services for the unemployed. Moreover, sanctions have been applied more often to those unwilling to take up work.[24] Other problems earlier identified concern the disincentives to look for work in the social assistance scheme (*revenu minimum garanti*, RMG), where the transition to work might leave people in some cases worse off. The government has announced a review of the RMG, including a revision in the calculation of the housing assistance, which will reduce the high marginal effective tax rate for people in this scheme.

Enhance active labour market policy

Active labour market policies for older unemployed have not been very successful. In 1997, only 150 people used wage subsidy programmes for older and long-term unemployed (*aide à l'embauche de chômeurs âgés et de longue durée*), although more than 1 000 registered unemployed would have qualified for these programmes. The lack of skills has been often an obstacle for employers to take on a long-term unemployed. Hence, the, the National Action Plan emphasises the improvement of skills and competences. As part of the Plan, a new training scheme (*stage de réinsertion professionnel*) will offer trainee positions for long-term and older unemployed in enterprises, lasting for up to a year. Participants will receive a benefit equal to the statutory minimum wage, 50 per cent of which will be paid by the Employment Fund (or 65 per cent in the case of women) and will get priority in recruitment if a suitable position in the enterprise arises.

Although youth unemployment does not seem to be a serious problem, the authorities have also decided to strengthen programmes targeted at this group (*Stage de préparation en entreprise*, Division d'auxiliaires temporaires (DAT), and *stage-initiation*), by increasing wage subsidies for employers to 50 per cent (or 65 per cent for women). But, the duration of the DAT contracts will be reduced from two years to one year, to prevent people staying in these programmes for long periods. These programmes could offer young people a chance to enter the labour market, and 70 per cent of participants have found regular employment through them. However, the dead-weight costs of these programmes are likely to be relatively high: given the short unemployment spells of youngsters, many of them would have probably found a job without these programmes.

Increase employment flexibility

Progress in this area – which in Luxembourg falls in the first instance within the purview of the social partners – has been painstakingly slow. Social partners have been able to agree only on the necessity of modernising the current strict legislation concerning working hours.[25] The government has announced the relaxation of rules on part-time work. Working hours will now be calculated on the basis of the minimum reference period of four weeks. However, this measure will only be applied on a temporary basis to verify its impact on the labour market. In addition, the government has submitted a new law on collective agreements to Parliament, including a minimum reference period of four weeks for all workers. The law will also offer the possibility to fix longer or shorter reference periods (with a maximum of a year) by collective agreement. Furthermore the government will examine the possibilities of supporting the transition from full-time to part-time work. This is already the case for older workers in the part-time early retirement scheme. In addition, the government has undertaken to provide financial incentives in the case of collective agreements that seek to reduce working hours and, at the same time, to recruit unemployed workers. If registered unemployed workers are hired, the Employment Fund pays their social security contributions – ranging from 22.4 per cent to 32.1 per cent of the gross salary – for five years. Although it is too early to assess the effectiveness of this scheme, experiences in other countries suggest that the costs of such programmes can be very high, and their effectiveness in terms of aggregate employment limited. Dead-weight losses could be large, if employers and employees would have agreed on reducing working hours, even without the subsidy. In addition, it is not clear what will happen after five years when the wage subsidy expires and the employer is confronted with a substantial increase in labour costs.

The Public Employment Service (ADEM) and temporary employment agencies signed an agreement for closer co-operation from the beginning of 1998. The aim is to make it easier for job seekers registered at ADEM to contact employers using the services of temporary employment agencies. The temporary employment agencies will notify ADEM of work offers, initially lasting a minimum of two weeks; they will also be involved in the administrative monitoring of employment offers. Meanwhile, ADEM will notify these firms of job offers that are clearly identifiable as temporary.

Improving labour force skills and competences

In the framework of the National Action Plan, the apprentice scheme will be reorganised to improve co-operation between schools and enterprises. In addition, the number of apprentice places will be substantially increased, especially for craftsmen. Links between the different courses in the general education and vocational education systems will be improved to facilitate the reorientation of pupils. Furthermore, the number of two-stage apprenticeship courses, that were set up for pupils with learning difficulties, will be enlarged. Finally, the apprentice scheme – which mainly addresses youngsters between 15 and 18 years – will be opened to adults.

The government has reached agreement with the social partners concerning the regulation of lifelong learning schemes and introduced a bill in parliament. A recently opened centre for professional training (*Centre national de la formation professionnelle continue*, CNFPC) will unfold new initiatives for lifelong training programmes. In addition, the government continues its support to schooling activities by branch organisations, and organisations of employers and employees. The government and social partners are also studying new projects to improve the employability of the unemployed, by providing financial support to schemes where the unemployed are temporarily taken on to replace workers that take leave of absence for reasons such as maternity, parental, and sabbatical leave. Although such schemes may be useful in upgrading the skills of the workforce, it is questionable if they should be subsidised. In general, the financing of paid-leave schemes should be settled in the private sector – as is the case with other working time arrangements – and be part of the negotiated wage agreements. Furthermore, the Danish experience with such publicly-financed schemes has been mixed. The generosity of the system encouraged many people to take paid-leave, thereby creating shortages in some segments of the labour market. As a result, the Danish authorities have abolished some of the schemes and scaled back the generosity of others.

Increasing product market competition

The European articles on competition policy, and in particular article 85 and 86, have been implemented in the Luxembourg legislation. Although strict licensing laws may have limited the entry in various professions, which could have hindered the dynamism of certain sectors, the openness of the economy and the proximity of foreign suppliers may have provided a check on abuses of market power. To promote entrepreneurship, the government has embarked on a policy of relaxing existing regulations and reducing administrative burdens. The relaxation of the establishment law in 1997, has allowed enterprises to widen their activities and has resulted in an improvement in their management. The authorities are preparing a relaxation of the strict rules on certificates in certain branches and abolition of limitations on the number of subsidiaries a person can own. Instead, some minimum certificate requirements will be introduced for managing a subsidiary. Furthermore, the government is intending to relax working-hour regulations for bakeries. In the area of reducing administrative burdens, a pilot scheme is currently underway to streamline procedures for setting up enterprises by introducing a one-counter system for administrative declarations. In addition, the burden of statistical data collection for Intrastat and Statec will be reduced. Finally, attached to every legislative proposal will be an evaluation of its impact on small and medium-sized enterprises (SMEs).

Administrative reform

In 1996, the government approved a major administrative reform programme, which focused on externally and internally oriented reforms. The externally oriented reforms aim at improving the quality of the public service. The government is focusing on a number of practical measures to be implemented in the short and medium term, such as the publication of a users' charter and the improvement of information to the public. The internally oriented reforms aim more at improving the internal organisation of the administration and its managerial methods, in order to improve the quality of the service. The most noteworthy initiatives in this field are the overhaul of public accounting and financial management procedures, the creation of a computerised personnel management system, merging of the *Gendarmerie* and the police force, revision of existing mechanisms for the recruitment into the civil service and improving the integration of trainees in the administration. Furthermore, the government is in the process of opening up the public service to nationals from other EU countries, following a judgement by the European Court of Justice in 1996.

Assessment and scope for further action

As economic growth has been robust and labour market conditions have remained satisfactory, the government has not engaged in a broad structural reform programme. Indeed, the good macroeconomic performance over the past fifteen years does not seem to indicate that the economy is lacking in dynamism. However, despite the current buoyancy, unemployment has only slightly come down. Labour market reform has been slow as decisions in this area are taken on the basis of consensus between the social partners. This consultation process between social partners is an essential element of the Luxembourg model, and has been a guarantee for social peace.

Given that unemployment remained relatively high at the low-wage end of the labour market, the National Action Plan rightly put the emphasis on raising the productivity of low-skilled workers by education, training, and lifelong learning programmes. However, such programmes will have an effect only in the medium term. Moreover, these programmes will not reach all low-skilled people. Therefore, in the short term, the government should consider reducing non-wage labour costs for the lower skilled or encouraging lower (minimum) wages for certain groups, such as for young people above the age of 17.[26] The reported success of subsidised youth training schemes is a clear indication that the high minimum wage for this group, often lacking in sufficient experience, is a handicap in finding a job. Also evidence from other OECD countries suggests that young people face less employment opportunities if a high minimum wage exists (OECD, 1998b). More generally, a lower minimum wage combined with in-work benefits may create new jobs, enhance incentives to work, and keep the standard of living of low-skilled workers at a socially accepted level. In terms of aggregate employment creation, this may be more effective than wage subsidies targeted at specific groups: studies in other countries show that such schemes have high dead-weight and substitution effects as employers may release people who do not get a subsidy and replace them with people who do.[27] However, the effectiveness of an in-work benefit depends on several features of the labour market, the wage distribution and benefit systems. The extra finance needed for the benefits could be quite substantial. If it is to be raised through income taxes, a large group of workers – depending on the wage distribution – may experience an increase in marginal tax rates, thus encouraging them to reduce their hours of work. If the financing needs are reduced through a high claw-back rate, this may lead to very high marginal effective tax rates for certain income ranges. Hence, poverty traps could spread to new segments of the labour market.

In addition, priority should be given to increasing participation in the labour market and in particular by women and older people. In this context, the authorities could proceed more forcefully in taking measures to promote part-time work, by further removing obstacles. Given that most part-time work is done by women, such an approach may be more effective – in terms of costs and net employment gains – than subsidies for women in training schemes, given the high dead-weight and substitution effects usually associated with such programmes. However, for reasons mentioned above, promoting part-time work arrangements through subsidised schemes should be avoided. Furthermore, the authorities should maintain the recently introduced tighter control and access to the disability schemes. Although the proposed legislation in this area broadens the scope of eligibility, the reform is welcome as it allows people in the new professional disability scheme to participate in the labour market. However, the authorities should continue to carefully monitor the growth of the number of beneficiaries in both schemes and consider further measures to limit the schemes to those in genuine need.

IV. The Luxembourg health system

Introduction

The quality of the Luxembourg health service is high and access is universal. Although health care spending, as a percentage of GDP, is modest compared with other OECD countries, it is very high in absolute terms, especially when considering the favourable age structure of the population. While the Luxembourg health system shows similarities with systems operating in Belgium, Germany and France, its specific traits are the cover it provides for a large group of non-residents – essentially cross-border workers – and the use of health services in neighbouring countries. In 1992, some cost containment policies were introduced but they did not result in a deceleration of health expenditure and further reforms seem necessary to contain expenditure pressures due to technological progress and population ageing. The first section focuses on the size of the Luxembourg health system and overall resource use. The second section describes the main features of the system and identifies potential inefficiencies and inappropriate incentives. The third section concludes with some recommendations for further policy initiatives to improve the efficiency of the system.[28]

The size of the health sector

Luxembourg national health spending[29] as percentage of GDP – at 7 per cent – is below the OECD average, but spending per head is one of the highest among the OECD countries (Table 7).[30] The statutory health insurance – to which almost the entire population belongs – finances around two-thirds of national health expenditure. As in many other OECD countries, health expenditure is rising sharply. During the period 1990-1997, nominal health expenditure rose by more than 8 per cent a year on average, more or less in all areas of medical care, raising its share in GDP by 0.5 percentage point.

Traditional explanatory factors for health expenditure, such as the size of the insured population, the number of elderly and price of health care, do not seem to provide an explanation for the rapid increase in spending. Concerning

Table 7. **Health expenditure in relation to GDP and per capita, 1997**

	As a percentage of GDP	Per capita (dollars, using PPP exchange rates)
Luxembourg	**7.1**	**2 340**
Belgium	7.6	1 747
France	9.6	2 051
Germany	10.4	2 339
United Kingdom	6.6	1 347
United States	13.5	4 090

Source: OECD Health Data 98; OECD Purchasing Power Parity Statistics.

demographic pressures, the Luxembourg health system seems in a better position than those elsewhere since the average age of the insured population is relatively low and falling. One of the reasons for the favourable age structure is the large number of foreign workers (residents as well as cross-border workers). This has two effects: first, their average age is lower than that of the Luxembourg residents and second, in accordance with EU rules, those foreign nationals who return to their country of origin will often be at the charge of their national insurance system.[31] Hence, many older people with high medical costs leave the Luxembourg health system. Medical expenditures have been rising in many OECD countries with very different types of health care systems, suggesting common factors such as technical progress (see, for example, Newhouse, 1992); but in the case of Luxembourg, the particular institutional structures (and associated incentives) for funding and providing health care may also have been conducive to the rapid increase in spending.

In general, the quality of health services has been high. In a recent European survey, about 70 per cent of Luxembourg respondents expressed satisfaction with the health system, which is substantially higher than the average level of satisfaction in the European Union (50 per cent).[32] Moreover, the life expectancy at birth, at 73 for men and 80 years for women, ranks among the highest in the OECD area. In addition, infant mortality – at 4.9 per thousand births – is very low by international standards. However, indicators for resource use point to relatively high inputs, in particular for hospital services. The number of hospital beds – at 10.7 per 1 000 persons – is well above the OECD average and the average hospital admission rates and duration of stay have also been higher than in most other countries.[33] Besides, one has to take into account that Luxembourg residents also use hospitals in neighbouring countries for treatments which are not available in their own country. In addition, the consumption of pharmaceuticals per head – outside the hospital sector – is about 10 per cent above the OECD average.

Problems with the institutional setting

Main features of the system[34]

The Luxembourg social insurance model for the provision of health care shows similarities with systems operating in Belgium, France and Germany. There is only one public scheme, administered by the Union de caisse de maladie (UCM), whose board is made up of representatives of employers and employees, with a single government representative having the casting vote.[35]

Universal coverage is a key aspect of the statutory health system. Affiliation to the scheme is obligatory for anybody who exercises a professional activity in Luxembourg, people receiving an income-replacing benefit, or students if they are not already covered.[36] The system also provides coverage for a large group of non-residents such as cross-border workers and their dependants. This group has grown substantially in recent years and currently accounts for around 20 per cent of those insured.

Solidarity is another major feature of the health-care system. Contributions are linked to taxable income and independent of health risk, and with household dependants co-insured without additional contributions. The insurance aspect of the system has thus been very limited. The contribution rate – set by the UCM – is dependent on expected health expenditures and the legal obligation to maintain reserves between 10 and 20 per cent of actual expenditures. The current contribution rate is 5.1 per cent of taxable income, equally divided between employees and employers.[37] Almost 40 per cent of the public insurance system is funded by the central government in two ways. First, the government pays for certain benefits, such as normal maternity benefits. Second, it pays an extra premium of 250 per cent on contributions from pensioners and 10 per cent on contributions from the active population.

Each medical act which is covered by the insurance is noted down in the so-called nomenclature with its corresponding reimbursement. The nomenclature is jointly decided by the Ministers of Health and Social Security, on the basis of recommendations from the Commission de nomenclature, the medical college and the Conseil supérieur des professions de la santé.[38] Acts which are not included in the nomenclature can be reimbursed on advice from the medical inspection of the social security. Given the size of the country, it would not be feasible to offer treatment for all pathologies in Luxembourg. Hence, the insurance reimburses treatment received abroad, although conditional on permission from the medical inspection. Such permission cannot be refused if treatment is not available from a Luxembourg health institute.

Medical treatment is mainly provided on a fee-for-service basis. As health services are almost completely covered by insurance, a meaningful market price cannot be observed. Hence, the UCM concludes conventions with organisations of health practitioners, which are legally binding for all medical practitioners in Luxembourg. The law sets minimum requirements for these conventions, such as the determination of fees for all medical acts covered by the insurance. The Minister of Social Security can submit the convention to the *Conseil supérieur des assurances sociales*[39] if it contravenes existing laws and regulations. The law also sets a calendar for negotiations, including mediation procedures if the negotiating parties cannot reach agreement. A mediator can be nominated and in case mediation fails, the *conseil supérieur des assurances sociales* can ultimately determine the convention. Medical fees are negotiated individually – mostly without comparison with fees for other medical procedures or similar acts in neighbouring countries – and are adjusted annually according to the average wage increase in the economy, taking into account the increase in the total volume of medical acts. Only in the case of new medical treatments, do fees in neighbouring countries and Germany in particular, serve as a guideline.

Patients have complete freedom of choice of physician and hospital, and rationing of health services, such as hospital waiting lists, has been avoided. To reduce over-consumption, co-payments – up to a certain ceiling – have been introduced for prescription drugs and doctor visits.[40] Co-payments represent about 10 per cent of total medical consumption (excluding non-reimbursable drugs) and the average co-payment for reimbursable prescription drugs is about 20 per cent.

Because of the relatively high reimbursement rate and the comprehensive package of the compulsory health scheme, the role of private health insurance is very limited. The main health insurance company outside the public health scheme is the *Caisse médico-chirurgicale mutualiste* (CMCM). The CMCM insures mainly supplements for medical treatment in hospitals in Luxembourg or abroad. Although 50 per cent of persons in the public scheme are members of the CMCM, the benefits reimbursed by the CMCM amount to only 2.2 per cent of those reimbursed by the public health scheme. However, lack of competition does not seem to have resulted in administrative inefficiencies and may even have some advantages. The UCM has used its monopsonistic powers to obtain information from health providers, and improve the efficiency of health spending through benchmarking, limiting unnecessary care and challenging unjustified claims. Moreover, as a single insurer, the UCM has been able to take a broader view of health care by participating in preventive health care programmes.

Problems and challenges

As in many OECD countries, the major problems facing the Luxembourg health system are the control of expenditure and the reduction in the oversupply of medical services. The authorities have taken several initiatives to slow down health expenditure, mainly related to an improved control of medical expenditure and pressure on doctors with high prescription records. One of the results of the 1992 reform of health insurance has been the setting up of medical data banks by the UCM, thus enabling them to monitor health expenditure better, and in particular the consumption of reimbursable drugs. Furthermore, the reform altered the financing of the hospital sector by the introduction of a prospective budget system in 1995.

However, control possibilities are limited as a large and still growing proportion of insured persons is not resident in Luxembourg. They are reimbursed for consulting health practitioners in their own countries, which are not bound to Luxembourg health conventions. The control mechanisms of the UCM have been further undermined by the European Court of Justice, which recently ruled that restrictions by the Luxembourg health system on buying health services from non-domestic providers are against the free movement of goods and services in the European Union, and thus illegal.[41] Given the proximity of foreign health practitioners for Luxembourg residents, these court rulings may have serious consequences for the current health system.

Medical care

Although negotiated doctor's fees have risen only moderately, spending on medical care has progressed rapidly as the increase in the number of medical interventions has outpaced the growth of the number of insured (Figure 5). This development may be partly attributed to technical progress, but also the financing method for medical care – mainly a fee-for-service system – and the growing number of medical practitioners may have induced an increase in the number of treatments. The Luxembourg health system does not have the possibility to regulate the supply of doctors, as every physician practising in the country is by law accredited to the health system. Concerning the remuneration system, research in other countries shows that fee-for-service systems tend to lead to a substantial oversupply of health care, and may even go against the best interests of the patient.[42] Patients – not facing the full marginal cost for their decisions – may easily consume more than is strictly necessary and even get reimbursed if they consult several doctors for the same sickness episode. Moreover, lacking sufficient information to make an informed choice, they depend on the decision of medical professionals, who also provide the services required, thus creating a potential conflict of interests. In addition, patients can directly consult a specialist, without prior consultation with a general practitioner. Thus, specialists are in direct competition with general practitioners for patients. Furthermore, the ambulatory sector is not strictly separated from the hospital sector and specialists often continue the treatment of their patients in the hospital sector. Given an oversupply of hospital beds and the lack of incentives to select the most cost-effective treatment for their patients, doctors may too easily opt for hospital treatment instead of cheaper out-patient care. The UCM has tried to curb expenditure by

Figure 5. **Growth of medicals acts**

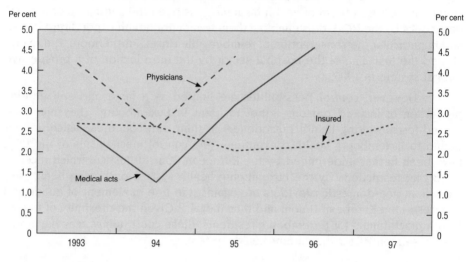

Source: Inspection générale de la sécurité sociale, UCM.

setting up data banks to monitor medical treatments more closely. This approach was initially quite successful, and the number of interventions decelerated sharply in 1994, when the system was put in place. However, its effectiveness has faded over time. Moreover, it may only have eliminated the most obvious cases of abuse of the system.

Hospital sector

Hospital care has been a major cost component and has risen quickly. As noted earlier, several indicators – such as the number of beds per head – point to substantial over-capacity in this sector. In addition, many of the hospitals are relatively small. Until 1994, hospitals received a flat-rate fee per occupied bed, thus giving them an incentive to prolong length of stay. As this fee was relatively low, hospitals would try to recuperate their costs by overcharging for ancillary hospital services and increase the output of their laboratories to balance the books. Hence, the reimbursement system encouraged unnecessary expenses and distortions in hospital management. Nevertheless, the hospital sector was heavily in deficit by the end of 1994.

The financing of the hospital sector was drastically changed in 1995 by the introduction of a budget system based on prospective spending. Hospitals receive an annual budget to cover their fixed and variable costs. However, all services by physicians remain on a fee-for-service basis.[43] The budgets are nego-tiated between the UCM and the 16 hospitals, on an individual basis. Further-more, the UCM paid off the past debts of the hospital sector, the so-called *Altlasten*.

According to the authorities, the aim of the new system was not primarily to reduce costs, but essentially to improve transparency in hospital funding. Although it may enable the UCM to put more pressure on hospitals with above-average costs to increase efficiency, the current approach provides few incentives for producers to improve the efficiency of their operations, as funding is not contingent on the quantity and quality of output, and little information on relative prices of treatment is generated or used. As negotiated contracts are based on historical costs, the current process even penalises efficient producers and puts little pressure on inefficient providers to improve. Furthermore, budgets are automatically adjusted for wage-cost increases, *i.e.* increases resulting from the wage indexation and collective labour agreements. However, hospital budgets are not automatically adjusted for changes in staffing and skill mix of hospital workers, as they are negotiated between the hospital and the UCM. In fact, in these negotiations trade union representatives are on both sides of the table: they negotiate with the hospital management on the size and composition of hospital staff, while their representatives in the UCM negotiate with the hospital manage-ment on the size of the budget. Thus in 1997, labour costs in the hospital sector increased by 6 per cent, compared with 3 per cent in the overall economy.

The authorities have been engaged in restructuring the hospital sector, but closing or merging regional hospitals have proved to be difficult. Currently the 1994 national hospital plan is in the process of being revised. However, the Social Economic Council has already criticised the updated hospital plan as it does not fix objectives nor establishes norms in relation to the country's needs (*Conseil économique et social*, 1998). Big investment projects in the hospital sector (currently above LF 120 million) are for 80 per cent financed by the state. The remaining 20 per cent are paid by the UCM, included in the annual hospital budget. These projects are the responsibility of the Minister of Health, advised by the *Commission permanente pour le secteur hospitalier*, which includes representatives of the Ministry of Social Affairs and the UCM, and the decisions often depend on the presence of the necessary medical expertise in Luxembourg and socio-political considera-tions. However, financial aspects do not seem to play an important role and the Ministry of Social Affairs and the UCM are only involved in these decisions through their membership of the *Commission hospitalier*. The financing of smaller investment projects are directly negotiated between the UCM and the hospitals.

Pharmaceuticals

The consumption of pharmaceuticals has been relatively high compared with other countries. The authorities have taken several measures to try to dampen the growth. First, co-payments have been in place for a long time. Prescription drugs have been classified in four categories, ranging from complete reimbursement to zero reimbursement, with the majority of drugs in the 80 per cent reimbursement category. Second, the UCM has set up a data bank, specifying all partly or completely reimbursable medicines outside the hospital sector by patient and prescribing physician and bought in Luxembourg. The UCM has used this data bank to monitor the prescription behaviour of physicians and, if necessary, uses pressure to correct it. In individual cases, the insurance fund may even approach the patient. Despite these measures, the consumption of drugs has increased rapidly, especially for completely reimbursable drugs.

The increase in spending on pharmaceuticals is also due to price increases, well ahead of the rate of consumer price inflation. The authorities fix prices for pharmaceuticals on the basis of producers' (or importers') sales prices in their domestic markets. At the moment, around 75 per cent of pharmaceuticals are imported from Belgium, and the rest from Germany and France where prices are generally higher. However, the share of more expensive German pharmaceuticals is increasing.

Scope for further reform

So far the rapid growth in health expenditure has not posed a serious problem as the economy has been strong and the fiscal position remains favourable. However, given expected future expenditure pressures, due to technical progress and population ageing, more changes will probably be required to keep the system affordable. To reduce moral hazard, the UCM could consider setting limits on the current system in which patients have complete freedom to consult specialists and general practitioners. Although such a system may be advantageous in certain circumstances, there is some evidence that in general, it may be more costly than a system where the general practitioner acts as a gatekeeper, *i.e.* patients need a referral from the general practitioner to get access to specialist care or hospital care (see Gerdtham *et al.*, 1994). In conjunction with this, the remuneration system could be changed. The general practitioner could, for instance, be remunerated by a combination of capitation payment with a small fee-for-service component.[44] The UCM could monitor the system to avoid cream-skimming by doctors, trying to off-load costly patients.

The UCM could also consider an increase in co-payments. However, the effectiveness of such a measure partly depends on the price elasticity of health services, which is probably low. Moreover, the measure is not effective once a patient has reached the ceiling on co-payments or in cases where employers reimburse the co-payments to their employees. Employers have only limited means to reduce health spending by their employees (and their dependants) and an increase in co-payments may only result in higher labour costs.

The UCM has made a start by introducing prospective budgets in the hospital sector. However, these measures have hardly been used to encourage greater efficiency and effectiveness by hospitals. Nevertheless, the current budget system has been an improvement by giving the health fund more insight into hospital spending. As a next step, the health fund could start benchmarking hospitals and introduce lump-sum payments based on the Diagnostic Related Groups-based system.[45] Similar systems have already been implemented or considered by other OECD countries.

The over-supply of hospital beds is a serious problem. Decisions to close hospitals are always politically sensitive, especially in a small country such as Luxembourg. A tighter budgetary system may go some way to forcing hospitals to co-operate, and may result in the merger of some smaller hospitals. Moreover, important savings could be made if co-operation between hospitals were not only restricted to Luxembourg but also involved those in neighbouring regions, the so-called *Grande région transfrontalière*. As a starting point, the Ministry of Social Affairs and the UCM need to be more closely involved in major investment decisions in the sector. In such a way, cost arguments could be incorporated in decisions on introducing new technologies in Luxembourg or buying therapies from hospitals in neighbouring countries.

Finally, many arrangements in the health sector are determined between the health fund (UCM), health practitioners, trade unions and employers' organisations. In some cases, the same negotiating parties are even on both sides of the table, such as in negotiations about hospital budgets. To avoid such situations, the authorities could consider revising the tripartite structure of the UCM or at least reducing the role of the social partners in the health sector.

Notes

1. In the Luxembourg version of the National Accounts, imputed bank services to non-residents are treated as exports of services and not – as in the 1968 SNA version – as intermediate consumption of resident industries.

2. The interest margin is the difference between the effective interest rates on bank deposits and bank lending.

3. Foreign exchange earnings were 4 per cent of gross earnings in 1997.

4. The acceleration in approved investments also reflected modifications to the diversification law at the beginning of 1997.

5. The majority of cross-border workers comes from France (52 per cent), followed by Belgium (30 per cent) and Germany (18 per cent).

6. The change in definition lowered unemployment by 0.3 percentage point.

7. The European Employment Observatory has calculated its own version of "broad unemployment" (or "extended unemployment") for all EU countries (European Commission, 1998). For Luxembourg, this concept adds to registered unemployment, people participating in active labour market programmes and other programmes to reduce the size of the economic active population (early retirement and disability pensions, parental leave etc.). On this basis, Luxembourg's broad unemployment rate was – at 12.2 per cent in 1996 – still the lowest of all EU countries.

8. The French departments of Meurthe-et-Moselle and Moselle, the German state Saar and the Trier region, and the Belgian provinces of Luxembourg and Liège.

9. Resident Luxembourg nationals earn on average 8.8 per cent more than cross-border workers for similar work and resident foreigners earn 2.6 per cent more (Statec, 1997a).

10. The competitiveness indicator shown in Figure 4, Panel A, is equal to the effective exchange rate, deflated by unit labour costs relative to foreign producer prices (for details see Krecké and Pieretti, 1997).

11. Krecké and Pieretti (1997) estimate that the almost 75 per cent of production in the manufacturing sector follows world market prices.

12. The surplus on the current account overstates the national wealth accumulation as – in the absence of reliable statistics – it is not possible to determine the portion of assets that is owned and controlled by Luxembourg citizens.

13. This is also caused by a reclassification of expenditures for railway maintenance following a change in the statutes of the national railway company.

14. In the absence of consolidated government accounts, it is difficult to assess whether general government spending – as a share of GDP – has increased, as part of the increase in central government spending was due to higher transfers to the social security sector.

15. The OECD Forum on Harmful Tax Practices recently established criteria for the identification of preferential tax regimes. Member countries have a 2-year period for self-reviewing their tax regimes.

16. A broad overview of the development of the Luxembourg financial centre can be found in Statec (1995).

17. For further discussion on acceptable versus harmful tax regimes see OECD (1998a).

18. Switzerland also decided to abstain from approving the OECD Report or its Recommendations.

19. The rest of the social security sector's receipt are made up by government transfers (45 per cent) and interest receipts (5 per cent).

20. The last time, the institutionalised wage indexation was suspended was between April 1982-September 1984.

21. However, the person may receive a complete disability pension in case of unemployment for a maximum period of 18 months or for an unlimited duration if the person is older than 55.

22. The *préretraite progressive* allows older workers (over 57) to work part-time, if an employer hires a previously unemployed person for the rest of the time.

23. Moreover, only a limited number of unemployed receive an unemployment benefit. In August 1998, only 38 per cent of unemployed received such a benefit.

24. Annually 300 to 400 sanctions are imposed, compared with an annual average of around 2 000 unemployment benefit recipients. Moreover, it has been decided also to apply sanctions to people, who do not receive an unemployment benefit by suspending the treatment of their file for two months, which may delay the start of their benefit.

25. Current legislation on working time, dating back to the early 1970s, provides for normal working time of eight hours a day and 40 hours a week, although collective agreements may specify shorter hours. Deviations are possible under the strictly regulated compensation dispensation scheme and overtime scheme for which Ministerial authorisation may be required.

26. The full social minimum wage applies for workers above the age of 17. Reduced rates for younger workers exist: 17 years, 80 per cent; 16 years, 70 per cent; 15 years, 60 per cent.

27. Evaluations based on employment-subsidy programmes in Australia, Belgium and the Netherlands suggest combined dead-weight and substitution effects as high as 90 per cent.

28. Cash benefits to the sick and those on maternity leave, which are part of the Luxembourg health insurance scheme, are not covered in this chapter.

29. National health spending is estimated at LF 39.2 billion in 1997 (7.1 per cent of GDP). This includes health care expenditure by the resident population including resident officials of Luxembourg-based international institutions. It does not include health care expenditure for cross-border workers. Public health expenditure, including expenditures for cross-border workers, was LF 36 billion in 1997 (6.4 per cent of GDP), of which 80 per cent is spent by the public health insurance (UCM). Expenditures for cross-border workers and other insured residing outside Luxembourg by the UCM was – at only 9 per cent of health insurance spending – well below their share in the insured population (21 per cent, excluding co-insured dependants). In addition, 4 per cent of health insurance spending was for treatment of Luxembourg residents abroad.

30. Luxembourg GDP substantially overestimates the income of the population, given the substantial input of foreign resources in production (cross-border workers and foreign-owned businesses).

31. According to EU rules, non-residents who also receive a pension from their country of residence, are covered by the health system of that country. Therefore, of the 30 000 non-residents who currently receive a Luxembourg pension, only 11 per cent are covered by the Luxembourg health system.

32. Mossialos (1997).

33. The number of acute care beds per 1 000 persons was 5.96 in 1997.

34. An historic overview of the system can be found in OECD (1994).

35. There are in fact nine sickness funds, organised according to sector or profession. These sickness funds only act as intermediaries between the insured and the UCM for the reimbursement of direct payments by the insured members to the providers. The main sickness funds are: the blue-collar workers' sickness fund (*Caisse de maladie des ouvriers*), the private-sector white collar workers' sickness fund (*Caisse de maladie des employés privés*), the civil servants' and public employees' sickness fund (*Caisse de maladie des fonctionnaires et employés communaux*) and the self-employed workers' sickness fund (*Caisse de maladie des professions indépendantes*).

36. International civil servants have their own health insurance and are not in the Luxembourg scheme.

37. The total contribution for the health insurance scheme (including cash benefits for the sick) is 5.4 per cent for white-collar workers and 10.1 per cent for blue-collar workers. This includes a temporary increase of 0.8 percentage point (0.2 percentage point for white-collar workers) to re-stabilise the funds' reserves. It is the intention to lower contributions again in 1999.

38. The *Commission de nomenclature* is a tripartite commission, consisting of representatives of the government, health funds and medical practitioners.

39. The *Conseil supérieur des assurances sociales* consists of a presiding judge and two magistrates, nominated by the Grand Duke for a period of three years.

40. Under current co-payment regulation, the insured are required to pay: 20 per cent for the first medical visit within 28 days and 5 per cent for all other ambulatory medical visits or consultations; 20 per cent for dental care and physiotherapy (maximum of eight visits); 0, 20, 60 or 100 per cent for prescription drugs; Lfr 220 per day at a hospital.

41. In the first case, the Luxembourg health insurance refused to reimburse a pair of glasses that were bought in Belgium, as the person had not asked permission in advance. The Court judged that the Luxembourg rules were an infringement of the free movement of goods and services, as it encouraged people to buy their glasses in Luxembourg (for which no permission is needed). The second ruling involved the treatment of a Luxembourg resident by a Germany based orthodontist. The Luxembourg health insurance did not want to reimburse the person as treatment was also available in Luxembourg. However, the Court judged that orthodontist treatment in the ambulatory sector is a service, and permission in advance would mean an infringement of the free movement of goods and services. The Court has not taken a decision on hospital treatment in another EU country.

42. Chassin *et al.* (1987) found, for the United States, that a sixth to a third of three commonly performed procedures in the fee-for-service system provided zero or even negative clinical benefit. Similar research in France revealed that 20 per cent of some components of medical care is clinically not justified (Béraud, 1992; CNAMTS, 1992).

43. The *Centre hospitalier Luxembourg* is the only hospital where medical practitioners are employed by the hospital.

44. In a capitation payment system, general practitioners receive a fixed payment for each patient on their list, sometimes adjusted for factors such as age and gender. In some countries, the system is combined with some fees or allowances for specific services.

45. In the Diagnostic Related Groups-based system, fees are set according to diagnosed medical conditions and standardised treatment costs.

List of acronyms

ADEM	Public Employment Service
CMCM	*Caisse médico-chirurgicale mutualiste*
CNFPC	*Centre national de la formation professionnelle continue*
DAT	*Division d'auxiliaires temporaires*
EMU	European Economic and Monetary Union
ESCB	European System of Central Banks
EU	European Union
IML	Luxembourg Monetary Institute
Intrastat	Data collection system for intra-EU trade
PPP	Purchasing Power Parity
R&D	Research and Development
RMG	General Assistance Scheme
SMEs	Small and Medium-sized Enterprises
SNA	System of National Accounts
Statec	Luxembourg Bureau for Statistics and Economic Studies
UCM	*Union de caisse de maladie*

Bibliography

Béraud, C. (1992)
   La sécu c'est bien, en abuser ça craint, report prepared for the CNAMTS, Paris.

Chassin, M. *et al.* (1987)
   "Does inappropriate use explain geographic variations in the use of health care services? A study of three procedures", *Journal of the American Medical Association* 258(17).

CNAMTS (Caisse nationale d'assurance-maladie des travailleurs salariés) (1992)
   "Bilan d'une année de contrôles menés par l'assurance maladie", CNAMTS, Paris.

Conseil économique et social (1998)
   L'*Évolution économique, financière et sociale du pays* 1998, Luxembourg.

European Commission (1998)
   Employment Observatory, SYSDEM, Trends, No. 30, summer.

Gerdtham, U-G., B. Jönsson, M. Macfarlan and H. Oxley (1994)
   "Factors affecting health spending: a cross-country econometric analysis", Annex to OECD *Economics Department Working Papers*, No. 149.

Krecké, Carine and Patrice Pieretti (1997)
   "Système d'indicateurs de compétitivité pour l'industrie luxembourgeoise", *Cahiers économiques* 89, Statec, Luxembourg.

Mossialos, Elias (1997)
   "Citizens' views on health care systems in the 15 Member states of the European Union", *Health Economics*, Vol. 6, pp. 109-116.

Newhouse Joseph, P. (1992)
   "Medical care costs: how much welfare loss?", *Journal of Economic Perspectives*, Vol. 6, No. 3.

OECD (1994)
   The Reform of Health Care Systems, Health Policy Studies No. 5, Paris.

OECD (1997a)
   Economic Survey of Belgium/Luxembourg, Paris.

OECD(1997b)
   The Tax/Benefit Position of Employees, Paris.

OECD (1998a)
   Harmful Tax Competition: An Emerging Global Issue, Paris.

OECD (1998b)
   Employment Outlook, Paris.

Statec (1995)
   Portrait économique du Luxembourg, Luxembourg.

Statec (1997*a*)

"Enquête sur la structure des salaires 1995", *Bulletin du Statec* 97-7, Luxembourg.

Statec (1997*b*)

"La politique de développement et de diversification économique", *Bulletin du Statec* 97-1, Luxembourg.

Statec (1998)

Note de conjoncture 1998/3, Luxembourg.

Annex

Calendar of main economic events

1997

January

At the biennial revision, the social minimum wage is increased by 3.2 per cent in line with past wage increases.

For the first time, the 4 000 blue-collar workers in the steel industry sign a separate collective agreement covering only 1996. This change reflects the restructuring of the labour force following the conversion to electric furnace steelmaking.

February

The diversification law is revised, following changes in EU guidelines on state aid for small and medium-sized enterprises and Research and Development projects.

Following the crossing of the threshold value (*cote d'échéance*) of the *échelle mobile*, wages and salaries and all indexed benefits are increased by 2.5 per cent. The previous automatic wage increase was in May 1995.

March

After the blue-collar staff, the 1 800 white-collar workers in the steel industry sign a collective agreement for the period 1996-1997. This includes the adoption of a new profit-sharing scheme.

A new telecommunication bill is adopted in line with EU legislation. One of the objectives of this law is to attract new activities in the area of communications services.

May

A new collective agreement is concluded in the banking sector. In contrast to the previous 1993 agreement, this accord is signed by all the sector's main trade unions. The new collective agreement provides for annual pay rises of 1.7 per cent, 1.6 per cent and 1.5 per cent for the years 1996, 1997 and 1998, respectively, together with a new bonus scheme.

A new electric furnace is put into service in Esch-Belval, which completes the LF 24 billion investment programme in the steel industry.

July

Luxembourg takes over the Presidency of the European Union from the Netherlands. Among its priorities are the ratification of the draft Amsterdam Treaty, pressing ahead with the final phase of European Economic and Monetary Union and making progress on enlargement of the European Union.

August

The government presents the 1998 budget to Parliament (Chapter II).

The last blast furnace is closed in Esch-Belval, following the starting up of an electric furnace in May.

October

A new collective agreement for blue-collar workers in the steel industry is signed for the years 1997-1998. The overall pay increase comes to 0.92 per cent.

November

The general assembly of the sickness fund (UCM) decides to temporarily raise employers' and employees' contributions for 1998 in order to restabilise the budget (Chapters III and IV).

Luxembourg, as President of the European Union, hosts the Employment Summit, which agrees to a framework for national action under the four "pillars" of employability, adaptability, entrepreneurship and equal opportunities.

December

The seventh satellite of the Astra system is successfully launched from the Cosmodrom in Baikonur (Kazakhstan).

The Public Employment Service (ADEM) and the Union of Temporary Employment Agencies (*Union luxembourgeoise des entreprises de travail intérimaires*, ULEDI), sign a co-operation agreement. The aim of this deal is to facilitate job-seekers, registered with ADEM, in contacting employers using the services of temporary employment agencies.

1998

January

The Public Employment Service (*Administration de l'emploi*, ADEM) changes the definition of employment, by removing all participants in labour market programmes from the national employment definition.

White-collar workers in the iron and steel industry sign a new collective agreement for 1998-1999, including an overall pay increase of 1.85 per cent spread over two years and acceptance of a previously agreed profit-sharing scheme.

February

A new collective agreement for the hospital sector is signed, including annual working time reductions from 2 080 to 1 976 hours by the year 2000. The statutory reference period of a month will become more flexible and adapted according to the needs of the enterprise or the wishes of the staff.

April

The Tripartite Co-ordination Committee adopts the National Action Plan for the Promotion of Employment (*Plan d'action national en faveur de l'emploi*) (Chapter III).

The European Court of Justice rules that restrictions by the Luxembourg health system on buying health services from non-domestic providers are against the free movement of goods and services in the European Union (Chapter IV).

May

The Luxembourg airline company Cargolux puts two new aircraft into service.

June

As part of the process towards monetary union, the Luxembourg Monetary Institute becomes the Central Bank of Luxembourg (Chapter II).

July

Parliament adopts the pension reform bill for the public sector, bringing the scheme more in line with the less favourable regime in the private sector (Chapter II).

August

The government presents the 1999 Budget to Parliament.

The eighth satellite of the Astra network is successfully launched from the Cosmodrome of Baikonur in Kazakhstan.

September

The government presents to Parliament a law proposing a new supervisory authority for the financial sector. The *Commission de surveillance du secteur financier* (CSSF) should become operational from January 1999.

November

The stock exchanges of Amsterdam, Brussels and Luxembourg decide to co-operate, by giving their members direct access to each other's markets from January 1999.

BELGIUM

Statistical annex and structural indicators

Table A. **Belgium – Selected background statistics[1]**

	Average 1988-97	1988	1989	1990	1991	1992	1993	1994	1995	1996	1997
A. Per cent changes from previous year											
Private consumption[2]	2.0	3.2	3.7	2.9	2.9	2.2	-1.3	1.6	0.9	1.8	2.1
Gross fixed capital formation[2]	4.0	16.4	11.4	9.6	-4.7	1.3	-3.6	-0.1	4.2	0.5	5.4
Public[2]	0.1	4.6	-26.0	-4.7	8.5	5.1	9.3	6.0	-6.7	-14.9	19.2
Residential[2]	6.0	25.0	17.6	8.2	-9.1	5.0	1.7	5.5	5.5	-4.0	4.9
Business[2]	4.1	15.4	15.3	11.8	-4.2	-0.5	-7.1	-3.4	5.1	4.6	4.2
GDP[2]	2.2	4.7	3.6	3.0	1.6	1.5	-1.5	2.6	2.3	1.3	3.0
Implicit price deflator											
GDP	2.8	2.1	4.6	3.1	3.1	3.7	4.0	2.3	1.5	1.6	1.4
Private consumption	2.6	1.2	4.0	3.3	3.2	2.4	3.2	2.8	2.1	2.3	1.8
Exports of goods and services	1.5	3.7	6.9	-1.5	-0.7	-1.2	-1.2	1.3	0.9	2.5	4.5
Imports of goods and services	1.3	2.2	6.5	-1.5	-0.6	-2.9	-2.6	1.9	2.1	2.9	5.2
Industrial production	1.9	5.8	3.4	3.8	-2.0	0.0	-5.2	1.9	6.5	0.8	4.4
Employment	0.3	1.5	1.6	1.4	0.1	-0.4	-1.1	-1.0	0.5	0.4	0.4
Compensation of employees	4.5	3.5	6.9	7.6	7.9	5.1	3.1	2.7	3.2	1.7	3.1
Productivity (GDP[2]/employment)	1.9	3.2	2.0	1.6	1.4	1.9	-0.4	3.6	1.8	0.9	2.6
Unit labour costs (comp. of employee/GDP[2])	2.2	-1.2	3.2	4.4	6.2	3.6	4.6	0.1	0.8	0.4	0.1
B. Percentage ratios											
Gross fixed capital formation as % of GDP[2]	18.7	17.7	19.0	20.3	19.0	19.0	18.6	18.1	18.4	18.3	18.7
Stockbuilding as % of GDP[2]	0.1	0.4	0.3	0.0	0.1	0.2	0.1	0.3	0.2	0.0	-0.3
Foreign balance as % of GDP[2]	3.1	3.1	2.6	2.2	2.5	2.1	2.2	3.1	4.0	4.0	4.8
Compensation of employee as % of GDP	51.8	51.5	50.8	51.4	52.9	52.9	53.2	52.1	51.8	51.1	50.5
Directs taxes as % of household income	12.8	13.5	12.5	12.8	12.2	12.3	11.9	13.0	13.2	13.1	13.4
Household saving as % of disposable income	17.3	15.3	16.2	16.6	18.2	19.1	20.4	18.4	17.8	16.1	15.2
Unemployment as % of civilian labour force	11.1	11.5	10.4	9.4	8.8	9.4	10.4	12.1	13.1	13.1	12.8
C. Other indicator											
Current balance (BLEU) (billion US$)	8.8	3.5	3.6	3.6	4.9	6.6	11.3	12.5	14.3	14.1	13.7

1. All variables including statistical discrepancies.
2. At constant 1990 prices.
Source: National Accounts Institute and OECD Secretariat.

Table B. **Belgium – Gross domestic product**[1]

Billion francs

	1988	1989	1990	1991	1992	1993	1994	1995	1996	1997
	Current prices									
Private consumption	3 633.2	3 919.1	4 166.1	4 423.6	4 629.5	4 714.9	4 924.0	5 071.2	5 282.0	5 488.0
Public consumption	857.2	884.0	917.7	987.4	1 027.6	1 088.3	1 139.5	1 181.9	1 205.4	1 251.6
Gross fixed capital formation	1 013.7	1 178.7	1 328.0	1 292.7	1 348.0	1 321.1	1 349.1	1 430.2	1 449.8	1 539.9
Change in stocks	16.1	19.6	-2.9	5.7	7.4	1.4	24.0	32.6	21.5	2.8
Total domestic demand	5 520.2	6 001.4	6 408.9	6 709.3	7 012.5	7 125.7	7 436.6	7 715.9	7 958.7	8 282.4
Exports of goods and services	3 758.1	4 347.6	4 464.4	4 573.0	4 677.8	4 591.7	5 042.6	5 394.6	5 649.4	6 326.4
less: Imports of goods and services	3 588.8	4 181.6	4 318.9	4 413.4	4 461.7	4 312.2	4 710.3	5 042.4	5 303.0	5 933.3
Gross domestic product at market prices	5 689.5	6 167.4	6 554.4	6 868.9	7 228.6	7 405.2	7 768.9	8 068.1	8 305.1	8 675.5
	1990 prices									
Private consumption	3 902.8	4 046.9	4 166.1	4 285.2	4 380.9	4 322.4	4 392.6	4 430.3	4 510.2	4 603.3
Public consumption	931.2	922.3	917.7	937.7	941.0	952.8	968.8	975.2	988.8	997.0
Gross fixed capital formation	1 087.3	1 211.1	1 328.0	1 265.7	1 282.4	1 236.4	1 235.1	1 286.7	1 293.1	1 363.1
Change in stocks	27.4	17.7	-2.9	6.5	12.5	3.3	21.3	16.3	2.4	-20.5
Total domestic demand	5 948.8	6 198.0	6 408.9	6 495.1	6 616.8	6 514.9	6 617.8	6 708.5	6 794.4	6 942.9
Exports of goods and services	3 955.9	4 280.9	4 464.4	4 605.0	4 765.5	4 734.1	5 130.8	5 437.9	5 556.6	5 953.3
less: Imports of goods and services	3 763.6	4 117.5	4 318.9	4 440.9	4 623.7	4 589.3	4 917.6	5 155.7	5 270.1	5 602.7
Gross domestic product at market prices	6 141.1	6 361.4	6 554.4	6 659.2	6 758.6	6 659.7	6 831.0	6 990.7	7 080.9	7 293.5

1. Including statistical discrepancies.
Source: National Accounts Institute.

Table C. **Belgium – Income and expenditure of households and private non-profit institutions**

Billion francs

	1988	1989	1990	1991	1992	1993	1994	1995	1996	1997
Compensation of employees	2 929.5	3 132.9	3 369.7	3 637.0	3 822.7	3 941.5	4 046.2	4 175.7	4 247.2	4 380.0
Income from firms received by individuals	1 147.2	1 181.1	1 262.6	1 294.5	1 359.0	1 390.3	1 517.9	1 570.2	1 645.6	1 704.9
Household property income[1]	741.8	848.7	943.8	1 035.9	1 134.7	1 193.9	1 186.1	1 151.3	1 133.3	1 154.5
Current transfers from government	1 485.3	1 572.3	1 670.7	1 814.1	1 942.0	2 013.1	2 063.0	2 151.4	2 215.8	2 279.3
Current transfers from the rest of the world	46.3	51.4	58.1	59.9	64.0	66.8	67.8	83.2	93.9	111.3
Household income	6 350.1	6 786.4	7 305.0	7 841.4	8 322.4	8 605.6	8 881.0	9 131.8	9 335.9	9 630.1
less:										
Direct taxes	859.7	847.8	938.3	957.1	1 019.8	1 028.3	1 153.7	1 201.7	1 226.9	1 289.4
Social security contribution by wage-earners and self-employed	864.4	916.4	984.6	1 066.1	1 140.3	1 190.1	1 209.9	1 241.5	1 256.7	1 301.4
Current transfers to the rest of the world	54.2	58.6	81.5	80.4	86.8	90.6	96.4	118.7	138.4	139.6
Other current transfers	280.9	284.4	305.5	329.3	350.8	375.5	385.5	403.5	421.6	424.4
Disposable income	4 291.0	4 679.2	4 995.0	5 408.6	5 724.8	5 921.1	6 035.6	6 166.5	6 292.3	6 475.3
Households savings	657.8	760.1	828.9	985.0	1 095.3	1 206.2	1 111.5	1 095.2	1 010.3	987.3

1. Including statistical discrepancy.
Source: National Accounts Institute and OECD, *National Accounts.*

Table D. **Belgium – Income and expenditure of enterprises**

	1988	1989	1990	1991	1992	1993	1994	1995	1996	1997
	Billion francs									
1. Gross operating surplus excluding subsidies	842	997	994	961	1 013	1 002	1 093	1 216	1 260	1 379
2. Subsidies	176	158	187	203	192	195	188	196	200	176
3. **Gross operating surplus** (1 + 2)	1 018	1 155	1 181	1 164	1 205	1 197	1 280	1 412	1 460	1 555
4. Net property income payable	177	204	258	306	323	284	278	284	285	295
5. **Gross primary income** (3 – 4)	841	951	923	858	883	913	1 003	1 128	1 175	1 260
6. Current transfers pais to other sectors	139	147	126	135	137	158	181	216	221	260
7. **Disposable income** (5 – 6)	702	805	797	722	746	755	822	913	954	1 001
8. Capital transfers (net)	30	21	25	25	32	39	21	–5	31	41
9. **Capital resources** (7 + 8)	731	826	822	748	778	794	843	907	985	1 042
10. Gross capital formation	581	710	798	799	811	755	762	827	858	877
11. Other[1]	17	20	18	20	16	22	29	42	50	42
12. **Net lending**	133	96	6	–71	–48	18	52	39	77	122
	Per cent of GDP									
Gross operating surplus (including subsidies)	17.9	18.7	18.0	16.9	16.7	16.2	16.5	17.5	17.6	17.9
Disposable income	12.3	13.0	12.2	10.5	10.3	10.2	10.6	11.3	11.5	11.5
Capital resources	12.9	13.4	12.5	10.9	10.8	10.7	10.8	11.2	11.9	12.0
Gross capital formation	10.2	11.5	12.2	11.6	11.2	10.2	9.8	10.2	10.3	10.1
Net lending	2.3	1.6	0.1	–1.0	–0.7	0.2	0.7	0.5	0.9	1.4

1. Change in mathematical retirement pension reserves and net purchases of land and intangible assets.
Source: National Accounts Institut and OECD, National Accounts.

Table E. **Belgium – Government revenue and expenditure**

Billion francs

	1988	1989	1990	1991	1992	1993	1994	1995	1996	1997
Current revenue	2 227.8	2 289.2	2 464.2	2 630.6	2 715.4	2 832.2	3 085.9	3 284.3	3 431.1	3 647.9
Income froms property and firms	56.9	70.8	78.1	90.2	84.7	85.3	68.5	76.0	89.7	70.1
less: Interest on public debt	-568.2	-629.1	-685.5	-691.6	-771.1	-793.8	-778.5	-719.1	-704.5	-679.4
Indirects taxes	689.4	749.4	801.4	832.8	876.5	918.7	988.7	992.1	1 052.7	1 111.2
Directs taxes	859.7	847.8	938.3	957.1	1 019.8	1 028.3	1 153.7	1 201.7	1 226.9	1 289.4
Social security contributions by wage-earners and self-employed	864.4	916.4	984.6	1 066.1	1 140.3	1 190.1	1 209.9	1 241.5	1 256.7	1 301.4
Imputed social contributions	113.6	119.7	125.5	138.8	146.6	158.8	167.0	173.2	181.2	186.8
Direct taxes on compagnies	157.1	173.8	160.2	165.9	155.5	180.8	213.1	251.6	265.9	305.8
Other current transfers	55.0	40.3	61.5	71.4	63.2	63.9	63.6	67.2	62.6	62.6
Current expenditure	2 483.7	2 577.6	2 725.6	2 961.3	3 102.8	3 236.3	3 346.0	3 474.8	3 580.4	3 684.1
Public consumption	857.2	884.0	917.7	987.4	1 027.6	1 088.3	1 139.5	1 181.9	1 205.4	1 251.6
Subsidies	175.7	158.5	186.6	202.6	192.4	195.4	187.8	196.1	199.7	176.1
Social security transfers to wage-earners and self-employed	1 063.8	1 115.4	1 182.0	1 287.8	1 375.8	1 428.9	1 462.3	1 527.6	1 582.2	1 621.2
Other current transfers (net) to households	136.8	155.5	164.3	170.9	182.8	182.9	197.0	205.6	210.7	221.3
Social benefits corresponding to imputed contributions	119.4	124.8	130.7	143.9	151.6	164.1	171.6	177.7	185.4	190.4
Other current transfers	130.8	139.3	144.2	168.6	172.6	176.8	187.9	185.9	197.0	223.5
Saving of general government	-255.9	-288.4	-261.4	-330.7	-387.4	-404.2	-260.1	-190.5	-149.3	-36.2
Consumption of fixed capital	19.6	21.7	22.2	23.4	24.3	24.9	25.5	26.2	26.5	27.0
Gross saving of general government	-236.4	-266.7	-239.2	-307.3	-363.1	-379.3	-234.6	-164.3	-122.8	-9.1

Source: National Accounts Institute, and OECD, National Accounts.

Table F. **Belgium – Area breakdown of foreign trade for the BLEU**

Million $US

	1992	1993[1]	1994	1995	1996	1997
Exports, fob	122 987	117 687	134 301	168 003	168 175	165 104
OECD	108 106	101 875	116 575	145 363	146 136	141 881
EU	96 059	88 434	100 374	126 913	126 492	121 041
of which:						
Germany	28 150	24 650	27 848	36 330	34 439	31 792
France	23 763	22 172	25 288	30 855	30 140	27 936
Netherlands	16 605	15 339	17 563	22 262	22 550	20 625
United Kingdom	9 621	9 850	11 277	13 677	15 356	16 708
Italy	7 250	6 444	6 876	9 300	9 165	9 110
United States	4 773	5 655	6 855	6 721	7 414	8 509
Other OECD	7 275	7 787	9 345	11 729	12 230	12 330
Non-OECD	14 045	15 233	17 082	22 005	21 299	22 571
Ex-COMECOM	1 780	1 272	1 562	884	958	978
OPEC	2 624	2 510	2 146	2 689	2 425	2 670
Other	9 641	11 451	13 374	18 432	17 916	18 924
Unspecified	836	579	645	635	741	652
Imports, cif	124 967	105 427	122 007	153 232	157 916	150 806
OECD	110 354	93 145	106 508	136 108	139 894	131 376
EU	96 045	80 129	91 110	116 087	119 256	108 795
of which:						
Germany	29 872	22 720	24 089	32 202	31 400	27 986
France	20 602	17 090	19 410	23 893	24 216	21 303
Netherlands	21 884	18 430	21 614	27 317	29 323	26 999
United Kingdom	9 624	9 941	11 551	13 566	14 352	13 722
Italy	5 665	4 680	5 184	6 566	6 664	5 885
United States	5 402	5 601	6 468	8 795	9 718	11 628
Other OECD	8 907	7 415	8 930	11 226	10 920	10 953
Non-OECD	14 548	12 161	14 457	16 953	17 952	19 363
Ex-COMECOM	2 087	742	1 206	661	723	900
OPEC	3 309	1 212	1 582	1 415	1 574	1 843
Other	9 153	10 207	11 669	14 876	15 655	16 621
Unspecified	65	121	1 042	172	71	67

1.   Following the abolition of customs within the EU on 1 January 1993, data on intra-EU trade are no longer based on customs declarations but on INTRASTAT.
Source: OECD, *Foreign Trade Statistics*, Series A.

Table G. **Belgium – Commodity breakdown of foreign trade for the BLEU**

Million US$

	1990	1993[1]	1994	1995	1996	1997
Exports, fob	118 281	120 631	134 662	168 124	168 375	166 723
SITC sections						
0. Food and live animals	9 852	11 382	12 293	15 138	14 976	14 837
1. Beverages and tobacco	787	1 069	1 206	1 340	1 360	1 313
2. Crude materials, inedible, except fuels	2 692	2 422	2 930	4 030	3 781	3 918
3. Mineral fuels, lubricants and related materials	4 127	4 093	4 072	4 395	5 380	5 038
4. Animal and vegetable oils, fats and waxes	481	403	531	756	696	787
5. Chemicals and related products, n.e.s.	14 756	16 836	20 679	29 697	28 968	29 941
6. Manufactured goods	36 289	32 694	36 078	46 159	43 508	42 041
7. Machinery and transport equipment	32 287	33 012	37 958	45 950	47 894	47 139
8. Miscellaneous manufactured articles	9 701	10 936	11 296	14 291	15 260	14 782
9. Commodities and transactions, n.e.s.	7 309	7 784	7 620	6 368	6 551	6 926
Imports , cif	120 304	111 037	123 499	153 415	157 967	153 220
SITC sections						
0. Food and live animals	9 426	9 808	10 971	13 780	13 507	12 678
1. Beverages and tobacco	1 305	1 581	1 600	1 913	1 883	1 745
2. Crude materials, inedible, except fuels	6 861	5 034	6 324	7 776	7 058	7 017
3. Mineral fuels, lubricants and related materials	9 800	8 309	8 528	9 431	11 155	10 860
4. Animal and vegetable oils, fats and waxes	405	438	608	727	713	773
5. Chemicals and related products, n.e.s.	13 362	14 213	15 863	21 647	22 196	23 316
6. Manufactured goods	28 095	24 701	27 840	34 687	34 378	33 184
7. Machinery and transport equipment	30 706	27 953	31 552	40 306	44 916	45 606
8. Miscellaneous manufactured articles	12 633	12 665	13 340	15 758	16 634	16 487
9. Commodities and transactions, n.e.s.	7 711	6 335	6 873	7 390	5 527	1 554

1. Following the abolition of customs within the EU on 1 January 1993, data on intra-EU trade are no longer based on customs declarations but on INTRASTAT.
Source: OECD, Foreign Trade Statitics, Series C.

Table H.   **Belgium – BLEU balance of payments**
Million US$

	1988	1989	1990	1991	1992	1993	1994	1995	1996	1997
Exports										
Goods	87 257	92 008	109 939	107 559	116 869	106 340	122 389	155 048	154 700	150 601
Services	21 041	21 820	28 266	30 511	33 568	33 443	40 289	35 358	35 535	34 891
Income	33 101	48 211	65 322	75 178	88 157	82 961	89 392	72 995	61 114	55 764
Imports										
Goods	84 584	89 734	108 270	105 466	113 186	100 516	115 587	145 500	145 808	142 429
Services	18 938	21 310	26 441	28 766	30 875	30 062	36 314	33 040	32 924	31 947
Income	32 609	45 523	62 970	71 920	85 242	78 049	84 185	66 193	54 068	49 420
Balance										
Goods	2 673	2 274	1 670	2 093	3 683	5 824	6 802	9 548	8 892	8 171
Services	2 102	510	1 825	1 745	2 694	3 381	3 975	2 318	2 611	2 944
Incomes	492	2 688	2 352	3 258	2 915	4 912	5 206	6 802	7 046	6 344
Transfers										
Other transfers, balance	−144	−168	−1 032	−825	−1 123	−970	−1 001	−1 161	−1 312	−908
General government, balance	−1 615	−1 718	−1 188	−1 405	−1 559	−1 815	−2 504	−3 248	−3 126	−2 872
Current balances	3 508	3 586	3 626	4 865	6 610	11 332	12 477	14 259	14 111	13 679
Capital account								377	158	400
Financial account										
Direct investment abroad	−3 766	−6 477	−6 208	−6 291	−11 357	−4 886	−1 204	−11 705	−8 070	−7 953
Portfolio investment, assets	−12 110	−14 391	−9 165	−29 703	−62 337	−58 005	−41 667	−27 793	−47 352	−55 810
Other investment, assets	5 352	−55 262	−64 356	−20 883	−49 300	−52 523	11 363	−22 167	−14 081	−48 189
Direct investment in the BLEU	5 069	7 031	7 953	9 294	11 301	10 776	8 314	10 804	13 784	12 002
Portfolio investment, liabilities	7 772	10 977	7 884	26 992	58 629	49 846	18 221	4 909	36 877	54 988
Other investment, liabilities	−5 077	55 488	62 333	17 201	45 256	41 096	−4 982	33 021	6 461	32 603
Reserve assets (nets)	−827	−312	−494	−515	−616	2 156	−281	−230	−576	−1 016
Errors and omissions (nets)	76	−640	−1 574	−960	1 814	208	−2 238	−1 474	−1 312	−705

Source: OECD Secretariat.

Table I. **Belgium – Structure of output and performance indicators**

I. Structure of output (1990 prices)

	Share of GDP							Share of total employment						
	1980	1985	1990	1994	1995	1996	1997	1980	1985	1990	1994	1995	1996	1997
Agriculture, hunting, forestry and fishing	1.9	2.2	1.9	2.1	2.1	2.0	2.0	3.0	3.0	2.5	2.3	2.3	2.3	2.3
Mining and quarrying	0.3	0.2	0.2	0.2	0.3	0.3	0.3							
Manufacturing	22.3	24.2	23.9	22.9	23.0	22.7	23.1	23.4	21.4	19.9	18.6	18.4	18.0	18.0
of which:														
Food products	4.3	4.4	4.0	4.0	4.0	4.0	4.0	3.0	2.9	2.7	2.7	2.7	2.7	2.7
Textiles	1.5	1.4	1.6	1.5	1.4	1.3	1.3	3.3	2.9	2.5	2.0	1.9	1.7	1.7
Paper	1.1	1.1	1.4	1.4	1.4	1.4	1.4	1.4	1.4	1.5	1.4	1.4	1.4	1.4
Chemicals	1.9	3.1	3.3	3.6	3.7	3.8	4.1	2.5	2.6	2.5	2.5	2.4	2.4	2.4
Metals	1.5	1.7	1.7	1.5	1.6	1.5	1.4	2.1	1.7	1.4	1.1	1.1	1.0	1.0
Metals products, machinery and equipment	6.9	7.9	6.9	6.1	6.0	5.9	5.9	9.6	8.4	8.0	7.5	7.5	7.4	7.4
Electricity, gas and water	2.5	2.5	2.5	2.6	2.6	2.7	2.7	1.6	1.5	0.9	0.9	0.8	0.8	0.8
Construction	6.6	4.5	5.2	5.1	5.1	4.9	5.0	8.1	6.1	6.6	7.3	7.1	7.0	7.0
Market services	47.5	48.6	49.2	51.1	51.1	51.4	51.1	42.1	45.0	47.9	49.4	49.8	50.6	50.6
Others[1]	5.8	4.5	5.4	3.9	4.0	4.1	4.3							
Total market sector	81.1	82.3	82.9	84.0	84.1	84.0	84.1	78.3	76.9	77.9	78.5	78.4	78.7	78.7
Non-market sector	13.1	13.2	11.7	12.0	11.9	11.9	11.6	21.7	23.1	22.1	21.5	21.6	21.3	21.3

1. Correction for investment from own resources, intermediate consumption of imputed interests (free services of financial intermediaries), VAT, statistical adjustment and net taxes on imports.

Source: National Accounts Institute; National Bank of Belgium and OECD, National Accounts.

Table I. **Belgium – Structure of output and performance indicators** *(cont.)*

2. **Economic performance** (1990 prices)

	Share of total investment							Productivity growth					
	1980	1985	1990	1994	1995	1996	1997	Average 1980-85	1990	1994	1995	1996	1997
Agriculture, hunting, forestry and fishing	2.0	2.5	1.9	1.1	1.0	1.2	1.2	4.2	-2.0	-4.3	3.3	0.4	
Mining and quarrying	0.4	0.5	0.7	0.3	0.3	0.3	0.3	5.2	1.5	7.6	3.0	2.0	
Manufacturing	13.1	21.1	27.7	20.6	21.5	23.4	23.4						
of which :													
Food products	2.1	2.7	3.4	3.0	2.7	2.9	2.9	2.6	-2.9	0.3	2.7	1.2	
Textiles	0.8	1.8	1.7	1.6	1.2	1.1	1.3	1.8	9.4	5.6	0.6	3.6	
Paper	1.0	1.5	2.1	2.3	2.1	2.0	1.9	2.5	-4.6	11.6	0.4	-1.0	
Chemicals	2.7	4.3	10.2	6.7	7.7	9.4	9.8	10.6	0.1	12.1	8.4	4.4	
Metals	1.6	2.3	1.7	1.6	1.6	1.6	1.5	7.9	1.8	15.5	7.4	-2.1	
Metals products, machinery and equipment	3.6	6.5	6.2	3.5	4.3	4.7	4.2	7.2	1.4	9.5	-0.7	0.8	
Electricity, gas and water	5.1	6.4	3.2	4.6	4.6	5.0	4.9	2.4	14.8	3.7	7.7	7.7	
Construction	1.5	1.7	2.2	1.8	1.9	1.8	1.9	0.0	1.4	0.6	3.8	-1.4	
Market services	57.4	59.7	58.9	61.9	62.3	62.1	62.6	0.6	-0.3	2.7	1.0	-0.2	
Other[1]	4.3	-4.9	-0.2	1.7	1.3	0.2	-1.5						
Total market sector	79.4	92.0	94.7	90.3	91.7	93.8	94.4	2.2	0.4	3.5	1.9	0.4	
Non-market sector	16.2	12.8	5.6	8.0	7.0	6.0	7.2	0.4	0.0	3.9	0.5	2.3	

1. Statistical adjustments and increase in stocks.
Source: National Accounts Institute; National Bank of Belgium and OECD, *National Accounts.*

Table I. **Belgium – Structure of output and performance indicators** *(cont.)*

3. **Other indicators** (current prices)

	1985	1986	1987	1988	1989	1990	1991	1992	1993	1994	1995	1996	1997
R&D as a per cent of GDP in manufacturing sector	4.9	5.0	5.3	5.1	4.8		5.1			4.8	4.8		
Total R&D expenditure as a per cent of total GDP	1.65	1.65	1.65	1.61	1.66		1.63		1.58	1.57	1.59		
Government funded R&D as a per cent of total	31.6	28.7	27.6	26.7	32.0		31.3		32.5	26.9	26.4		
Breakdown of employed workforce by size of establishment:													
1 to 9 employees	14.7	14.9	15.1	16.0	16.1	16.0	16.1	16.3	16.4	16.7	16.7		
10 to 49 employees	20.0	20.4	20.8	21.5	21.8	22.1	22.4	22.5	23.3	23.3	23.3		
50 to 199 employees	20.9	21.0	21.6	21.6	21.4	21.3	21.7	21.8	22.4	22.5	22.7		
200 to 499 employees	14.8	14.4	14.7	14.6	14.9	15.0	14.5	14.8	14.6	14.3	14.2		
500 to 999 employees	9.5	9.6	9.6	9.4	9.4	9.2	9.3	9.3	9.3	9.5	9.3		
1 000 employees or more	20.2	19.8	18.2	17.0	16.5	16.4	15.9	15.4	14.0	13.7	13.8		
Total	100.0	100.0	100.0	100.0	100.0	100.0	100.0	100.0	100.0	100.0	100.0		
Workforce (thousands)	2 844.6	2 862.5	2 888.7	3 002.6	3 082.0	3 145.3	3 153.5	3 158.9	3 156.2	3 142.0	3 188.0		

Source: National Social Security Office and OECD, *Main Science and Technology Indicators.*

Table J.   **Belgium – Labour market indicators**

	1980	1985	1990	1994	1995	1996	1997
A. Trend							
Standardised unemployment rate	8.3	10.3	6.7	10.0	9.9	9.7	9.2
Unemployment rate	7.9	12.3	8.7	12.9	12.9	12.7	12.5
Male	4.6	8.8	5.9	9.8	9.8	9.6	..
Female	13.5	17.7	12.8	17.1	17.0	16.6	..
Youth (15-24 years old)		23.6	14.5	21.8	21.5	20.5	21.3
Share of long-term unemployment[1]	..	68.9	68.7	58.3	62.4	61.3	60.5
Unfilled vacancies (thousands)	5.9	18.3	18.8	19.0	19.7	21.3	24.6
B. Structural and institutional features							
Labour force (per cent change)	0.3	–0.5	0.8	0.2	0.5	0.1	0.2
Participation rate[2]	63.0	61.7	62.6	63.9	64.2	64.2	64.3
Male	78.8	74.2	72.7	72.1	72.1	71.9	71.5
Female	47.0	49.1	52.4	55.5	56.1	56.5	57.0
Employment as a per cent of population aged 15 to 64	58.0	54.3	57.2	55.6	55.9	56.1	..
Employers, self-employed and family and family workers (as a per cent of total employment)	16.4	17.8	17.9	18.9	18.9	19.0	18.8
Employees (as a per cent of total employment)	83.6	82.2	82.1	81.1	81.1	81.0	81.2
Civilian employment by sector (as a per cent of total)							
Agriculture	3.2	3.1	2.7	2.5	2.5	..	..
Industry	34.7	30.2	28.3	27.0	26.5	..	..
Services	62.1	66.7	68.9	70.5	71.0	..	..
of which: General Government	19.2	20.7	20.0	19.1	18.8	..	..
Total	100.0	100.0	100.0	100.0	100.0	..	..
Non-wage labour costs[3]	21.1	24.0	26.8	27.1	27.0	27.0	26.9
Unemployment insurance benefits[4]	33.3	28.8	32.8	..	..	..	..

1.   People who have been looking for a job for one year or more as a percentage of total unemployment.
2.   Labour force as a percentage of the corresponding population aged between 15 and 64 years.
3.   Employers' social security contributions as a percentage of totale wages.
4.   Average unemployment benefit as a percentage of compensation per employee.
Source: National Institute of Statistics; *Annuaire statistique de la Belgique,* 1994; Ministry of Finance, *Note de conjoncture* 1996/6/131; OECD, *Labour Force Statistics* (Parts II and III) and *Main Economic Indicators.*

Table K. **Belgium – Public sector**

	1975	1980	1985	1990	1994	1995	1996	1997
Budgetary indicators: general government accounts (as a per cent of GDP)								
Primary receipts[1]	45.0	47.9	51.0	47.3	49.1	49.2	49.4	49.6
Primary total expenditure[1]	47.2	51.3	50.5	43.0	44.6	44.6	44.4	43.9
Primary balance[1]	−2.2	−3.4	0.5	4.2	4.5	4.5	5.0	5.7
Net interest payments	2.9	5.3	9.6	9.7	9.4	8.5	8.1	7.6
Net lending	−5.0	−8.7	−9.1	−5.4	−4.8	−3.9	−3.1	−1.9
Structure of expenditure and taxes (as a per cent of GDP)								
General government expenditure	45.9	52.7	58.0	52.0	53.1	52.0	51.6	50.3
of which:								
Transfers	23.0	25.5	26.8	24.7	26.0	26.0	26.2	26.0
Subsidies	3.1	3.7	3.7	2.8	2.4	2.4	2.4	2.0
Tax receipts	41.7	43.8	46.9	44.0	45.9	45.7	45.8	46.2
Personal income tax	13.5	16.0	16.8	14.3	14.9	14.9	14.8	14.9
Corporate taxes	3.1	2.3	2.6	2.4	2.7	3.1	3.2	3.5
Social Security contributions	13.5	13.2	15.3	15.0	15.6	15.4	15.1	15.0
Consumption taxes	11.7	12.4	12.2	12.2	12.7	12.3	12.7	12.8
of which: Value added tax	6.5	6.8	6.7	6.4	6.4	6.3	6.4	6.5
Other indicators								
Income tax elasticity	1.8	0.6	0.9	1.4	3.8	1.5	0.9	1.6
Income tax as per cent of total tax	39.8	41.6	41.4	38.1	38.3	39.4	39.3	39.8
Gross general government debt (as a per cent of GDP)	58.3	77.1	120.2	125.5	133.3	131.0	126.8	121.9
Net general governemnt debt (as a per cent of GDP)	48.6	68.1	110.1	115.9	124.1	123.8	120.6	116.5

	Prior to		After
Tax rates (per cent)			
Personal income tax rates			
Top rate	72	1 January 1989	55[2]
Lower rate	17	1 January 1989	25[2]
Number of brackets	13	1 January 1989	7
Corporate tax rates	41	1 January 1991	39[2]
Standard VAT rate	20.5	1 January 1991	21.0

1. Excluding interest charges.
2. Excluding the solidarity tax surcharge (*contribution complémentaire de crise*) which has increased the tax rates by 3 per cent since 1 August 1993 (to 56.65,25.75 et 40.17 respectively).
Source: National Bank of Belgium; National Accounts Institute; OECD, *National Accounts* and OCDE Secretariat.

Table L. **Belgium – Financial markets**

1. **Sector and Structure of financial assets and liabilities**

	1975	1980	1990	1993	1994	1995	1996	1997
Sector size								
Sectoral employment[1]/total employment	..	1.8	2.1	2.0	2.0	2.0		
Non-financial agents' accumulation of financial liabilities/GDP	16.7	21.2	18.7	16.0	10.7	10.1		
Non-financial agents' accumulation of financial assets/GDP	17.5	16.8	18.6	21.7	14.7	14.9		
Stock-market capitalisation/GDP	16.0	9.2	31.6	38.5	34.9	37.6		
Density of banking network[2]	35.9	39.0	36.3	34.8				
Density of banking network: credit institutions[3]	..	..	90.2	78.1	76.9	75.6		
Structure of financial assets and liabilities								
Share of intermediated financing in total financing[4]	..	..	69.0	67.6	68.1	65.3	63.9	62.2
Financial institutions' share of financial assets of non-financial sectors	..	..	49.8	50.5	50.1	49.6	49.0	48.8
Share of securities issues in financial flows of non-financial agents	..	..	52.1	56.1	57.0	57.7	59.3	60.3
Structure of private non-financial sector's portfolio[5]								
Deposits	..	..	29.0	26.0	26.9	26.3	25.8	25.1
Bonds and bills	..	..	25.1	23.7	23.9	23.7	22.5	20.6
Equities	..	..	34.7	39.0	38.1	38.2	40.0	42.6
Non-financial corporate financial structure:								
Equity	..	..	34.7	36.5	36.5	37.4		
Short-term debt	..	..	40.3	38.9	58.3	38.2		
Long-term debt	..	..	21.1	20.3	20.9	20.2		

1. Only financial institutions.
2. Number of deposit banks' branches and head offices per 100 000 population.
3. Number of bank branches and head offices per 100 000 population.
4. Share of financial institutions in total external financing of non-financial agents.
5. The private non-financial sector includes corporations as well as households and non-profit institutions. The total differs from 100 because certain items, such as loans and trade credit, are excluded.

Source: National Bank of Belgium.

Table L. **Belgium – Financial markets**
2. Internalisation and efficiency of markets

	1975	1980	1990	1993	1994	1995	1996	1997
Internationalisation of markets								
Foreign business of the banking sector:[1]								
Assets	38.4	46.8	48.6	35.2	35.2	35.2		
Liabilities	43.6	56.1	59.6	40.8	40.2	40.2		
International banking network:								
Foreign banks in Belgium[2]	40	51	63	80	78	78		
Belgian bank branches abroad	..	..	52[3]	69	..	..		
Share of cross-border transactions:								
Net purchases of foreign securities by residents[4]	25.6	11.1	16.7	76.3	45.3	60.4		
Net purchases of domestic securities by non-residents[5]	9.6	19.4	18.9	49.5	42.5	33.9		
Efficiency of markets								
Cost of bank intermediation[6]	3.1	2.5	1.7	1.9	1.7	1.8		
Bank productivity[7]	73.6	74.6	69.3	67.6	71.6	66.9		
Interest margins[8]	2.5	2.0	1.3	1.2	1.3	1.2		

1. As a percentage of deposit banks' balance sheets.
2. Number of branches and subsidiaries.
3. Number of deposit banks' branches and head offices.
4. Purchases of foreign shares and other securities, equity participations in foreign entreprises as a percentage of total purchases of domestic and foreign securities by the private non-financial sector.
5. Purchases of Belgian shares, foreign equity participations in Belgian entreprises and other purchases of securities issued by residents as a percentage of domestic securities issues.
6. Gross benefit margins as a percentage of the annual average balance sheet of deposit banks.
7. Operating costs as a percentage of the gross benefit margins of deposit banks.
8. Difference between interest receipts and interest payments divided by the annual average balance sheet of deposit banks.
Source: National Bank of Belgium.

LUXEMBOURG

Statistical annex and structural indicators

Table A. **Luxembourg – Selected background statistics[1]**

	Average 1988-97	1988	1989	1990	1991	1992	1993	1994	1995	1996	1997
A. Annual percentage change											
Private consumption[2]	3.2	4.6	5.1	5.7	6.3	-0.9	1.7	2.4	2.4	1.9	2.5
Gross fixed capital formation[2]	7.7	15.0	7.0	2.7	31.6	-9.0	28.4	-14.9	3.5	-1.7	14.1
GDP[2]	5.8	10.4	9.8	2.2	6.1	4.5	8.7	4.2	3.8	3.0	4.8
GDP price deflator	2.5	0.7	4.4	5.2	2.3	2.6	0.6	4.7	0.3	2.2	2.5
Industrial product	2.4	8.7	7.8	-0.5	0.3	-0.8	-4.3	5.9	1.4	-1.9	7.2
Employment	3.0	3.0	3.5	4.1	4.1	2.5	1.7	2.5	2.6	2.7	3.2
Compensation of employees	7.8	7.1	12.2	11.2	9.9	9.3	5.7	7.4	4.2	5.2	5.4
Productivity (GDP[2]/employment)	2.7	7.2	6.1	-1.9	2.0	1.9	6.9	1.6	1.1	0.4	1.6
Unit labour costs (compensation of employees/GDP)[2]	2.3	-3.0	2.1	8.2	4.9	3.6	-1.5	2.7	1.2		
B. Percentage ratios											
Gross fixed capital formation as % of GDP[2]	25.3	24.0	23.4	23.5	29.2	25.4	30.0	24.5	24.5	23.3	25.4
Stockbuilding as % of GDP[2]	0.8	2.9	-0.4	1.2	4.6	2.8	2.1	-0.6	-1.1	-1.8	-1.7
Foreign balance as % of GDP[2]	8.5	4.8	6.0	5.1	2.9	8.2	7.8	11.6	12.2	13.2	13.2
Compensation of employees as % of GDP	54.9	54.2	53.1	54.6	56.0	56.5	55.4	54.3	54.8		
Number of unemployed	3 718	2 483	2 269	2 060	2 298	2 734	3 526	4 643	5 130	5 680	6 354
Unemployment as % of civilian labour force	2.2	1.6	1.4	1.3	1.4	1.6	2.1	2.7	3.0	3.3	3.6
C. Other indicator											
Current balance (million US$)	2 022	1 221	1 602	1 753	1 475	1 944	1 760	2 714	2 875	2 809	2 072

1. Throughout this Survey, GDP is on a SNA basis.
2. 1990 prices.
Source: STATEC, preliminary constant data price and Note de conjoncture No. 3/98; OECD, National Accounts and OECD Secretariat.

Table B. **Luxembourg – Gross domestic product**

	1988	1989	1990	1991	1992	1993	1994	1995	1996[1]	1997[1]
					Current prices					
Private consumption	179.2	192.0	206.3	225.6	229.2	239.0	253.7	262.6	270.8	281.7
Public consumption	37.7	41.6	45.9	49.1	52.6	56.7	60.3	66.5	71.3	72.8
Gross fixed capital formation	68.5	73.1	84.5	103.1	98.5	114.7	107.2	116.9	115.1	134.5
Change in stocks	2.4	1.6	4.1	3.3	1.7	0.5	1.9	4.7	2.6	3.8
Total domestic demand	287.8	308.4	340.8	381.1	382.1	410.9	423.1	450.6	459.8	492.8
Exports of goods and services	295.2	347.4	365.8	392.0	407.6	453.5	501.7	514.4	539.5	594.2
less: Imports of goods and services	291.6	321.7	347.6	383.2	371.9	407.6	426.2	446.2	453.0	500.0
Gross domestic product at market prices	291.5	334.1	359.0	389.9	417.8	456.8	498.6	518.8	546.3	587.0
					1990 prices					
Private consumption	185.7	195.2	206.3	219.3	217.3	220.9	226.3	231.7	236.1	242.0
Public consumption	42.8	44.5	45.9	47.7	48.4	50.2	51.2	52.3	54.1	56.2
Gross fixed capital formation	76.9	82.3	84.5	111.2	101.2	129.9	110.6	114.5	112.5	128.4
Change in stocks	9.2	–1.4	4.1	17.5	11.1	9.0	–2.7	–5.1	–8.6	–8.4
Total domestic demand	314.6	320.5	340.8	395.7	378.0	410.0	385.4	393.4	394.1	418.1
Exports of goods and services	327.4	353.8	365.8	390.1	408.7	420.1	438.4	457.6	468.2	496.2
less: Imports of goods and services	311.9	332.6	347.6	378.9	375.9	386.5	385.9	400.6	404.7	429.3
Gross domestic product at market prices	319.9	351.4	359.0	381.1	398.1	432.8	451.0	468.0	482.3	505.4

1. Estimates.
Source: STATEC, Note de conjoncture No. 3/98 and preliminary data; OECD, National Accounts and OECD Secretariat.

Table C. **Luxembourg – Labour market**
Thousands

	1988	1989	1990	1991	1992	1993	1994	1995	1996	1997[1]
Labour force[2] (A + B)	176.1	182.0	189.2	197.1	202.4	206.7	212.9	218.9	225.3	232.8
A. Unemployed	2.5	2.3	2.1	2.3	2.7	3.5	4.6	5.1	5.7	6.4
B. Total employment	173.6	179.7	187.1	194.8	199.7	203.2	208.3	213.8	219.6	226.5
Employees	156.3	162.7	170.4	178.4	183.4	187.0	192.2	197.5	203.1	209.9
Agriculture	1.3	1.4	1.5	1.5	1.5	1.5	1.6	1.6	1.6	1.6
Industry	35.6	36.2	36.0	36.2	35.7	34.1	33.1	32.5	32.2	32.0
of which: Iron and steel	13.5	13.1	12.3	11.6	10.9	10.0	9.4	8.9	8.3	7.7
Energy	1.5	1.5	1.5	1.6	1.6	1.6	1.6	1.7	1.8	1.8
Construction	15.9	16.8	18.3	20.2	21.6	22.1	21.9	22.1	22.4	22.6
Market services	76.0	80.5	85.9	90.8	94.1	97.8	102.8	107.4	111.9	117.6
Non-market services	26.0	26.4	27.1	28.1	28.9	29.8	31.2	32.2	33.2	34.4
Self-employed and family helpers	17.3	17.0	16.7	16.4	16.3	16.2	16.1	16.3	16.4	16.6
Unemployment rate (per cent)	1.6	1.4	1.3	1.4	1.6	2.1	2.7	3.0	3.3	3.6
Participation rate (per cent)	61.2	61.8	62.1	62.1	61.7	61.3	61.8	61.7	62.1	62.5
Job vacancies[3]										
Unfilled vacancies (monthly average)	216.3	201.0	177.7	153.8	159.0	125.6	271.3	437.7	1 107.3	931.4

1. Estimates.
2. Including cross-border workers, nets.
3. In units.
Source: STATEC; OECD, Main Economic Indicators and OECD Secretariat.

Table D. **Luxembourg – Structure of output and performance indicators**

1. Structure of output and economic performance (1990 prices)

Structure of output

	Share of GDP						Share of total employees					
	1985	1990	1994	1995	1996[1]	1997[1]	1985	1990	1994	1995	1996[1]	1997[1]
Agriculture, forestry and fishing	2.0	1.6	0.9	0.9	0.8	0.8	0.9	0.9	0.8	0.8	0.8	0.7
Energy and water	1.9	1.6	1.5	1.5	1.5	1.4	1.0	0.9	0.8	0.8	0.9	0.9
Mining, quarrying and manufacturing	23.1	21.3	15.1	15.1	14.5	14.3	25.8	21.1	17.2	16.4	15.9	15.2
of which: Ores and metals	10.1	6.4	2.8	2.6	2.6	2.9	10.8	7.2	4.9	4.5	4.1	3.6
Construction	4.5	7.0	6.6	6.5	5.8	5.5	9.2	10.8	11.4	11.2	11.0	10.8
Market services[2]	58.0	56.3	64.0	64.0	65.1	65.8	46.1	50.4	53.5	54.4	55.1	56.0
of which: Financial institutions and insurance companies	9.8	13.3	15.0	15.0	15.3	15.3	7.7	9.9	9.5	9.5	9.4	9.2
Non-market services[3]	10.5	12.1	11.9	12.1	12.2	12.2	17.0	15.9	16.2	16.3	16.4	16.4
Total	100.0	100.0	100.0	100.0	100.0	100.0	100.0	100.0	100.0	100.0	100.0	100.0

Economic performance

	Share of total investment						Productivity growth[4]					
	1985	1990	1994	1995	1996[1]	1997[1]	1985	1990	1994	1995	1996[1]	1997[1]
Agriculture, forestry and fishing							2.8	0.9	-1.3	8.8		
Energy and water							3.4	1.6	2.1	3.1		
Mining, quarrying and manufacturing							7.0	-1.6	0.6	4.9		
of which: Ores and metals							6.4	2.2	-9.5	1.6		
Construction							1.2	-2.7	-0.6	2.0		
Market services[2]							5.0	1.7	0.9	0.5		
of which: Financial institutions and insurance companies							4.5	-2.5	0.6	3.5		
Non-market services[3]							0.7	0.8	-0.6	-2.6		

1. Estimates.
2. Wholesale and retail trade; restaurant and hotels; transport, storage and communications; finance, insurance, real estate and business services.
3. Community, social and personal services.
4. Average for 1985-89 instead of 1985.

Source: STATEC, *Note de conjoncture* No. 3/98 and preliminary constant price data and OECD, *National Accounts* and OECD Secretariat.

Table D. **Luxembourg – Structure of output and performance indicators** *(cont.)*

2. Other indicators

	1980	1985	1988	1989	1990	1991	1992	1993	1994	1995	1996	1997
Breakdown of employed workforce by size od establishment:[1]												
1 to 19 employees	13.6	14.4	13.9	13.9	13.7	15.0	14.9	16.1	16.8	16.7		
20 to 49 employees	9.2	10.2	11.5	11.9	12.7	13.0	14.4	14.2	14.6	15.3		
50 to 99 employees	8.5	9.2	10.4	11.7	11.2	10.1	10.4	12.0	11.4	10.5		
100 to 249 employees	14.3	16.0	14.9	14.8	15.0	17.1	15.8	17.4	17.2	18.3		
250 to 499 employees	12.0	11.9	9.6	8.7	10.1	10.8	12.5	11.0	10.9	12.2		
500 employees and over	42.3	38.3	39.7	39.0	37.3	34.0	32.0	29.3	29.0	27.0		
Total	100.0	100.0	100.0	100.0	100.0	100.0	100.0	100.0	100.0	100.0		
Workforce (thousands)	57.4	52.0	55.0	56.0	56.5	59.8	60.3	59.8	58.4	59.2		

1. Only industry and construction.
Source: STATEC.

Table E. **Luxembourg – Public sector**

	1985	1990	1993	1994	1995	1996	1997
Budget indicators: general government accounts (as a per cent of GDP)							
Primary receipts [1]	49.6						
Primary expenditure [1]	46.0						
Primary balance [1]	3.6						
Nets interest payments	−1.2						
General government budget balance	4.8	5.0	1.7	2.8	1.9	2.9	3.0
Structure of expenditure and taxes (as a per cent of GDP)							
General government current expenditure	47.1						
of which:							
Subsidies	3.5	3.2	3.0	3.0	2.2		
Social security benefits	24.4	24.0	25.5	25.0	25.5	26.1	
Investment	4.4	4.6	5.4	4.4	4.7	4.9	
Tax receipts	46.7	43.4	43.9	44.3	44.1	44.4	
Personal income tax	12.0	10.2	9.1	9.5	9.4	9.8	
Corporate tax	8.3	6.9	7.1	7.5	7.7	7.2	
Social security contributions	12.3	11.8	12.3	11.8	11.8	11.6	
Consumption taxes	11.4	10.8	12.0	12.1	12.0	12.4	
of which: Value added tax	5.8	5.9	6.3	6.0	6.2	6.7	
Other indicator							
Income tax as a per cent of total tax	43.3	39.4	37.0	38.5	38.8	38.3	

	Prior to		After	
Tax rates (per cent)				
Personal income tax rates				
Top rate	56	6 December 1990	50	
Lowest rate	10	6 December 1990	10	
Number of brackets	25	6 December 1990	18	
Corporate tax rates	34	6 December 1990	33	
VAT rates				
Lower reduced rate		1 January 1992	3	
Reduced rate		1 January 1992	6	
"Parking" rate		1 January 1992	12	
Standard rate	12	1 January 1992	15	

1.   Excluding interest charges.
Source: STATEC, *Rapport annuel 2/98* and *Annuaire statistique 1997;* Ministry of Finance and OECD, *Revenue Statistics* and *National Accounts.*

Table F. **Luxembourg – Financial markets**

	1980	1985	1990	1991	1992	1993	1994	1995	1996	1997
Sector size										
Sector employment[1]/total employment	4.8	6.3	8.7	8.8	8.8	9.1	9.5	9.4		
Financial assets/GDP[2]	26.7	33.7	36.3	34.4	36.2	36.4	36.8	35.8		
Stock-market capitalisation/GDP	30.9	59.5	99.5	99.0	94.4	177.1	220.3	216.3		
Density of banking network[3]	30.5	32.2	46.7	48.6	54.6	55.2	55.4	53.7		
Structure of financial flows										
Share of credits granted to non-financial sector in total banking assets	35.1	33.4	24.0	24.4	24.7	23.8	18.4	18.1		
Internationalisation of markets										
Foreign business of the banking sector:[4]										
Assets	84.2	86.1	88.1	87.9	86.6	81.5	81.9	80.8		
Liabilities	78.4	77.6	76.5	75.9	73.7	73.4	73.0	72.4		
International banking network:										
Foreign banks in Luxembourg[5]	100	107	158	169	205	210	214	212		
Luxembourg bank branches abroad[6]	74	70	55	6	6	7	7	11		
Efficiency of markets										
Interest margins[7]	0.8	1.2	0.8	0.8	0.8	0.7	0.7	0.7		
Bank productivity[8]	40.5	27.9	37.3	40.5	39.4	38.0	44.8	46.3		
Cost of bank intermediation[9]	0.9	1.4	1.2	1.2	1.1	1.2	1.1	1.1		

1. Credit institutions until 1990, credit institutions plus other intermediaries from 1991.
2. Ratio of banks' balance sheet total to GDP.
3. Number of saving and banking institutions per 100 000 population.
4. As a percentage of deposit banks' balance sheets.
5. Number of foreign saving and banking institutions.
6. Number of regional offices, agencies and branches abroad.
7. Interest margins divided by total assets.
8. Operating expenses as a per cent of gross earnings.
9. Gross earnings as a per cent of total assets.
Source: OECD, Bank Profitability 1985-1994; STATEC, Rapport annuel 1995 and data provided by the Institut monétaire Luxembourgeois.

BASIC STATISTICS

BASIC STATISTICS:

INTERNATIONAL COMPARISONS

	Units	Reference period [1]	Australia	Austr...
Population				
Total	Thousands	1996	18 289	8 0...
Inhabitants per sq. km	Number	1996	2	...
Net average annual increase over previous 10 years	%	1996	1.3	0...
Employment				
Total civilian employment (TCE)[2]	Thousands	1996	8 344	3 7...
of which: Agriculture	% of TCE	1996	5.1	7...
Industry	% of TCE	1996	22.5	33...
Services	% of TCE	1996	72.4	59...
Gross domestic product (GDP)				
At current prices and current exchange rates	Bill. US$	1996	398.9	228...
Per capita	US$	1996	21 812	28 3...
At current prices using current PPPs[3]	Bill. US$	1996	372.7	172...
Per capita	US$	1996	20 376	21 39...
Average annual volume growth over previous 5 years	%	1996	3.9	1...
Gross fixed capital formation (GFCF)	% of GDP	1996	20.3	23...
of which: Machinery and equipment	% of GDP	1996	10.2 (95)	8...
Residential construction	% of GDP	1996	4.6 (95)	5...
Average annual volume growth over previous 5 years	%	1996	5.6	2...
Gross saving ratio[4]	% of GDP	1996	18	21...
General government				
Current expenditure on goods and services	% of GDP	1996	17	19...
Current disbursements[5]	% of GDP	1995	35.6	48...
Current receipts	% of GDP	1995	34.9	47...
Net official development assistance	% of GNP	1995	0.36	0.3...
Indicators of living standards				
Private consumption per capita using current PPPs[3]	US$	1996	12 596	12 15...
Passenger cars, per 1 000 inhabitants	Number	1994	460	43...
Telephones, per 1 000 inhabitants	Number	1994	496	46...
Television sets, per 1 000 inhabitants	Number	1993	489	47...
Doctors, per 1 000 inhabitants	Number	1995	2.2 (91)	2...
Infant mortality per 1 000 live births	Number	1995	5.7	5...
Wages and prices (average annual increase over previous 5 years)				
Wages (earnings or rates according to availability)	%	1996	1.7	5...
Consumer prices	%	1996	2.4	2...
Foreign trade				
Exports of goods, fob*	Mill. US$	1996	60 288	57 87...
As % of GDP	%	1996	15.1	25...
Average annual increase over previous 5 years	%	1996	7.5	7...
Imports of goods, cif*	Mill. US$	1996	61 374	67 37...
As % of GDP	%	1996	15.4	29...
Average annual increase over previous 5 years	%	1996	9.7	5...
Total official reserves[6]	Mill. SDRs	1996	10 107	15 90...
As ratio of average monthly imports of goods	Ratio	1996	2	2...

* At current prices and exchange rates.
1. Unless otherwise stated.
2. According to the definitions used in OECD *Labour Force Statistics*.
3. PPPs = Purchasing Power Parities.
4. Gross saving = Gross national disposable income minus private and government consumption.
5. Current disbursements = Current expenditure on goods and services plus current transfers and payments of property income.
6. End of year.

EMPLOYMENT OPPORTUNITIES

Economics Department, OECD

The Economics Department of the OECD offers challenging and rewarding opportunities to economists interested in applied policy analysis in an international environment. The Department's concerns extend across the entire field of economic policy analysis, both macro-economic and microeconomic. Its main task is to provide, for discussion by committees of senior officials from Member countries, documents and papers dealing with current policy concerns. Within this programme of work, three major responsibilities are:

- to prepare regular surveys of the economies of individual Member countries;
- to issue full twice-yearly reviews of the economic situation and prospects of the OECD countries in the context of world economic trends;
- to analyse specific policy issues in a medium-term context for the OECD as a whole, and to a lesser extent for the non-OECD countries.

The documents prepared for these purposes, together with much of the Department's other economic work, appear in published form in the *OECD Economic Outlook, OECD Economic Surveys, OECD Economic Studies* and the Department's *Working Papers* series.

The Department maintains a world econometric model, INTERLINK, which plays an important role in the preparation of the policy analyses and twice-yearly projections. The availability of extensive cross-country data bases and good computer resources facilitates comparative empirical analysis, much of which is incorporated into the model.

The Department is made up of about 80 professional economists from a variety of backgrounds and Member countries. Most projects are carried out by small teams and last from four to eighteen months. Within the Department, ideas and points of view are widely discussed; there is a lively professional interchange, and all professional staff have the opportunity to contribute actively to the programme of work.

Skills the Economics Department is looking for:

a) Solid competence in using the tools of both microeconomic and macroeconomic theory to answer policy questions. Experience indicates that this normally requires the equivalent of a Ph.D. in economics or substantial relevant professional experience to compensate for a lower degree.

b) Solid knowledge of economic statistics and quantitative methods; this includes how to identify data, estimate structural relationships, apply basic techniques of time series analysis, and test hypotheses. It is essential to be able to interpret results sensibly in an economic policy context.

c) A keen interest in and extensive knowledge of policy issues, economic developments and their political/social contexts.

d) Interest and experience in analysing questions posed by policy-makers and presenting the results to them effectively and judiciously. Thus, work experience in government agencies or policy research institutions is an advantage.

e) The ability to write clearly, effectively, and to the point. The OECD is a bilingual organisation with French and English as the official languages. Candidates must have excellent knowledge of one of these languages, and some knowledge of the other. Knowledge of other languages might also be an advantage for certain posts.

f) For some posts, expertise in a particular area may be important, but a successful candidate is expected to be able to work on a broader range of topics relevant to the work of the Department. Thus, except in rare cases, the Department does not recruit narrow specialists.

g) The Department works on a tight time schedule with strict deadlines. Moreover, much of the work in the Department is carried out in small groups. Thus, the ability to work with other economists from a variety of cultural and professional backgrounds, to supervise junior staff, and to produce work on time is important.

General information

The salary for recruits depends on educational and professional background. Positions carry a basic salary from FF 318 660 or FF 393 192 for Administrators (economists) and from FF 456 924 for Principal Administrators (senior economists). This may be supplemented by expatriation and/or family allowances, depending on nationality, residence and family situation. Initial appointments are for a fixed term of two to three years.

Vacancies are open to candidates from OECD Member countries. The Organisation seeks to maintain an appropriate balance between female and male staff and among nationals from Member countries.

For further information on employment opportunities in the Economics Department, contact:

Management Support Unit
Economics Department
OECD
2, rue André-Pascal
75775 PARIS CEDEX 16
FRANCE

E-Mail: eco.contact@oecd.org

Applications citing ''ECSUR'', together with a detailed *curriculum vitae* in English or French, should be sent to the Head of Personnel at the above address.

Where to send your request:

In Austria, Germany and Switzerland

OECD Centre Bonn
August-Bebel-Allee 6,
D-53175 Bonn
Tel.: (49-228) 959 1215
Fax: (49-228) 959 1218
E-mail: bonn.contact@oecd.org
Internet: www.oecd.org/bonn

In Latin America

OECD Centre Mexico
Edificio INFOTEC
Av. San Fernando No. 37
Col. Toriello Guerra
Tlalpan C.P. 14050,
Mexico D.F.
Tel.: (52-5) 528 10 38
Fax: (52-5) 606 13 07
E-mail: mexico.contact@oecd.org
Internet: rtn.net.mx/ocde/

In the United States

OECD Center Washington
2001 L Street N.W., Suite 650
Washington, DC 20036-4922
Tel.: (202) 785 6323
Toll free: (1 800) 456-6323
Fax: (202) 785 0350
E-mail: washington.contact@oecd.org
Internet: www.oecdwash.org

In Asia

OECD Centre Tokyo
Landic Akasaka Bldg.
2-3-4 Akasaka, Minato-ku,
Tokyo 107-0052
Tel.: (81-3) 3586 2016
Fax: (81-3) 3584 7929
E-mail : center@oecdtokyo.org
Internet: www.oecdtokyo.org

In the rest of the world

OECD Paris Centre
2 rue André-Pascal, 75775 Paris Cedex 16, France
Fax: 33 (0)1 49 10 42 76 **Tel:** 33 (0)1 49 10 42 35
E-mail : sales@oecd.org
Internet : www.oecd.org
Online Orders: www.oecd.org/publications *(secure payment with credit card)*

OECD PUBLICATIONS, 2, rue André-Pascal, 75775 PARIS CEDEX 16
PRINTED IN FRANCE
(10 1999 29 1 P) ISBN 92-64-16970-9 – No. 50423 1999
ISSN 0376-6438